Praise for
Open Wide the Freedom Gates

"Rich with historic details, [*Open Wide the Freedom Gates*] is a humble account of a magnificent life's work." —*Essence*

"Befitting her generation of strong women, [Dr. Height] reveals herself to be made of grace and a titanium backbone ... Put her inspiring memoir on your daughter's summer reading list—and your own."
—*Baltimore Sun*

"[*Open Wide the Freedom Gates*] gives a poignant short course in a century of African-American history." —*The New York Times Book Review*

"A long-awaited memoir from a veteran freedom fighter and witness to history ... in this personal and inspiring story of [Dorothy Height's] life-long fight for civil rights, she reflects on her life of service and leadership, from her childhood encounters with racism, the thrill of college life during the Harlem Renaissance, her marches against lynching, her place on stage with Dr. Martin Luther King Jr. during his pivotal 'I Have Dream' speech and her diplomatic counsel sought by U.S. presidents from Eisenhower to Clinton." —*Ebony*

"If Hillary Clinton weren't already making such good use of it, *Living History* would be an apt title for Dorothy Height's memoirs ... a long-awaited event for those who have badgered Height for years to tell her story." —*New Orleans Times-Picayune*

"In its foreword Maya Angelou describes Height, now 91, as a giant among mighty women. And, indeed, she is a gentle, persistent giant for human progress." —*Detroit Free Press*

"The history of the civil rights movement is made fuller and more complete by [Dorothy Height's] compelling memoir." —*The Miami Herald*

"Ms. Height brings women's roles and projects [in the civil rights movement] out of the shadows with this crisp, clear reflection on her work as she toiled alongside such legendary figures as Eleanor Roosevelt and Mary McLeod Bethune, as well as everyday women of all races."
—*Dallas Morning News*

"Her sheer conviction makes the book more readable than most memoirs. The pearls of insight, wisdom and courage she graciously shares should draw and satiate anyone who wants to better understand America's 20th century, the race and gender dynamics we still grapple with today, and how one woman has walked and talked a mantra of diversity throughout her long and distinguished life." —*The Crisis*

"A straightforward tale, full of information—and yet underlying it all, beneath the unemotional recitation of history, it tells a triumphant and amazing story." —*Deseret News*

"As an activist and woman of great significance to the preservation of American democracy, Dorothy Height has experienced America at many crossroads.... This [book] is a tribute to the legacy of intelligent womanhood. It is a thought-provoking story about what it takes to enact change and embody the spirit of liberation. It is a privilege, indeed an honor, to experience this journey with Dorothy Height." —*Black Issues Book Review*

"For the reader who is seeking an autobiography that is well written and witty, but also offers humanity and a personable style, pick up ... *Open Wide the Freedom Gates.*" —*Chicago Defender*

"Dorothy Height is the most prominent civil rights leader you've probably never heard of ... 'While Rosa Parks is the mother of the civil rights movement,' noted Pennsylvania activist C. DeLores Tucker once said, 'Dorothy Height is the queen.'" —*Pittsburgh Post-Gazette*

"For decades, Dr. Dorothy Height has been an unsung heroine. But not anymore. At 91, Height finally tells her life story in this eloquent memoir, which chronicles her life and her historic role in the civil rights movement ... *Open Wide the Freedom Gates* provides an intriguing history lesson." —*San Antonio Express News*

"Height's book is not just a remarkable account of her role in some of the 20th century's most defining moments. It is also the story of her unflagging courage in the face of its heady battles ... Height is a woman of many gifts, not the least of which is her inspiring legacy of altruism and activism, as detailed in this important memoir." —*The Virginian-Pilot*

"An important resource for anyone with an interest in the long and continuing struggle for equality and social justice ... The memoir reveals a woman with the capacity to learn and grow continuously, a woman passionate about doing good." —*Milwaukee Journal-Sentinel*

"[*Open Wide the Freedom Gates*'] value for historians of the civil rights era and of black women's organizations is central." —*Publishers Weekly*

"An intimate and extended vision of the Civil Rights movement, from a very special black women's perspective. This memoir by a recipient of the Presidential Medal of Freedom is essential for any collection on civil rights, black women, or 20th century U.S. history." —*Library Journal* (starred review)

"Height walks us step-by-step through a remarkable lifetime of witnessing every significant event in the fight for racial equality . . . Amusingly, Height's matter-of-fact tone recounting her experiences belies the magnitude of their historical significance . . . What is most striking about this book is Height's recurring insistence (and proof!) that a sincere commitment to excellence is the tool that can afford remarkable opportunities to everyone." —*Booklist*

"This book will make sure you understand just how important Dorothy Height is to America's history. Dorothy Height has spent over ninety years moving the mountains of racial and human injustice. You'll understand why Dorothy Height has never taken the time to promote herself, to elbow her way into photo-ops, to say controversial things, and grab the headlines. No, instead, this book tells you how Dorothy Height got some extremely important things done by staying out of the limelight. Mountains move very slowly—that's why you maybe never noticed Dorothy Height." —Bill Cosby

"With her clarity of vision, her eloquent voice for justice and human decency and her courageous and determined leadership, Dr. Dorothy Height has been a great inspiration to me. In the early days of the Civil Rights Movement, she was the only woman in the decision-making councils of the male leadership. Dorothy was always there, and she has continued to be there, before and after. As this wonderful memoir reveals, she has been in the forefront of the major struggles for civil and human rights in our times as a compelling advocate. Her historic contributions on behalf of women and families, the poor, the victims of racial and sex discrimination, the disadvantaged, downtrodden and forgotten people of our country have made America a more just and compassionate nation." —Coretta Scott King

"[Dr. Height is] a legend in her own time. . . . Some say life is in the breath we take. I believe life is in the moments that take our breath away. Every time I'm in the presence of Dr. Dorothy Height is a moment that takes my breath away." —Tavis Smiley

PublicAffairs *New York*

OPEN WIDE THE
FREEDOM GATES

A Memoir

DOROTHY HEIGHT

WITH A FOREWORD BY MAYA ANGELOU

Dedicated to my loving mother,
Fannie Burroughs Height,
and her great expectations

———

Book design by Mark McGarry, Texas Type & Book Works
Set in Caslon 540

Library of Congress Cataloging-in-Publication Data
Height, Dorothy I. (Dorothy Irene), 1912–
Open wide the freedom gates: a memoir / Dorothy Height : with a foreword by Maya Angelou.
p. cm. Includes index.
ISBN 1–58648–286–6 (PBK)
1. Height, Dorothy I. (Dorothy Irene), 1912– 2. African American women civil rights workers—Biography. 3. Civil rights workers—United States—Biography.
4. National Council of Negro Women—Biography. 5. African Americans—Civil rights—History—20th century. 6. African Americans—Social conditions—1964–1975.
7. African Americans—Social conditions—1975– I. Title.
E185.97.H444A3 2003   323'.092—dc21   [B]   2003046581

10 9 8 7 6 5 4 3 2 1

Contents

Foreword

by Maya Angelou

Mighty women have been with us and for us from the beginning of time. This is patently true or as a species we would have become extinct centuries before we learned how to use fire or store water. The Empresses and Queens of Western Literature have been portrayed as greedy, indulgent vixens, or tyrannical old hags who manipulated everyone and everything for their own selfish purposes, to reach their own selfish ends.

When Westerners wrote of women of other cultures, they showed them as cruel monarchs in ancient China or submissive Indian maidens in early America—or sexually insatiable slave girls of the American South.

Hale and Theresa Woodruff, Susan B. Anthony, Mother Jones, Sojourner Truth, Harriet Tubman, and their kind, somehow have been elevated beyond this mortal coil. In fact, when we read of them today, it is difficult to believe they ever really inhabited human form, they were so noble, so fierce, so long ago, and so fictional.

Now, one of the giants has presented herself as herself with some little explanation, but totally without apology.

In *Open Wide the Freedom Gates*, Dr. Dorothy Irene Height gives an account of her life, her struggles, her failures, and successes, which makes the reader stop, put the book down, and ponder. Could one African American woman, born in the early twentieth century, bound on all sides by the seeming immutable laws of racial and sexual discrimination escape being devastated? How could she go further and achieve such an impressive curriculum vitae?

This book is an historical and social resource of gargantuan proportions. The reader is introduced to the flesh and bones of people who had only been shining names on antiquitous pages. W. E. B. Du Bois, Dr. Martin Luther King Jr., Mary McLeod Bethune, Adam Clayton Powell, Sr. and Jr., Marian Anderson, Eleanor Roosevelt are among them. In these pages, the legends live as real people, as influences on the life of Dorothy Irene Height. For all the clarity brought to those of olden days, Height has been most successful and courageous in unveiling her own character to the reader.

We see an African American woman in her early twenties asked by city officials to cope with and quell the Harlem riots of 1935. We see her commitment to a lifetime of advocacy for human rights. In this book we are able to follow her work for the desegregation of the armed forces and her work to gain access for all people to public accommodation.

Her dedication to Mary McLeod Bethune and the National Council of Negro Women began in the late 1930s and continued into this century.

It is fortuitous that *Open Wide the Freedom Gates* is being offered here and now. Now when each of us is asking ourselves why am I here and what can I do to make this a safer and better world.

Mari Evans in her poem "I Am A Black Woman," describes

Dorothy Irene Height and helps us to see how we can use the life
Height has lived and is living to improve our own.

I
am a black woman
tall as a cypress
strong
beyond all definition still
defying place
and time
and circumstance
assailed
impervious
indestructible
Look
on me and be
renewed.

Chapter One

A "Little Old Lady"

I THINK OF my life as a unity of circles. Some are concentric, others overlap, but they all connect in some way. Sometimes the connections don't happen for years. But when they do, I marvel. As in a shimmering kaleidoscope, familiar patterns keep unfolding.

I was born in Richmond, Virginia, on March 24, 1912, to Fannie Burroughs and James Height. My mother was over forty—I was, as some say, a "second life" baby—so for me, she was never really young. Perhaps that is why I have always enjoyed being around older people. Even as a young child, I found it interesting to talk with them, and they seemed to enjoy me. They took me seriously because I took life seriously. I was shy, and I loved to get off by myself to read. I never enjoyed doing nothing. I always liked a challenge. If it was jumping rope, I wanted to go on to Double Dutch. My older sisters explained me by saying I was an "old folks" child.

My grandparents died long before I was born, so I knew little about them, but I'm told that my father's family was part Native American, from North Carolina, and my mother's people were from Virginia. Both my parents had been twice widowed, and both had children from their previous marriages. I have known two of my father's children well—his daughters Golden and Minnie. And all my mother's children were very close to me. She had three by her first marriage: Willie, the oldest, Bennie, and Jessie. In her second marriage, there was Josephine. My sister Anthanette and I were her two Heights. Although we were actually half-sisters to the rest, I always felt we were "whole" sisters and brothers. It seemed to me that I came up in a large, loving family.

Josephine had to look after me when I was small because Momma worked long hours as a nurse in a Negro hospital in Richmond. A friend of Josephine's also had the care of a younger sister, and Josephine used to tell how we two little ones always seemed to be in the way of our older sisters' fun. So one day they took us to a nearby bridge with the idea of simply dropping us out of sight into the James River. When they got to the bridge, they saw a neighbor coming toward them and made a beeline back home. Josephine often said she was glad they thought better of it.

When I was four years old, we moved to Rankin, Pennsylvania, part of the Great Migration of southern Negroes to the North. At the time of my birth more than three-quarters of the black population of the United States was still providing cheap labor in rural areas of the South. Nearly fifty years after the Civil War, the ravages of slavery remained. But by 1916 that was beginning to change. Booming industry in places like Chicago, Detroit, and Pittsburgh drew great waves of Negroes—along with immigrants from Europe—to work in the mines, mills, and factories that promised a better life.

Though our family had no relatives to receive us up North, my parents, like thousands of others, were willing to risk everything for a new start. As a building and painting contractor, my father knew that Pennsylvania would be much richer territory for him. It was a different story for my mother. While many northern hospitals admitted Negro patients, none would employ a Negro nurse, so she had to make do with household work. But she made that transition with a grace that was a wonderful example to me. And eventually, through her own ingenuity as a household worker and the relationships she established with her employers, she was able to put her nursing skills to use taking care of private patients.

Rankin was a lucky choice. My parents had heard a great deal about the appalling living and working conditions that many were forced to endure in Philadelphia, New York, Chicago, and Detroit. Housing often was the worst kind of tenement, with more than one family crowded into a unit. What were called "multiple dwellings" were really just plain slums, usually owned by wealthy absentee landlords.

Rankin was different. It was a small borough of Pittsburgh, nestled in the rolling hills along the Monongahela River. The low land along the river made a perfect place for steel mills, as well as for the railroad tracks that had come into the area in the 1850s. Most people counted on the mills for their livelihood, though many worked in the nearby coal mines. As World War I drove up the demand for steel, Rankin flourished.

The population was largely foreign-born. On almost any evening in our neighborhood, you could hear Italians singing on one side of the street and Croatians or Germans on the other side. The one prominent Jewish family owned the butcher shop. I have many happy memories of being together with people who were so different from one another. My date for the high school junior prom, for instance, was a Croatian boy who was the president of our class when I was the class secretary.

But with all the joyous celebrations that we shared, there was always the struggle to earn a living—and that meant certain economic tensions among all those groups searching for a better standard of living. There was a clear hierarchy. First in line and always on top economically were American-born whites, though they were a minority. Then came the foreign-born—the Italians, the Croatians, the Hungarians, the Polish, the Czechoslovakians, and the Yugoslavs who had fled war-ravaged Europe and comprised the bulk of the population. Negroes from the South were the last in line. Whites born in America looked down on white Europeans. And with the Great Migration, thousands of white ethnic families collided with the influx of southern Negro families.

During the First World War, when the steel industry desperately needed more laborers, the steel and mining companies would make deals with the railroads to offer southern Negroes free railway passage north. They called it "the Transportation." It wasn't exactly slave labor, but the wages were only marginally better than what the Negro workers could earn in the South. Even so, since the North was perceived as the region of opportunity, folks didn't think twice about moving, and our house became a meeting ground for many who came after us, especially those from Virginia and North Carolina. Many were willing to work twelve hours a day under terrible conditions. As a young child, I saw "last hired, first fired" in living reality.

I was eight years old when my aunt, Sally White, came up from Virginia to visit her son, Lincoln, who worked in a nearby mine. She was the oldest of my mother's three sisters, and she was the only one among the four who never learned to read or write, although she spoke perfect English. Unlike her sisters, she had little schooling because she had become a wage-earner as a very young woman. She was a great pastry cook, working her magic touch with flour, shortening, and sugar for wealthy white families in Prince William County, Virginia.

Lincoln sent his mother a train ticket to Pennsylvania, hoping that after a good visit he could convince her to come live with him. Aunt Sally had barely arrived when Western Union delivered a telegram to our house. She could not read it, so when I came home from school, she handed it to me. The telegram said that Lincoln had been lost in a cave-in at the mine where he worked. I didn't know what to do, but I knew this was shocking news. I also knew that Aunt Sally couldn't read it, and that she probably thought a child my age couldn't read it either. I folded the telegram and told Aunt Sally that I would give it to my mother to read to her.

When my mother came home, she sat Aunt Sally down and read the telegram to her. Through her tears, Aunt Sally let me know that she appreciated how I tried to protect her from the awful news. An instant bond developed between us. Aunt Sally told my mother lovingly that she had a "little old lady" in me.

It was a terrible moment when Aunt Sally had to go to the mine to identify Lincoln's body. It was so final. Everything they had planned together and waited for was suddenly gone. I learned then the risk and impact of the coal mines on families all around us. Families had such feelings of hopelessness after each cave-in, yet they went back to work, knowing they had to make a living. Many accidents never made the news, but word got around the community. Whole families were devastated by their losses. Years later no one ever had to convince me that John L. Lewis and the United Mine Workers Union were fighting a crucial fight. Whenever I heard his voice staking his claim on behalf of the workers, I remembered Lincoln and that day with Aunt Sally.

McClintock Marshall was the largest steel mill in Rankin. Every day it belched out red-hot flames and smoke that floated like clouds above us and then rained down iron-ore dust over our backyard. My mother insisted on washing our curtains every other week just to get the soot out. No one had heard of antipollution laws then! When we studied anthracite, iron, or bituminous coal in school, it was very real to me.

The whistle of the steel mill seemed to control our lives. It blew at seven in the morning, at noon, at three, at seven in the evening, and at eleven at night. In good weather, we children would sit out on our back porch in the evening and play a great game. We counted the mill workers. The winner was the one who could count to the highest number before the last man on the evening shift came out of the mill. When the mills were flourishing, the numbers were so great that the men looked like ants, all moving in the same direction. As jobs began to disappear, we realized that the numbers were dwindling. And then there came a time when it was easy to count those who came through the gate. There were no bright flames gusting out of the stacks. The smoke diminished, the ore dust settled. It was the post–World War I depression.

My father was always self-employed. Highly skilled, he was a building contractor, a master at house painting, decorative painting, several kinds of refinishing, carpentry, and building, and he was much in demand. He was acclaimed for his stencil work on the walls of the Syrian Mosque as well as for his work on the less glamorous walls of the morgue in downtown Pittsburgh. He even had the contract to paint the yellow lane-divider lines down the middle of Rankin's streets. He often tested his paints on our porch, so I never knew what color it would be when I got home from school. For my father, it was not just a test but also an advertisement.

My father provided work for many young men coming up from the South, and as the depression deepened, more and more young men came to our house seeking employment. My father did what he could, but he had to turn many away. Men out of work often would stop me on my way home from school and say, "Please, tell your father that if he needs help, I can do anything he needs." I knew some of these young men and came to see how precious work is for people. I understood that what I had seen from the back porch was connected to what was happening on the front porch. People were desperate. As a woman in Harlem said to me later, "This was a time when a dollar was a dollar and Negroes didn't have any."

My father was also active in Republican politics. After all, those were the days when the Republicans were still the party of Abraham Lincoln. Our dining room table could tell many stories of decisions made, of candidates chosen or nixed. In truth, however, neither of the political parties offered much advancement for the Negro, for whom unemployment and lynching were realities of everyday life. On the local, state, and national levels, Negro Americans gained ground through the kind of self-help that had characterized our struggle since slavery—by creating our own organizations to meet our needs. My mother was very active in the Pennsylvania Federation of Colored Women's Clubs, founded in 1895. She took me to every state and national meeting. There I saw women working, organizing, teaching themselves. I heard a lot about uplifting the race. Years later I would have a better appreciation of how much women had done through those clubs to provide basic services that white people took for granted.

It was in Williamsport, Pennsylvania, when I was thirteen years old, that I saw and heard for the first time a Negro woman who was an elected official. Her name was Maude Coleman, and she was a member of the state legislature. Her address to the girls' group of the state federation kept me awake most of the night. The words haunted me, so I found a way to get them from Representative Coleman. To this day I go back to the poem she recited at the end of her speech:

> *To every man there openeth a high way and a low,*
> *And every man decideth the way his soul shall go.*
> *Some Souls climb the high way, others grope the low,*
> *And in between, on the misty flats, the rest drift, to and fro.*
> *To every man there openeth a high way and a low,*
> *And every man decideth the way his soul shall go.*

I went to these meetings because my mother wanted me to, although I didn't like the fact that many were held on holiday weekends. One Fourth of July, when all my playmates were getting ready to shoot their fireworks, I was packed off to a women's church meeting. I never admitted to my mother that the reason my eyes were so red that Saturday afternoon was because I had carried a Thunderbolt with me into the ladies' room and tried to set it off. I suppose it was fortunate for all that it simply backfired in my face and did not blow up the building. There was no water cold enough to stop the burning that stung my eyes all weekend. But most of the time I enjoyed whatever festivities the women of the Pennsylvania Federation of Colored Women's Clubs put on. Since those early days, I've never doubted my place in the sisterhood.

As a household worker, my mother earned three dollars a day plus carfare. The carfare was important because Rankin was almost an hour away from downtown Pittsburgh. I remember best a family named Johnston, for whom my mother worked over the longest period. My mother felt very close to Mrs. Johnston and her daughter Mary, but my feelings were decidedly mixed: I both liked and hated Mary Johnston. On the one hand, it seemed that during every important event in my life, my mother had to be at Mary's house, and that bothered me. On the other hand, Mary was about my age and size and had beautiful clothes, many of which I inherited. Once, when I won an impromptu speech contest, Mrs. Johnston sent me a beaver coat that Mary had outgrown. Beaver coats were very elegant, and everyone at school knew that only rich girls could have them. That was one of those moments when I loved Mary Johnston!

In 1974, when the *Ladies' Home Journal* named me "Woman of the Year" in human rights, Mary Johnston saw the story and sent me a lovely letter. She told me of her work in the Presbyterian Church and said that she continued to feel that her life and mine were connected. Through my mother, her mother had made it a point to keep up with me—my good grades, awards, and scholarships in school. She had taken pride in my every achievement. At the end of the letter, Mary wrote, "I imagine that, even now, wherever they both are, our mothers are rejoicing in your success and are part of a heavenly committee watching over both of us."

*

I loved school. I liked learning. And I thought I had the best teachers in the world. They were drawn from the white ethnic groups that made up most of Rankin. Only in Sunday School, music, and later basketball did I have Negro teachers, who seemed rather special to me.

The one obstacle to my perfect school attendance was asthma, which was not helped by the industrial air of Pittsburgh. My father and I had severe cases. To get relief, we used a powder called Asthmador, which we would light on fire; then, with hoods over our heads, we would inhale the fumes to open our bronchial tubes. When I lay down, my breath would cut off, so I had to sit up night after night, sometimes for as long as two weeks, just to get rest and relief. To this day I get comfort by sleeping in a reclining chair before finally going to bed.

Despite the asthma, I almost always went to school. When I couldn't see through my tears what the teachers were writing, I memorized what I heard them say. My teachers knew it was hard for me, and every once in a while one of them, noticing my struggle to breathe, would encourage me to put my head down on my desk. Sometimes, having sat up in a chair most of the night, getting little real rest, I would fall asleep. I never wanted my classmates to feel sorry for me, so I braved it out until the end of the day.

As I began to outgrow the asthma, I developed a strange ailment—a toe ache. My mother often had it too, and sometimes we had it together. Her concern about me took us to many places to try to find out what was wrong: to Johns Hopkins Hospital in Baltimore and to St. Luke's and Columbia Presbyterian Hospitals in New York. When I was twelve, Mrs. Johnston referred my mother to a specialist in downtown Pittsburgh. After examining me, the doctor excused me and spoke to my mother. On the streetcar going home, I saw her eyes filling with tears, although she kept her head turned, hoping I wouldn't notice. After a while, I told her I had heard what the doctor said—that I would not live to be sixteen.

"He was wrong," I told her. "I'm going to live a long time." She put her arms around me, and we continued back to Rankin.

Whatever the specialist prescribed seemed to have little effect, until one day when I was trying to memorize a very long poem. A terrible toe ache just wouldn't let me concentrate. I had to be ready for a concert the following Sunday, so I went into the kitchen and got a piece of string, which I tied as tightly as I could around the aching toe. After a while, the pain disappeared. After that, I did the same thing every time the toe aches came on—and eventually I outgrew them, just as I had outgrown the asthma.

Perhaps some of the doctors we consulted could have been more helpful had I not grown so very tall before I was ten years old. I was exceptionally thin, and I had little or no appetite. I remember a fourth-grade teacher, Ruth Marks, who worried about me. She would say, "Dorothy, you just rest. Put your head down and rest." Although she was my favorite teacher, I hated to hear her say that. As time went on she could see that despite my wheezing and tearing, I was ready to answer her questions when called upon, but I was very shy about raising my hand. If she knew I had the answer and wanted me to give it, she would call on me anyway. That was a great help.

Because the majority of children in the school were first-generation Americans, most of them spoke their parents' language at home. The English language was drilled into us at school. But we had our own collection of colloquialisms that grew out of so many different languages and speech patterns. One favorite was "you-uns," which we used when speaking to more than one person. The teachers scolded us when we used it. Add to that "y'all," which southern Negro children used, and the teachers were always on a language warpath. We were drilled every day to say "you" or "all of you" or "all of us" or "we." The teachers were tough. If someone said "ain't," we would all have to practice every proper alternative. I got so bored going over and over the same thing. Recently a staff member asked me why I always say "do not" or "will not" and seldom say "don't" or "won't." I had never noticed it, but I suppose it's because those speech forms were drummed into me every day so early in life.

At the end of World War I, a war memorial to the fallen soldiers from Rankin was to be unveiled on the school grounds. An Italian girl, Maria, and I were chosen to do the unveiling. Both of us learned our little speeches. When our teacher heard us at practice, she tried to get Maria to use the correct English accent. Maria had the opening remarks. She was to say, "The Armistice Day, just past . . . ," and then go on with the rest. But she never got through the first sentence because she kept saying "thearmisticedayjustpast," as if it were one word. The comma meant nothing to her. Finally, wanting her students to make a good showing at this important event, the teacher said, "Maria, if you can't do it, I'll have to get someone else." Maria was reduced to tears.

We wanted to do this together. We asked for another chance. Over the weekend I went down to Maria's house, and we sat together on her porch to practice and practice so she finally got so she could say it right. As her mother fed us cookies she told Maria, "You listen to Dorothy and say it just like she does." We sat on the porch for hours, both of us saying that phrase over and over. Maria had no trouble with the rest of her speech; it was just something about her accent on the word "armistice" that got her.

On Monday, when we rehearsed, the teacher was so proud that she gave Maria a big hug. When the moment came, here was an Italian girl and a Negro girl representing our school, making the speeches, and drawing the curtain on the memorial to the war dead. Rankin had its strangeness, but it was a marvelous place to grow up.

In fact, in those early years I knew little about prejudice. I remember my first real hint of what it was all about. When I was eight years old, my best friend was Sarah Hay. She was Irish Catholic, blond and blue-eyed, and I thought she was very pretty. We lived next door to each other on a hill, and we walked back and forth to school together. In good weather we held hands and ran down the hill. In the wintertime snow and ice we would crawl up the hill together and slide down it, shrieking with laughter.

One day as we were ready to run down the hill, Sarah turned away and said, "I can't go down the hill with you."

"Why not?" I asked.

"Because you're a nigger," she said.

"What?" I asked, stunned.

"You're a nigger," she repeated, and ran down the hill by herself.

I was crushed. I had heard the word before, and I knew it wasn't supposed to be used, at least not by anyone who had manners.

I stumbled to our house, trying to hide my tears. I could hardly wait for my mother to get home from work. When she arrived, she looked at my crumpled face and asked what was the matter. I told her Sarah Hay wouldn't go down the hill with me because, she said, I was a "nigger." "Am I really a nigger?" I asked.

My mother, always so gentle and so firm, put her arms around me. "You are a nice girl, Dorothy. You are a smart girl, and there are many things that you can do. If Sarah Hay doesn't want to play with you, just think of all the friends you have who do want to play with you."

"But she called me 'nigger,'" I cried.

"I don't think Sarah Hay knows what that means," my mother said. "She just doesn't know. She doesn't know who you are."

The sting stayed with me for days, but Momma was right. I did have plenty of other friends, and I found them.

Chapter Two

Keeping the Faith

W E LIVED right next door to the Emmanuel Baptist Church, where there was always a lot going on, and everyone connected with the church took it for granted that they could call on me to be a "go-fer." In the wintertime, for instance, the janitor would call my mother to ask whether I could light the furnace to warm up the church before everyone else arrived.

My father was a deacon, superintendent of the Sunday School, and choirmaster, and as a result, some Sundays we spent all day in church. Father believed that whatever we did had to start promptly. Sunday School was at 9:30. Even if he and I were the only ones there on time, as sometimes happened on rainy or snowy mornings, we'd start the devotional. By the time others arrived, he would be far into his agenda and the latecomers would just have to figure out what was going on. He did not believe in repeating himself.

He had a beautiful, high tenor voice, and he lectured us about the importance of singing a hymn all the way through. "It isn't just the tune and the rhythm that are important," he would say. "If you sing only the first and last verses, you miss all that's in between!" He always stressed that the hymnist was communicating an important message and you could not just take his work and make it yours. To this day it troubles me when people sing only the first and last verses.

Often the Church Missionary Society held chicken dinners to raise money. A Mrs. Reynolds was in charge. Women on the committee would bring a turkey or a ham, or they would bake rolls, a pie, or a cake. My job was to help get the food organized, and sometimes, if the church oven was already full, I would take anything that needed to be warmed up next door to our house.

Mrs. Reynolds was easily annoyed. If the woman who was supposed to bring rolls came late, or if she had not brought enough, everyone knew we were in for trouble. Mrs. Reynolds would throw up her hands and sigh, "Jesus, if I can just make it in." If a woman promised to bring a homemade cake and showed up with a store-bought version, Mrs. Reynolds was furious. And while everyone was trying to eat, she would get people stirred up about helping the starving children in Africa, insisting that you should clean your plate—and never take what you could not eat. She was a perfectionist about church dinners. Nothing was too good for God.

During those years I learned a lot of lessons I didn't fully understand until much later. Because I was a quick learner, for instance, I often got impatient with other people. One time in church we children were rehearsing for the Easter exercise. We wore our new Easter outfits, and children made little speeches and sang songs. Mrs. Ford, the pastor's wife, was directing us. Afterward she called my mother to complain that I had giggled all the way through the rehearsal and that other children had followed my lead. When I got home, my mother was waiting for me, impatient to hear my side of the story.

I told her that Herbert, one of the boys, had a short speech. He started saying, "He is risen, He is risen...," and he couldn't remember the rest, which was "...from the dead." "He had so little to remember," I said, "and that sounded funny!"

My mother saw nothing funny about it. "And what about you?" she asked.

"Oh, I knew mine," I assured her. "I had a long piece, I had learned it, and I had already said it."

"Well," Mother said, "if you are all that smart, why didn't you help Herbert? If you cannot do that, then I think you had better not be in the Easter exercise." I could not bear missing the show. So from that point on I offered to help. I became the unofficial prompter, giving cues if any child hesitated.

My mother helped me understand how not to show off what I knew, but how to use it so that others might benefit. She always kept before me my responsibility to other people, and she taught me the importance of being cooperative instead of competitive. But she did make me compete with myself and always made me perform upward. When I brought home my report card, she would ask, "What happened? Last time you made 92. This time you made 90." I'd protest that 90 was the best grade in the class. "I did not ask what other people did," my mother would reply. "I want to know about Dorothy Height. What happened that she didn't do as well as she did last time?" Even today, after I make some kind of public presentation, I have to evaluate it for myself. I want to give everything my best because when you do that, you get much more than you give. That's one of my mother's lasting legacies.

Because I was so eager to help out, Mrs. Ford asked me to work with her when she had practices for plays and pageants. I loved showing the younger ones how to do things. One day Mother came home from work to find a sign in our front window: "Music Lessons—25 cents." What in the world, she asked, did that sign mean? I replied that I was giving music lessons. She pointed out that I didn't know all that much about music. A little hurt, I explained that I could teach what I did know. And I did. I just tried to stay about five lessons ahead of my pupils. One of them went on to study music more formally and became a concert pianist.

There were fifty-seven students in my eighth grade class in 1925. Billy Bodner, a Croatian boy, was class president and I was secretary—and we had an idea. We wrote to the H.J. Heinz Company of Pittsburgh, telling them about our class and hoping they would recognize us in some way. To our surprise, the company invited the class to visit a Heinz plant and to have lunch at a downtown hotel. When we told our teachers, they insisted on some preparation—etiquette classes to teach us how to handle the silverware and properly express our thanks. We had a great time. And that preparation, along with my home training, has helped me move comfortably and dine with anyone, anywhere.

When I was still quite young, a white woman named Luella Adams was sent by the American Baptist Home Mission Society to establish the Rankin Christian Center. The idea was to "save underprivileged souls" in our town. At first the center was just a small frame building across the street from my house, and it featured "Americanization" classes for the foreign-born. Many days, after school, I would stop by and talk with Miss Adams. We had a very warm relationship despite the difference in our ages.

After a few years Miss Adams had raised enough money to build a modern brick building to house the center. Its doors opened in 1923, and inside there were a chapel, a gym, and a nursery. It seemed like a skyscraper to me, the most beautiful structure I had ever seen. Its purpose was "to bring the 'more abundant life' to the crowded, underprivileged communities created by our modern industrial order." And though its official policy stated that it was available to all, without discrimination as to faith or race," six days a week it was opened exclusively for European whites.

One of the daily activities at the center was a kindergarten. Every morning I'd hear those little white kids carrying on. One day, when the din was particularly deafening, I had an idea. I decided to present it to the center's director, my friend Luella Adams.

I told Miss Adams how much noise the children were making and suggested that they needed something to keep them busy—perhaps someone to come in and tell them Bible stories and help them make up plays that they could act out. Miss Adams thought this was a good idea. Then I told her I'd be glad to do it. At that moment, as Miss Adams reported in her memoir, she did not know how to say no to me. And at that moment—the last time I ever had to apply formally for a job—my life's work began.

I started teaching Bible stories to the white children. One day, when a group of children were gathered at my feet, listening intently, two distinguished guests stopped by. They were wealthy white American Baptist ladies for whom this was a mission center, and although I had no idea at the time who they were, one of them would later play a very important role in my life. A history of the Rankin Center dates the opening of the center to the Negro community to the start of my teaching. In fact, it was not until years later that the doors were opened wide enough to let in everyone every day.

As I grew older the weekly "Negro Day" at the Rankin Christian Center was my favorite after-school activity. One day Dr. Mary Jane Watkins, a dentist from downtown Pittsburgh, came to the center to teach hygiene and personal grooming and to coach a girls' basketball team. She was a charming person. Because the center basketball team played boys' rules, which I liked better than girls' rules, I was one of the first to sign up. Others were better players, but no one was more enthusiastic than I.

I also played on our Rankin High School team, which played by girls' rules. I can still feel the sting of the day the Rankin High School team traveled south, around the bend in the river, to play against McKeesport High School. When they discovered that three members of our team were Negroes, the McKeesport team would not play. Every member of the Rankin High team was upset, but there was nothing we could do. We returned home, feeling defeated. Marie Wall, another Negro player on the team, and I took the first chance we had to tell Dr. Watkins our story. She tried to help by telling us that she thought we were terrific players, but it still hurt deeply to have our team rejected simply because we were members.

Once the Rankin Christian Center was pretty well established, two representatives of the Pittsburgh Young Women's Christian Association (YWCA), Lula Johnson Howell and Edna Kincheon, came to visit. Their mission was to organize a Girl Reserves Club, the YWCA youth program. As usual, I was among the first to join. On any given Thursday we'd make full use of the center facilities. One member would make fudge, others would prepare snacks, still others might be rehearsing for some kind of play. That club made us feel we were linked with girls from all over the city.

When I was elected president of the club, Lula Howell encouraged me to attend the citywide Girl Reserves meetings in downtown Pittsburgh. Soon thereafter I was delegated to sing "Father of Lights" at the semiannual induction ceremonies. As new members marched in, each wearing a white middy blouse and a blue tie and carrying a lighted candle, I sang the verses until everyone was in her place. That was a magical evening for me, filled with beauty and inspiration and a sense of being part of something important.

Eventually I was selected to be photographed with two white girls, all of us in uniform, for a Girl Reserves poster for the Pittsburgh YWCA. The Rankin club was very excited. We were so elated that several of us decided to go to the Chatham Street YWCA in downtown Pittsburgh and learn how to swim.

When we arrived, we marched up to the front desk to ask for directions to the pool, and as we spoke the woman behind the desk got a curious look on her face. She told us that Negro girls could not swim in the YWCA pool.

I was only twelve years old. I had never heard of "social action," nor seen anyone engaged in it, but I barely took a breath before saying that I would like to see the executive director. Though she received us graciously, the director held to the stated policy. I let her know that we were Girl Reserves, that women from this YWCA had come out to Rankin to organize us, and that I was even going to be on the Girl Reserves poster. But nothing I said made any difference. Young women of color were not welcome in the Chatham Street YWCA pool.

We were crushed—and bewildered. In Rankin we were used to working and playing together interracially, and it was inconceivable to us that the YWCA could be so backward. In our community there was a cohesiveness and friendliness among different racial and ethnic groups. At that moment, as the director of the YWCA stood unyielding before us, we Rankin girls felt a transcendent sense of solidarity. The YWCA's discrimination seemed small and petty, but it struck a painful chord that reverberated in each of us long afterward.

When our YWCA advisers returned to Rankin the following week, I wasn't shy about asking why we could not swim in the YWCA pool. They encouraged us to be proud of being Girl Reserves, but even as they tried to help us conquer our feelings of rejection, it was clear that they had no satisfactory answers. As members of the Negro Wiley Avenue Branch YWCA of Pittsburgh, they could do no more than we to change the rules that denied us the opportunity. I never did learn how to swim.

Years later, when I was a speaker and honored guest at the Chatham Street YWCA, I told the swimming pool story. I was then an executive on the national staff of the YWCA, and most of the people in the audience could not believe what I was telling them. By then the segregated structure of the YWCA, in which cities had a "central" YWCA primarily for whites and a separate "branch" for Negroes, had long since disappeared. Everyone was welcome at Chatham Street. I was proud of that and other changes in the organization. I was asked then, as I have been asked so many times since, how I kept the faith and continued the struggle in the face of such deep humiliation. In reply, I mentioned the many times I witnessed or was part of progress simply because people of different races were determined to improve their lives.

We members of the Girl Reserves considered ourselves the "youth backbone" of the Emmanuel Baptist Church, and many of us were members of the Junior Missionary Society as well. One night we held a "pie social" at the home of Deacon Williams to raise money for missions in Africa. Deacon Williams's granddaughter, Peggy Lee, was a member of our group. Various people brought records so we would have some good music, and when everyone had gathered, someone wound up the Victrola. Forest Shields asked me to dance, but I confessed that I did not know how. He was about to show me when Deacon Williams opened the door. He was appalled. Dancing, of course, was forbidden in the church. He stopped the music and would listen to no explanation. That was the end of our pie social. I determined then and there to learn how to dance if it was all that exciting!

But there were repercussions. Deacon Williams said he would have us "silenced" in the church. We were scared to death. When I got home, I tried to explain to my father that Deacon Williams had not given us a chance. We felt we were doing nothing wrong. But my father, also a church officer, made it clear that there were no two ways about it: we had brought disgrace. Worse still, for us and our missions, we had not sold any of our pies.

Being "silenced" meant that we were not permitted to sing in the choir on Sunday morning. And to tell the truth, our voices were sorely missed. Then, after church, we were ordered to appear before the Deacon Board to confess our "sins." As the meeting opened, Deacon Williams reported our moral turpitude to the other members of the board. At that moment, perhaps because we had been so tense and because it was hard for us to see the error of our ways, we all started to giggle. We couldn't help it.

After several deacons had pronounced on the magnitude of our transgression, we were allowed to speak. One by one, we gathered our composure enough to say, once more, that we were having a pie social and we played a record, but we were not having a dance. Finally, each of us had to promise that we would not "sin" again. Two of the group refused to make that promise because they felt it was unfair. I made the promise and said I was sorry, even though I had not been dancing because I did not know how to dance. In the end Deacon Harris joined my father in saying that we should be given a warning and the silence should be lifted. I think the other deacons welcomed this way out, but they sternly admonished that this should never happen again.

Some of the young people never again had much enthusiasm for the church. Those who refused to make the promise dropped out entirely, feeling that the deacons were hypocritical. Several joined another church. Forest Shields, who was very smart, became a more aggressive and articulate member of the group that stayed. Years later, when he was a pharmacist in Washington, D.C., our paths crossed again. We laughed about the "sinful" pie social that never happened.

Though most of my extracurricular life revolved around the church and the Christian Center, Rankin High School was very special to me. For years there had been no high school in town; students had to go several miles to Braddock. But in 1925 the Rankin High School was built in the middle of town, and I was in the first class to graduate after four full years in the new building.

To celebrate our new school I wrote the alma mater along with another Negro student, Dolly Slaughter. I wrote the words, and Dolly chose the music. It was very exciting to have a sense of being at the beginning of something. When we presented our song to the students, everyone liked it. It is still being sung today even though the building no longer stands.

Dolly played the piano when we students sang in assembly.

The music teacher, who came only twice a month, had assigned me to lead the singing whenever she wasn't there. That was the routine until one day a new principal arrived. After seeing me lead the singing in the first assembly he attended, Mr. Straitiff told my homeroom teacher, Mary Mohr, that for the next assembly the students would sing without my coming to the platform to lead them. A few minutes before the next assembly Miss Mohr explained this to me. I saw tears in her eyes as she spoke.

As the students gathered in the auditorium Mr. Straitiff called everyone to stand and sing the alma mater. I was seated in the row with my class, and I stayed where I was, as I had been told. Dolly played the introduction, and a few teachers stood, as did I, but the other students remained seated. Dolly played the introduction again, but no one stood and no one sang. It was a very strange experience, almost as if it had been organized. Everyone seemed to feel that something was wrong. It was 1928. The student body was 95 percent white.

After Dolly played the introduction a third time, Mr. Straitiff beckoned me to the platform. When I got there, everyone stood and sang the alma mater as they never had before. As the principal was returning to his office, Billie Bodner, an officer of my class, said, "Mr. Straitiff, this is the way we always do it. Dolly plays the piano, and Dorothy leads us in the singing. We don't do it any other way." From then on Mr. Straitiff did not object. Over time he accepted many things that were new to him. Though his racial bias was clear at the beginning, eventually he became a good friend and supporter.

Music was always a passion. Peggy Lee, Dolly Slaughter, and I formed a trio in high school called the Jolly Three. Peggy was a contralto, Dolly a soprano, and I an even higher soprano than Dolly. Dolly played piano solos, Peggy and I sang solos and duets, and I recited poetry. It occurred to us that we might raise money for college by giving concerts at churches.

I wrote a letter to local churches and made an offer: the Jolly Three Trio would present a concert, and 60 percent of the proceeds would go to the church and 40 percent to our scholarship fund. We had a theme song, "Sweet and Low," and we were good at gospel and old favorites like "Whispering Hope." We had our own arrangements of a few popular songs too, but of course we didn't mention jazz. No one would dream of performing jazz in church. One evening Dolly called, quite excited. She had heard a group singing on station KDKA radio. "They're imitating us," she said. "They're syncopating the way we do!" When we learned that the group was the McGuire Sisters, we were very impressed.

Another of my favorite extracurricular activities was the debating team. My English teacher, Myrtle Peters, encouraged me to participate in speech contests wherever I could. I loved them. They bolstered my confidence and made me overcome my shyness. I enjoyed thinking about things, both abstract and practical, and debating important issues—war and peace, for instance, and capital punishment—that I might otherwise never have thought about because they did not come up very often in our little town.

One day I was on my way to downtown Pittsburgh to participate in a speech contest at another school. As the streetcar pulled to a stop at the corner of Third and Hawkins, our pastor's wife, Mrs. Ford, saw me. She demanded to know what I was doing out of school at ten o'clock in the morning. I stepped back and waited until she got close enough so that I could tell her I was on my way downtown to represent Rankin High School in a speech contest. By the time I finished explaining, the streetcar had gone. And by the time I got downtown, the time to enter the contest had long passed. I had to wait several weeks for another round. It took me considerably longer to find a way to feel kindly once again toward Mrs. Ford.

When I was fifteen, I won the Western Pennsylvania High School Impromptu Speech Contest. That meant I would participate in the state finals. They were to be held in Harrisburg, Pennsylvania's capital.

My Latin teacher, Mary Mohr, and the principal, Mr. Straitiff, kindly said they would drive me to Harrisburg. When they arrived at my house, my mother carefully placed on a hanger the white dress she had made for me to wear that evening. As I got into the car, she said, "No matter what happens, Dorothy, just hold *yourself* together."

When we got to Harrisburg, Mr. Straitiff drove to the hotel where he had reservations. After a few minutes he came back out and called for Miss Mohr to come with him. Miss Mohr was a lovely person, but she had rather homely buck teeth, and when she got upset, those protruding teeth would nibble in a peculiar way at her lower lip. When she came out of the hotel, her teeth were pulling away at her lip, and I knew something was wrong. She took a deep breath and said, "Dorothy, they say we cannot stay at this hotel. They say they did not realize that you were a Negro girl." She paused and nibbled for a moment. "I just don't know what we can do. We have to have a place for you to dress, but we also have to get on to Carnegie Hall to prepare for the contest." Mr. Straitiff didn't say a word, but he was as red as a beet.

I remembered my mother's words: "Dorothy, just hold yourself together." I told Miss Mohr not to worry. We should go straight to the hall. If we could find a delicatessen and get some milk, graham crackers, and bologna, I could make a sandwich, then dress in the Carnegie Hall ladies' room. That's just what we did.

There were seventeen students in the contest, and I drew position number 17. I would be last, which was both good and bad. It was good because I would be fresh in the judges' minds when they made their decision. But it was terrifying because I would have to wait forever to get my assignment. Each contestant drew the subject only ten minutes before going onstage. Until then, they were kept closeted while others were speaking, leaving plenty of time for anxiety. While I waited, I did some exercises a teacher had taught me to make me relax. Finally the time came to draw my subject: the Kellogg-Briand Peace Pact, a treaty among sixty nations, signed in August 1928, which called for the renunciation of war as an instrument of national policy.

Ten minutes later I stepped out onto the stage. I saw two or three thousand people in the audience but only one other person of color—a janitor, standing way in the back by an exit door. He smiled at me.

I had been struck by the assessment of the League of Nations by Aristide Briand, the French statesman who had been one of the key negotiators of the treaty. He argued that it was not the official structure of peace that was important. He said the world could not rely on any machinery to bring peace; machinery was needed to facilitate the process, but peace would come only when people truly wanted it.

I said that I believed that peace would come in the hearts of all people someday, but it would take time. I recalled that two thousand years before, the message of peace had been brought to the world, but there was not room at the inn for the messenger, who was turned away at his birth. His parents were turned away at the inn, just as my principal and teacher had been turned away that afternoon at the Harrisburg Hotel because I was with them and I was a Negro. "But the people at the hotel who turned us away did not know anything about me," I said. "They did not want me simply because my skin was colored."

I proposed that if we could follow Briand's idea, accepting the message that came to us two thousand years ago, we would learn to respect one another. We would try to live with one another and work together. Only as we began to see each other as human beings, I concluded, as part of the same human family, would we find lasting peace.

Several moments later the judges announced that I had won first prize. It was a unanimous judgment by a panel of all-white judges. The outpouring of applause was hard for me to believe, especially as there was no one of my race in the audience. I had just become the Pennsylvania State Champion in Impromptu Speech for the year 1928.

What a day it had been! In the afternoon white people had turned us away from the hotel. But that same evening white judges were fair enough to give me the decision. I had been turned away from a public facility because of my race, but so were my white principal and teacher. They shared my experience, and in that instant they were as black as me. I was representing Rankin High School, and they were responsible for me. They shared my humiliation. And they shared the glory that came with winning.

When it was all over, Mr. Straitiff, Miss Mohr, and I got in the car for the long drive back to Rankin. The next day the high school almost burst with pride. Mr. Straitiff called a special assembly to announce the news. My schoolmates embraced me with affection and admiration. I realized then how much I loved them. They gave me the sense that I could do anything.

When we graduated the following June, they wrote this about me in the Rankin High School yearbook:

> *In every class*
> *There is one apart,*
> *A student of great renown.*
> *And Dorothy, here, has a wonderful start*
> *To win an orator's crown.*

Of all the awards I have received, no citation has meant more to me than that one from my classmates.

Nearly fifty years later Principal Straitiff and I were honored at the first reunion of Rankin High School classes. Fourteen hundred graduates, representing an amazing spectrum of professional callings, came from thirty-nine states. Like a widely dispersed, joyous family coming back together, we all still had that amazing sense that Rankin was not an ordinary school. We sang the alma mater Dolly Slaughter and I had written, and as always, our shared sense of spirit transcended our differences. I felt blessed once again.

Chapter Three

Coming of Age in Harlem

I GRADUATED from high school in June 1929, at the start of the Great Depression, and came out with terrific grades. But you can't eat grades—or pay tuition with them. I needed help, and it came from an unexpected place.

Earlier that year I had gone to a basketball game at the Rankin Christian Center with a group of friends. On the way into the gymnasium, I saw a poster:

WOULD YOU LIKE TO GO TO COLLEGE?
ENTER AN ORATORICAL CONTEST
ON THE CONSTITUTION OF THE UNITED STATES
SPONSORED BY THE IBPO ELKS OF THE WORLD
WIN A FOUR-YEAR SCHOLARSHIP!

I knew nothing about the Independent Benevolent and Protective Order of Elks of the World, but I called the man whose name and telephone number were on the poster. Mr. W. H. Brooks of East Pittsburgh said the contest was open to all. I could hardly wait to tell my mother.

The next day after school, encouraged by Myrtle Peters, my English teacher, I went to the library and did some research on the Constitution. The Elks contest offered several choices of subject—Lincoln and the Constitution, for example. But I was particularly intrigued by the Thirteenth, Fourteenth, and Fifteenth Amendments. Known as the "Reconstruction Amendments," they were drafted after the Civil War by Republicans who wanted to invalidate attempts by southern states to perpetuate slavery under other guises. Together they ensured the basic rights of all persons born or naturalized as U.S. citizens and guaranteed that race could not be a barrier to voting rights.

The language of these amendments meant a lot to me. Already I had begun to discover the gaps between what the Constitution promised and what people of color experienced every day. It is sadly ironic to me that today, seventy-five years later, I am still working to ensure the enforcement of the Reconstruction Amendments.

I became absorbed in the Constitution and wrote volumes about what I was learning. Obviously I had to cut it down to a more manageable form, and there I had the help of Bert Logan, one of the young men from Richmond employed by my father. Bert was like a brother to me. He helped me sift through the material to produce a twenty-minute oration. Miss Peters helped me polish my essay to final form.

The Elks contest was nationwide but began at the local level. Just before the local contest, two of my teachers convinced Mr. Straitiff, our principal, to call a special assembly for me—my own dress rehearsal before a terrific audience of students. They made me feel I had done something really great.

I won the local contest, then those at the county and state levels. The next round, the tri-state, was in Pittsburgh, where finalists from Pennsylvania, Ohio, and West Virginia were to face off. But when I arrived in Pittsburgh, I was confronted with a very awkward situation. A young man named John Thornton was claiming that he, not I, was the Pennsylvania finalist.

Lethia Fleming, an Elks leader from Cleveland who had brought the Ohio winner to the contest, took charge. In a patronizing tone, she said, "It's very clear this young man was the state winner." Nothing I said seemed to get through. She ruled that I could not participate in the contest.

Without telling anyone my plans, I went into the audience and asked my mother for three dollars, then crossed the street to a drugstore and called Judge W. C. Houston, the commissioner of education for the Elks, in Washington, D.C. I reminded him that he had sent me a congratulatory letter after I won the state contest. Now, I explained, I was being told that I was not the winner. Commissioner Houston told me to inform Mrs. Fleming that I had won. If I was not allowed to participate, he would declare the entire contest out of order.

After what seemed to me hours of discussion, the officials decided to have both John Thornton and me present our orations. In the end, at the first ever tri-state contest with two contestants from one state, I was declared the winner.

Years later, John Thornton and I met again in Washington, D.C. He was a leader in the United Steelworkers' Union, and I was active in the National Council of Negro Women; we were often in the same meetings, lobbying for some piece of legislation. He teased me about how I bested him in Pittsburgh. But he always added that I had done a lot for him: "I made up my mind that nobody was going to beat me again after that."

From Pittsburgh I went to the national contest—the last hurdle between me and the four-year college scholarship I needed so badly. It was held in Chicago in an enormous armory, which could seat more people than lived in Rankin. A congressman named Oscar De Priest was the presiding officer. Never before had I seen a Negro in so powerful a position.

Shortly before the contest started, we were told that orations could be no longer than ten minutes. Up to that point the limit had always been twenty minutes, and I was devastated. Judge Houston explained firmly, but kindly, that I would disqualify myself if I did not stay within the time limit. In the short time before the presentation, I thought about what I had learned in impromptu speech contests. I remembered the feedback from classmates on my presentation—the ideas that were clearest and most important. I revised my speech, cut it to ten minutes, and came home with the scholarship.

Judge Houston later said he had never seen a student pursue a contest with such tenacity. He kept in touch while I was in college and invited me to the Elks' convention to speak about what the scholarship meant to me. For the rest of his life he was a wonderful supporter. And I have been thankful ever since to the Elks. Most of those who paid the per capita tax that funded my scholarship did not have the benefits of a college education. When I graduated, one of my first acts was to organize an Elks temple in Brooklyn, New York. I became the first Daughter Ruler of Rose of Sharon Temple Number 655 of the Independent Benevolent and Protective Order of the Elks of the World.

I wanted to become a doctor—a psychiatrist. My oldest brother, William Briggs, told me that New York's Barnard College, with its strong science programs, was my best choice. I applied, backed by a beautiful letter of recommendation from Mr. Straitiff, and took the entrance examination.

In the summer of 1929 my mother took Anthanette and me to New York City to visit William, who was terribly sick with tuberculosis (he would later die from it) and was then being treated at Bellevue Hospital. We returned to Rankin on a Saturday and found a telegram that had been sent the day before, asking me to report for an interview at Barnard the following Monday at 9:00 A.M. If only we had known this while we were in New York! Mother and I scurried to get ready, and she put me on a late Sunday night train back to New York. I was nervous all the way and slept fitfully. The train was twenty minutes late, and I rushed uptown to Barnard.

When I arrived, breathless, in the office of the dean, I was asked to have a seat. It seemed an eternity before the dean finally came to speak to me. I apologized for being late. It didn't matter, she said. Although I had been accepted, they could not admit me. It took me a while to realize that their decision was a racial matter: Barnard had a quota of two Negro students per year, and two others had already taken the spots. "You are young enough to wait for next year," said the dean, meaning, I suppose, to be encouraging.

But I couldn't believe my ears. I was devastated. Since childhood, school had been my love, my life. I wanted to get on with it. I pleaded with her, but she was adamant. Rules were rules, and two young women named Belle Tobias and Vera Joseph were holding the only two precious places for Negro women in Barnard's class of 1933.

I couldn't bear to call home and report that I wasn't going to college after all—that they didn't want me. Crushed and confused, I went to the Harlem apartment of my sister, Jessie Randolph. We called William, who said, in a positive tone, "There are other schools," and urged me to call New York University. Jessie took me to New York University in the Bronx—a mistake, since that branch of the school was for men only. We were referred downtown, to Washington Square in Manhattan. The registrar warned that this was the last day of registration and that the office would close at 8:00 P.M.

Racing, we got to Washington Square at seven. I finally got to see Dean Ruth Schaeffer. She asked to see my diploma, which I did not have with me. She asked whether I had an application to NYU. No. Then Jessie reminded me that the dean at Barnard had given me a letter about my acceptance. That letter was in my purse, along with the transcript of my high school grades and the results of the entrance exam.

Dean Schaeffer studied the letter. I'll never forget her eyes as she looked up. She said, "A girl who makes these kinds of grades doesn't need an application to enroll at NYU." A ray of hope crept into my heart. She gave me a form. When I filled it out, I was matriculated at NYU. From that day forward I have loved every brick of that university.

That fall I moved to New York and began classes at NYU. I took several elective courses in religion, thinking that I might want to work in the church. One day, after a favorite class, the professor, Dr. Samuel Hamilton, asked me to drop by his office. He told me that I was a very good student, but that the church was not ready for women, and the black church surely was not ready for me. "Study it as much as you want," he advised, "but find another field in which you can make a living." That was a revelation for me.

It was not long after the conference with Dr. Hamilton that my brother William died on the operating table at Bellevue. In the car coming back to the city from the cemetery, I sat quietly with my mother, William's wife, Fay, and her young son, Bill. I knew that without William's promised support, I would never be able to go to medical school. That realization—along with Dr. Hamilton's recent advice—led me to choose psychology and social work as my major fields of study.

Through my friend Nettie Berg, who was in my freshman science class, I got connected to a study group. There were seven of us: Nettie, five Jewish boys, and me. We prepared together for exams, each taking responsibility for leading the discussion about a particular part of the material. When we took exams, each agreed to finish in time to memorize at least one question so that we could discuss our answers afterward. This was the most intellectually satisfying and cooperative experience I ever had studying. Many times, when classmates were going to a party or a dance or a boat ride, they would invite me to go along with them. I always came up with some excuse, but the real reason was that I preferred to hold my place with the study group.

All during my college years signs of the deepening depression were everywhere. Men around Washington Square sold apples to students—for a nickel—just to survive. There were no jobs. I earned a bit of money by tutoring Negro teachers who had come to study at NYU from schools in the South. As the National Association for the Advancement of Colored People (NAACP) pushed for the equalization of salaries for Negro and white teachers in southern schools, many Negro teachers were in danger of losing their jobs. They came to northern universities for advanced degrees or special courses to make them more attractive hires. Every college credit counted. Harlemites could be quite disdainful of these teachers from the rural South. "She's at Columbia U. to take two points in penmanship" was the sort of comment you'd often hear.

One teacher with a poor educational background, Margaret Terry, wanted to improve her skills to teach mathematics. She would try to memorize what I was telling her. Again and again I would tell her that memorizing just wasn't enough; she had to understand how to get the answer. When she began to think along with me, we both learned more. She helped me appreciate how important it is to focus your attention when you study. I realized that in the study group I was learning how to learn. And as I taught what I learned I learned even more.

But I missed doing things outside of academics. Martin Harvey, a student I had met in Sam Hamilton's religion course, almost got us thrown out of a study hall one day when he was telling me about an exciting weekend at a youth retreat of the African Methodist Episcopal Zion Church. Older than me, Martin was in charge of the church's youth work. We became like brother and sister. He helped me get connected—and ultimately to become a founding member of the United Christian Youth Movement of North America.

Sorority rush season at NYU was exciting. Those who had the highest grades were chosen first. All grades were posted on the walls, identifying students only by our seat numbers. Through several postings I maintained a straight-A average. Suddenly I was getting sorority bids. I decided to go to one of the rush parties, held in a student lounge. When I got to the door, I was told I was at the wrong lounge. I showed them my invitation. While several flustered white students tried to decide what to do, I stepped into the room. No one approached me. One of the guardians of the door finally explained that I had been invited by mistake. Just for the fun of it, I accepted refreshments from a student who didn't know I was a "mistake." Then I left and went to a student lounge on another floor. My straight-A average kept the invitations coming, and it became a kind of game for me to see how the white sorority women reacted to my presence.

I never really felt rejected by the white sororities. Their members seemed too wrapped up in impressing each other. My real interest was in becoming a member of Delta Sigma Theta, a sorority that had been founded by and for women of color. Lula Howell and Edna Kincheon, the women who had organized the Girl Reserves program back in Rankin, had drilled that idea into me. The rushing experience heightened my desire to find Delta, but at the time there were no Negro organizations at NYU.

Imore Portrait Wright and I decided to change that. Along with twelve other students, we set out to organize an NYU chapter of Delta Sigma Theta. We did the necessary paperwork, and I was designated to take our proposal to the university officials. To be recognized as a sorority at NYU, a majority of the members had to maintain a B average or better. What I didn't know until the dean told me was that most of our group did not have the grades. I did not think of a sorority again until 1939, when I was pursuing advanced studies and finally initiated into Delta Sigma Theta.

But that didn't stop Negro students from getting together in other ways. There was a spirited camaraderie among us at NYU. With thousands of students on campus, it was hard to tell what percentage of the student body we represented, but it was small. Maybe that's why we stuck together and looked out for each other.

I remember Mary Tobias, whose sister Belle had been one of the quota of two barring me from Barnard. Their father, Dr. Channing Tobias, was a distinguished national leader in the Young Men's Christian Association (YMCA) and the National Association for the Advancement of Colored People. In later years he became a mentor and one of my greatest supporters. Marjorie Poole was a Pittsburgher. Thelma Goode had come from Mobile, Alabama, and was very active in social circles.

All of us were as much a part of Washington Square activities as we wanted to be. But we did want to do more together, and so we organized the Ramses Club. Similar organizations were being formed by black students all over town. At Columbia University a group including Kenneth Clark, who became a most distinguished psychologist, organized the Touchtone Club. Negro students at City College also put together a club. There was no partying as such; we simply enjoyed getting together, whether it was for a Sunday afternoon lecture by Dr. W. E. B. Du Bois, discussions of our own about selected topics, an hour with poets like Countee Cullen or Langston Hughes, or an evening with Paul Robeson. Hulan Jack and Carson De Witt Baker, who later became key political leaders in New York, were members of Ramses. The club formed lasting friendships. The intellectual stimulation that made our gatherings so lively helped me to feel at home with serious issues for the rest of my life.

We were incredibly lucky to be going to school right in the midst of the Harlem Renaissance. As an undergraduate, I lived in Harlem with my sister Jessie. She had been in New York for a number of years before Anthanette and I met her on a trip with our mother. She was a very private person, devoted to her family and her church. Her husband, Flannigan Randolph, a postal worker, and their children, Howard, Bernard, and Jean, all embraced me. Howard eventually joined the New York Police Department, becoming one of "New York's finest." Bernard would become an outstanding physician in St. Louis. And Jean would enjoy her own professional work and also her world travels with her husband, who was in the military.

Living with the Randolphs was a good vantage point as I found my place in the big city. Our address in Harlem was 323 Edgecombe Avenue. It was a marvelous time to be there. There was such a richness to the community—so many points of cultural interest. Among the celebrities who lived next door were the Mills Brothers, a legendary quartet, and the Nicholas Brothers, who were perhaps the greatest dancers in American theater at the time.

On Saturday nights Harlem came alive. I remember when the Savoy had two orchestras with continuous music. It was the heart of community life. White people came uptown to dance there and at the Cotton Club. A small restaurant at 135th Street and Seventh Avenue drew crowds with artists who waited tables and entertained after their performances downtown. A quartet might burst into an aria from *Rigoletto*. Fats Waller might play the piano. He could be followed by the likes of Noble Sissle or Eubie Blake. The restaurant was a kind of sanctuary where musicians could jam with each other while the patrons dined. The scene wasn't very competitive because no one was making much money. No matter how talented these musicians were, they were all poor. But no matter how poor they were, they loved their music and wanted to play.

In my graduate school years I lived with a family whose daughter, Frankie Dixon, I had met in a music appreciation class at NYU. Frankie and I were like sisters. Frankie was a concert pianist and later taught music at Howard University. Her mother, Maude Myers, was a designer and milliner, the widow of the composer Will Dixon. Mrs. Myers was very fair, with red hair. She moved in wide circles, long before they were open to Negroes.

The Myers home was an eight-and-a-half-room cooperative apartment at the corner of Seventh Avenue and 114th Street. This co-op building, as elegant as the finest on Park Avenue, was one of the first owned by Negroes. Among its prominent residents was Father Shelton Hale Bishop, the exceptional rector of St. Phillips

Episcopal Church on West 134th Street, a mainstay of the Harlem community.

On the first floor lived a Miss Allen, an outstanding teacher I came to know when I became the first black student teacher at the Little Red Schoolhouse, a private school in Greenwich Village that focused on progressive education. Though Miss Allen was professionally devoted to education in Harlem, she was willing to pay tuition at the Little Red Schoolhouse so that her niece June, who lived with her, could have the finest education possible. June was a beautiful child who looked white, but with her aunt's tutelage she was very proud of being black.

One evening Miss Allen came up to see me, quite disturbed. June had reported that she made Jello in school that day. Miss Allen thought it was a major waste of time and money. I hadn't been at the school long enough to know about Jello making, but I did know what headmistress Elizabeth Irwin told us from the beginning: "You never teach a subject, you always teach a child. You teach children in a way that they will learn, and then things will fall in place for them."

I asked Miss Allen to have June tell me more about the Jello. June was quite clear about what she had been doing, and then I understood: her class had been making *jelly* with various ingredients, and she was learning about measurement proportion. She knew that until she got the right proportions of all the ingredients, the mixture would not gel. Miss Allen was greatly relieved when I explained this approach to numbers and ratios.

After that June and her aunt seemed to involve me in whatever they were doing. I found it heartwarming to have a friendly face in the school where I was the only black adult.

Two doors down from the Myers's apartment was the home of the "Father of the Blues," W. C. Handy. Every so often Mr. Handy would take several of us under his wing and go out to the clubs to hear the great jazz players. Wherever we went, they would play "The St. Louis Blues," his most famous composition. When Mrs.

Handy was living, the couple often invited artist friends to their home. On any given night the great composer-lyricist Andy Razaf might come to try out a new song, or someone who had received accolades for a recording would show up to celebrate. We would listen and sing.

Life was hard during the Depression. But then came Franklin D. Roosevelt's New Deal, and the Works Progress Administration (WPA).* In his fireside chats, President Roosevelt told the country that what was needed was not only national security to protect the United States but social security to protect people's lives. The new WPA program would provide jobs so that people could take care of basic human needs. In those days jobs were so scarce that people grew angry when a job was "stolen" by an outsider. Harlem was no exception. Blacks tended to resent whites who found employment there.

The revival of the old Lafayette Theater on Seventh Avenue was a major WPA project that employed musicians and a wide range of technicians. Mrs. Myers and Frankie persuaded Jimmy Harris, who worked in their home as a caretaker, to apply for a job at the theater. He was taken on as a stagehand and trained to work in other capacities as well. Then one day he announced that he and the other recruits at the Lafayette were planning a strike because two of the main jobs at the theater had been given to white men. My instinctive reaction was to tell Jimmy to concentrate on what he was doing and forget the protest. I did not know anything about the two white men, but I knew that it was in Jimmy's best interest to hold on to his job.

A few days later we learned that the two men whose employment Jimmy was protesting were Orson Welles and John Houseman. The two, already greatly distinguished in the theater, had come to the Lafayette to help its revival, create more jobs, and

---

*The WPA, in operation from 1935 to 1942, was later renamed the Work Projects Administration.

encourage people in the neighborhood to acquire the skills they needed to qualify for bigger, better-paying jobs. Eventually the theater became a beacon of the future, introducing hitherto unknown local talent to appreciative audiences. By then we could all look back and see how funny Jimmy's protest had been. Forever after he would ask me, "Well, how did you know? How did you know that these two white men would help us so much?"

During those years I got to know something I suspect very few people realize about Harlem—that it was many communities of people from all walks of life. Its cultural heritage was complex, like an intricate mosaic. My love of Harlem grew naturally out of the ways my own roots went down, through myriad interests and the spirited people who touched and nurtured me. It was a joy to be there, to feel the exhilaration.

All through my college years I did little jobs to make up the difference between my scholarships and actual costs. My cousin Ethel Sayles, who later became the first black wardrobe mistress for Broadway shows, took care of the laundry for several performers. When she found out that I was good at ironing clothes, she let me assist her. I pressed Eddie Cantor's shirts and Simple Simon's bow ties. I also wrote obituaries at five dollars each for a Harlem mortician. An itinerant minister who officiated at funerals gave me the vital information, and I did the writing.

One day a fellow journalism student at New York University was offered a job as a proofreader on Marcus Garvey's newspaper, *The Negro World*. He didn't need the work, and I convinced him to give it to me. I have been thankful for that ever since. Garvey's Universal Negro Improvement Association was the largest organized movement in black history and a critical link in black America's struggle for equality, justice, and freedom. Although Garvey failed to realize all of his objectives, his movement still represents a liberation from the psychological bondage of racial inferiority. His drive for demonstrated excellence permeated every aspect of his work. That was clear at *The Negro World*, a widely disseminated weekly edited by William Merchant. Pride in excellence was instilled every day. I thrived in that atmosphere.

Not all of my jobs were so rewarding. When one of my school friends needed someone to hold her waitress position while she went on her honeymoon, she gave it to me. I was just the right height and color for this particular "old South" restaurant, where quaint uniforms set the tone. I did very well until one day two customers asked for Worcestershire sauce. I didn't know what it was. I brought them ketchup, mustard—anything I could think of—but nothing I did was right. Other waitresses, fearing competition from a new worker, would do nothing to help. Finally, the hostess showed me a bottle of Worcestershire sauce. After that episode, I decided it was more important to make my grades than to work at the restaurant.

For a while I had a job in a clothing factory on Thirty-seventh Street. I was assigned to put hooks and eyes on girls' collars. I produced many pieces but earned very few dollars because the factory paid just pennies for each one. As we sat on the fire escape eating our lunch one day, an older Italian woman whispered that I should ask the cutter to put me on women's dresses, which were decorated with flowers, because they paid more. For what I was earning, the struggle to compete with workers who knew the ropes just didn't seem worth the effort. Once again I felt it was better to focus on my studies.

NYU required 128 points, now called "credits," for an undergraduate degree, which was generally completed by taking sixteen points each semester for four years. After the first semester of my freshman year, I asked permission to carry twenty points each semester, plus eight points during the intercessions between May and June and eight during summer school. At first my adviser thought this schedule would be too rigorous. But when I presented a straight-A record for the entire year, he agreed to let me try. As a result, I finished my bachelor's degree in three years, graduating in the class of 1932.

Could I use the fourth year of the Elks scholarship for graduate study? When Judge W. C. Houston heard of my achievement, he made matters quite simple. "We called it a four-year scholarship, and that's what you will get," he declared. I could hear his pride over the telephone. "Just keep going," he said.

But even as I commenced my master's program in educational psychology at NYU, I had a lingering yearning to study medicine. I enrolled in two evening classes at the Columbia University School of Pharmacy. I had to get this desire to study medicine out of my system. It did not take long. The more I learned about pharmacy, the more I learned about myself: I would not survive, much less flourish, working with medications, weights, and measurements. My interest was not really in medicine but in serving people. It became clear that social work was the right field for me.

Since the very first day I taught Bible stories in Rankin, I had been drawn to Christian education, and at NYU I took a course in religious education for social workers. It was taught by Professor Ruth Boardman, who sent me on a field assignment to the Brownsville Community Center, established by the Brooklyn Church and Mission Federation in the Brooklyn neighborhood with the highest rates of delinquency and unemployment in all of New York City. Although the neighborhood was predominantly Jewish, there were a few Italians and quite a large Negro population. The center's director, the Rev. W. B. M. Scott, was a Baptist minister who had come to New York from Jamaica. Under him, the center had begun a major feeding program for the unemployed. It was one of the designated distribution points for American Red Cross food packages, and twenty WPA workers provided services and distributed the food.

The challenge of serving a needy population of seventy-five thousand was enormous. I soon became Reverend Scott's assistant, supervising the WPA workers, who earned more each week than I did in a month. Very quickly what had begun as graduate school field work became a real job for me.

The center was eager to have me stay on after I completed my master's degree, but there was no money for my salary. Reverend Scott appealed to the Brooklyn Church and Mission Federation, which arranged a meeting with Mrs. Orrin R. Judd, a principal officer. Reverend Scott described the center's work and the job I carried, making the case for my staying on after completing my master's degree.

Mrs. Judd asked me to tell her about myself. When I said I'd grown up in Rankin, she asked whether I knew of the Rankin Christian Center. I told her I had indeed known it, since I lived right across the street. A strange look came over her face. "Were you the girl who was telling Bible stories to the children in the nursery?" she asked. Amazed, I said I was. Instantly she declared that she would pay my salary at the Brownsville Center.

Although the pay was only twenty dollars a month plus car fare, this was my first real job. And I was immensely pleased. More important, I had found my life's work. I wanted to help people. And this was the perfect place to start.

Chapter Four

"Me Culled Too"

THE BROWNSVILLE Community Center was housed in a loft above a banana warehouse at 187 Osborne Street, Brooklyn, New York. There was terrible overcrowding in the neighborhood, and most people—many of them transplants from the West Indies and the American South—lived in mean, miserable quarters. Crammed together like animals, they felt a terrible sense of alienation and dislocation. They were adrift, cut off from home, washed up on inhospitable shores. I will never forget stepping around two dead bodies on the sidewalk the first day I arrived.

We tried to make the center a place where people of all ages and backgrounds would feel at home. The Reverend Scott was always in and out of court, helping families whose young were in trouble with the law. He persuaded attorneys just out of law school to volunteer their services. I worked with the young women.

Early in my time at the center I had a frightening experience. A group of young men who were well known as the neighborhood tough guys decided to test what I was made of. One summer evening, knowing that the other workers had already gone home, they waited until Reverend Scott left the building.

Except for a lavatory and a small kitchen, the center was one wide open space. To give it some form, Reverend Scott had built a platform at one end, in front of the windows, with a railing and a small gate. That evening I was working at a desk on the platform, alone in the enormous loft.

Suddenly the door opened, and in swaggered a gang of young men. They wore no shirts, and they were a terrifying sight. I recognized two, because Reverend Scott had just gotten them out of jail. They started firing questions at me: Who was I? Where did I come from? What did I think I was doing?

They grew more and more vulgar. I was only nineteen, and scared to death, but I felt I had to appear calm. I knew about some of the violence these boys had been part of, and how they treated their mothers and young women. I was too frightened to go to the telephone, or even to move from my seat. There was no one I could signal, no one I could call for help. My only defense was to be polite and pretend they were there for the serious business of the center.

I explained what the center was about—that we were there to be of help—and asked what I could do for them. I had accompanied Reverend Scott to the home of two of the young men, the Stubbs brothers, so I reminded them that I knew some of their families.

No matter what I said, their teasing became steadily rougher. Finally, one of the Stubbs brothers spoke up. "She's okay," he said. "Let's get on." And slowly he led the group out. I never really knew what they were after, or whether my terrified calm disarmed them. But after that incident those boys became my friends. They looked out for me as I went through the neighborhood.

Years later the show *This is the Army, Mr. Jones* played in Washington, D.C., where I was living. My cousin, Major Campbell C.

Johnson, executive director of the Twelfth Street branch of the YMCA, invited me to come to a special luncheon that the YMCA was giving in honor of the show's cast—and there among the dancing stars were the Stubbs brothers. One of them whispered, "Don't tell them you knew us as delinquents." I smiled. On the contrary, I said, I was there to show everyone that I knew celebrities. Underneath I was grateful to realize that perhaps some of what we had tried to do in Brownsville during those dark Depression days had been worthwhile.

Reverend Scott was concerned that so many who had migrated into Brownsville were adapting to the predominantly Jewish culture, forsaking their own. He noted, for instance, that church didn't matter to most of them, even though Sunday service had once been a central part of their lives. But this apparent abandonment of spiritual calling was as much about economics as anything else. One of the few "jobs" available to blacks in Brooklyn during the Depression was making fires and doing other small chores for Orthodox Jewish families from Friday evening, when their Sabbath started, until Saturday evening, when it ended. When you asked Negro men what they did, they'd reply, "I light fires." It took me a while to catch on to what that meant, and why so many followed the rhythm of the Jewish week.

Sunday, accordingly, had become the day to shop and do chores, just as it was for Orthodox Jews. Troubled by this, Reverend Scott decided to add some spiritual enrichment to our program of economic relief. Since few of our clients expected to participate in any formal religious activity on Sunday morning, we decided to start a Sunday School for children at 6:00 P.M. After a few months, we moved it to 4:00 P.M., then to 2:00 P.M., and finally to 10:00 A.M.

As the Sunday School got under way, Reverend Scott appealed to the adults in the community to join the church. As he had for the children, he started with a service late Sunday afternoon. Then, little by little, he moved the hour up to eleven in the morning. We called it the Universal Baptist Church, and even though the "church" was in our loft over the banana repository, people responded enthusiastically. Most were Baptist or Methodist, and we had a few Presbyterians as well, and even an Episcopalian or two. Reverend Scott encouraged marriages and offered baptisms and funerals, which many immigrants to the area had been missing since they left home. The Universal Baptist Church was popular because it responded to people's earthly needs.

They had spiritual needs as well, of course—and not only in Brownsville. When I was still a student of religion at NYU, I had met Horatio Seymour Hill, then director of Christian education at the Abyssinian Baptist Church in Harlem. He and others at that venerable church had been an important part of my student life. Mr. Hill introduced me to a church school teacher named Olivia Pearl Stokes, and through her I got to know the church's pastor, Adam Clayton Powell Sr. Dr. Powell was writing a book at the time, and he would invite Olivia and me to talk with him about it. He raised profound questions and expected thoughtful replies. He had a delightful sense of humor, and it was fun being with him.

Since those days, Mr. Hill had become the director of the Baptist Educational Center, and when he learned about my work at the Brownsville Center, he asked me to teach in the Columbia University extension program in religion. So in addition to my Brownsville duties, I started teaching classes for intermediate church school teachers and administrators. Mr. Hill also got me to teach a course for vacation Bible school teachers at the Friends Seminary on Saturdays. The pay was a great help.

In addition, I volunteered to work with the Brooklyn Bureau of Charities, especially on problems of youth. One of the supervisors liked my work and brought me to the attention of Jean Kallenberg in the personnel office of the New York City Welfare Administration. Miss Kallenberg decided to recruit me as an investigator for the Home Relief Bureau, a job that paid $27.50 a week.

This was so much more than I was earning at the Brownsville Center—just $20.00 a month!—that I had to give it serious consideration. I loved my work with Reverend Scott. I worked not only for the money but for the sense of mission. So many eager young people and their families had endeared themselves to me. And at the center I was free to do my extra teaching work on Saturdays, whereas the Home Relief Bureau strictly required a six-day work-week. But Miss Kallenberg was persistent. In the end I accepted her offer.

The Home Relief Bureau aimed to put unemployed people to work helping other unemployed people find jobs. The need was enormous. There were about 200,000 families with no employed member—more than a million New Yorkers in need of help with necessities such as food and shelter. Very few on the staff had any training in social work. My first position was as a caseworker in District 65 in Brooklyn. Ruth Kaunitz, the administrator, seemed very pleased to have someone who knew firsthand the problems of poor people and felt comfortable working with them.

Our unit was made up of eleven young men and me. Nine of the men were Jewish, two were black. They were very bright, all college graduates. Our supervisor, an immigrant from Ireland named Sylvia Croak, was smart, but she had no education beyond the eighth grade and no relevant work experience. She was extremely rigid, terrified of abrogating official policy, and confounded by any unusual situation. Not surprisingly, there was perpetual tension between Miss Croak and the aggressive young men under her supervision. Sometimes they poked fun at her; the rest of the time they simply ignored her.

From time to time, when I found myself struggling with Miss Croak's by-the-book mentality, I would think back to lessons from childhood. When I was scornful of children who didn't learn as fast as I, my mother would insist that if I was so much smarter, I should help the others. I suppose that is why I tried to get my fellow case-workers to stop harassing Miss Croak. I felt we should honor her position and help her, and Miss Croak appreciated me for it. She and I developed a warm relationship. She told me a little of her life since coming to the United States. She laughed at how surprised she had been to find money under the plates whenever she sat down at a restaurant table. She thought Americans were either very careless or unusually generous, she did not know which. It took a while before she learned not to take the change—to leave it for the server.

I worked in the Williamsburg section of Brooklyn, where the unemployment rate was exceptionally high. The Unemployment Council, an advocacy group for the jobless, made regular visits to our office, representing people on welfare or those who had been rejected. There was one man around whom the others seemed to rotate. He would storm in with a long list of demands and say, loud and clear, that he was not leaving until every one of them had been addressed.

I had been at the Home Relief Bureau for just six months when the administrator, Mrs. Kaunitz, proposed an unusual new assignment. The commissioner of welfare had asked that we study the role of administrator in selected district offices. In each one a staff member was to shadow the administrator every day for a month. Mrs. Kaunitz, a vivacious, outspoken person, had chosen me to take on this responsibility in her office because, she said, I had the "right temperament." She said she needed someone who was not easily upset under pressure.

I was immediately relieved of my caseload. Seated next to Mrs. Kaunitz at her desk, I recorded every activity of her day—every contact, every interview, every telephone call. It was a splendid opportunity to learn about the welfare system. I also got to know Mrs. Kaunitz personally. She lived on Central Park West, and often we met on the subway in the morning at the Ninety-sixth Street station and rode together to Brooklyn. On one of those rides she asked if I would be her personal representative and liaison to the Unemployment Council.

There had been no letup in the council's visits to our office. Sometimes they would bring in as many as fifty people and tie up the entire office. More than once, when the situation got very tense, Mrs. Kaunitz asked me to act as her representative. I developed enough rapport with the disgruntled council members to allow us, at least, to keep order. It was not always possible to produce what they demanded, but often there was a compromise that was acceptable, so long as they felt that their needs were acknowledged and their demands not simply ignored.

I particularly remember a woman named Rose Ganz. She was on welfare, and she had no teeth. She had gone to a clinic to get false teeth and had been refused because she couldn't pay for them. The Unemployment Council made Rose Ganz's teeth an issue, but there was no provision in the welfare system for dental assistance. Mrs. Ganz would settle for nothing short of a full set of false teeth, however, and so week after week I would tell her that the matter would be considered. The situation got hotter and hotter. Then I learned that dental students at a local hospital were taking on a few clients on a pro bono basis. Imagine my relief when I was able to refer Mrs. Ganz to the aspiring dentists to get new teeth!

My encounters with council representatives taught me the importance of really listening and giving people the sense that their concerns are being heard. I learned to deal with conflict without intensifying it, to understand why saying things like, "We don't have a policy on that question," or, "There's nothing we can do to help you," is inflammatory. If you listened to people, then figured out what the welfare system, limited though it was, could do to help, you could get a little respect from them even though they were hungry, frustrated, and angry because "the system" seemed so hopelessly inadequate. As a representative of the Welfare Administration, no matter what I thought or how much more I wished we could grant, I would not denounce the system as long as I believed that it offered channels through which you could work for change.

Several weeks after my study of the role of the administrator was completed, the commissioner announced that, among all of the office surveys that had been undertaken, the report of Mrs. Kaunitz's operation was best. Mrs. Kaunitz was very pleased by that and began to think that I could handle a bigger job. Not too long after that I was invited by the borough office to become a special investigator.

The principal job of special investigators was to examine allegations of fraud. In poignant testimony to public desperation, people were constantly filing complaints about each other. Seeing a neighbor well dressed and going out, an observer would write a letter to the Welfare Administration, saying, "They have a job and yet they're on welfare." Or if someone saw a man coming back and forth into a neighbor's apartment, she would write, "Mrs. So-and-so is cheating. She's getting welfare for her children, and she says there is no man in her house, but that is not true." And so on. It was sad how disconnected and distrustful people felt. Most of the letters were written by welfare recipients, but some were from people who resented the idea of welfare: "I'm going to work every day, and they are sitting home and getting taxpayers' money." With or without work, people were hurting because jobs were so scarce, and those who did find work labored hard and long for little pay.

In those early experimental days of the welfare system, New York City Mayor Fiorello LaGuardia had made it official policy that every complaint was to be investigated. Eligibility requirements were very stringent, and we had to do our utmost to see that they were observed. Since many of the complaints were anonymous, it was an enormous task. Sometimes our search involved hunting for responsible relatives to try to get them involved in supporting their family members.

Several members of the special investigators unit had legal training. They had—and used—the authority to search for all kinds of resources through banks, businesses, and industry. Many of my colleagues in the special investigation unit demonstrated detectives' zeal as they approached the alleged ne'er-do-wells, determined to eliminate wasteful misappropriation of scarce city resources. But despite the effort to serve in good faith, there seemed to be no way

to escape the climate of distrust within the community and the pervasive assumption that *all* people on welfare were chiselers or con
artists.

When I arrived at the borough office, I was assigned to make a
study of the first one hundred families accepted for relief in Brooklyn—to find out where they were and whether they had found jobs
or were still on welfare. These questions rarely could be answered
easily. Real money was so scarce that often people stayed on welfare a little while after they got a job so they could buy some
clothes and get on their feet. If you had been on welfare for a year
and didn't have decent clothes, how could you go into the work-
force? The system failed to provide for this transition. I had trouble
faulting people who took into their own hands what the law should
have done.

Sometimes when I'd call to set up an appointment to investigate a family's situation, the head of the household would say, "You
needn't come. We're going off welfare. Go ahead and close our
case." That meant they probably had stretched the system a bit
and were overdue for closure.

In the Red Hook section of Brooklyn, there were many people
who had come from Puerto Rico with no English and no employ-
able skills. It was almost impossible to figure out what was happening with them. So many people crowded together into living
quarters that it was hard even to identify who was who. Neighbors
protected one another, as I'd seen people do in Harlem and in
other poor areas. But people often were very helpful too, and I
grew to appreciate some of the difficulties faced by welfare recipients—the constant surveillance, the loss of control over your life,
and, at the bottom, the loss of self-esteem. I was often irked when
I witnessed the disrespect shown to heads of families as they came
to get help. I saw relief for what it was—temporary help—but I
came to realize that the way we gave the help was more important
than what was given. The bureau was always being accused of
"fostering dependency." Few people took the time to see that it

was the way we treated our clients, rather than the basic structure of the welfare program, that got in the way of their independence.

One of the cases I examined got me mixed up with the notorious Adamowitz brothers, who had been indicted for smuggling whiskey across state lines. One of their workers had carelessly poured hot mash into a container of ashes, causing an explosion that injured several people next door. When one of the injured reported the incident, he claimed that a young Hispanic man was the culprit. Moreover, he asserted, the offender was receiving welfare for which he was ineligible because he was employed. As the young Hispanic was a member of one of the first one hundred welfare families I'd been asked to review, the investigation fell to me.

When I went to the young man's home, his family denied his existence. I had no choice but to go to his alleged place of employment, way over on the other side of Brooklyn. It was near dusk by the time I got to the Adamowitz brothers' plant. It appeared deserted, but when I tapped on a door, a man flung it open. I jumped back in fright. The man asked me to identify myself. It turned out they were FBI agents, casing the place. The Adamowitz brothers had fled to Europe but were expected to return, and the authorities were preparing an ambush for their arrest. Unintentionally, I had wandered into the middle of a crime scene.

A few weeks later I was called to prepare testimony and identify the young Hispanic worker in court. The poor man! He spoke very little English and clearly did not realize what he had been doing when he emptied the mash into the container of ashes. He seemed a pathetically small figure in a very big, complicated case. He had to have special representation because of the larger FBI investigation. In addition, he had not reported any employment, was still receiving his relief payments, and therefore had to answer to the Home Relief Bureau as well. I was greatly relieved the day this matter was removed from my hands because of the larger litigation in progress.

When I started the study of the first one hundred Brooklyn families on welfare, sixty-six cases were still active. Most of the others had either found work or had given up. By the time I ended my investigation, I concluded that thirty-seven of the original one hundred cases would not close in the foreseeable future. Ten or twelve others were families who seemed to have pretty good prospects and were looking forward to getting off the relief rolls. The majority of my original one hundred cases were closed.

Mrs. Kaunitz was pleased to have me return to the district office, and strangely enough, so were the members of the Unemployment Council. I was promoted to unit supervisor and put in charge of a group of special investigators.

It was 1935. A sense of entrenched desperation had taken root across the city, especially in black and Hispanic neighborhoods. Harlem was by far the largest and most dense. In a geographic area of no more than three and one-half square miles, some 200,000 Negroes lived, crowded into largely substandard housing, accorded woefully inadequate educational and health facilities, and denied employment by local white merchants, who generally charged them terrible prices for inferior goods. Jobs were hard to find for anyone, but people of color faced blatant discrimination even when they qualified for the few jobs available. Negroes, only 8 percent of the city's population, made up 42 percent of the unemployed on welfare. They were even denied positions on work projects set up by the welfare system. There was not a single person of color in a position of authority on the management staff of the Welfare Administration.

On March 19, 1935, it took no more than a rumor—that a black youth suspected of shoplifting had been struck by a white policeman on 125th Street—to start a riot. As the rumor spread and grew, people streamed into the streets, repeating increasingly dramatic accounts of a brutal, racist murder. Looters roamed the streets, breaking store windows, attacking buses, and shouting at police. By nightfall it hardly mattered what the original provocation actually had been.

No story about the disturbance was more poignant than that of the Chinese laundry on Seventh Avenue. As storefronts were being systematically smashed, the laundry owner scribbled across his windows, "ME CULLED TOO." People laughed, but his building was not touched. It stood out proudly amid the rubble of white-owned storefronts around it. The next day the *New York Post* editorialized, "It would have been impossible to inflame Harlem residents had there not been discrimination in employment and on relief and justifiable complaints of high rents and evil living conditions."

On the second day of the riot Mayor LaGuardia appealed for calm and announced that he was appointing a special committee headed by the Reverend John Johnson of St. Martin Episcopal Church to look into the cause of the riot. Reverend Johnson's biracial Citizens Committee on Harlem made many crucial recommendations, including a stipulation that black professionals be appointed to some of the policymaking positions in the central office of the Home Relief Bureau. There were a few black administrators in the district offices, especially in Harlem, but the committee said this was not enough.

Shortly after the committee issued its report, Anna Arnold Hedgeman, a widely respected social activist in Harlem, was appointed special adviser to the city's welfare commissioner, Charlotte Carr. Anna also was to serve as the minority representative in the Welfare Administration, but neither of these moves fully satisfied the Citizens Committee. They insisted that a black professional be appointed to a senior position in the personnel office because what really mattered was recruiting and placing blacks in key staff positions out in the district offices. When Commissioner Charlotte Carr asked district office administrators to name staff who might qualify, Ruth Kaunitz proposed me.

During the summer after the Harlem riot, while the committee was making its study, I attended the Conference of the United Christian Youth Movement at Lakeside, Ohio, using part of my vacation. When I returned to the Home Relief Bureau, I found a notice summoning me to meet with Commissioner Carr. Such a summons always suggested the possibility of a reprimand. But I was well fortified by the conference I had attended to face almost anything. Bravely, I went to the central office.

Charlotte Carr was an impressive woman with a no-nonsense attitude. She said that the recommendations for me had been so strong that she had decided to make me a personnel supervisor in the central office. Her only hesitation was that she was aware that I was very active in the union in the district office. She stressed that a personnel supervisor always had to represent management.

I felt overwhelmed by the enormous responsibility I was being asked to carry, but I knew that my previous assignments had prepared me well for this new one. I also felt tremendous gratitude for all those who had helped me along the way, especially Mrs. Kaunitz, who had so much faith in me. When I called to thank her, I was told that she had been stricken and hospitalized. She was dying. I owed Ruth Kaunitz so much. How I wished that I could have told her what she meant to me.

Placed in charge of all central office services, I was responsible for recruiting and employing specialists in health, nutrition, home economics, ophthalmology, insurance, and various other fields. I was also responsible for several thousand workers in two district offices and all the major special services the Welfare Administration provided citywide. I represented the administration at hearings on cases of discrimination or dismissals that were being challenged, for any reason, and I was often called upon by the commissioner and by my colleagues as a resource on issues that concerned relations among people of different races. I was all of twenty-three years old.

More than once I thanked God for Anna Hedgeman, the welfare commissioner's special adviser on minority affairs. Anna and I spent many hours in earnest consultation and became treasured friends. She had a perspective on overall policy, and I could tell her what was happening on the ground. Sometimes she'd anticipate policy changes and alert me so that I could see what practical steps had to be taken to make them work. Other times I would advise her about an issue, and together we would work out how to tackle it, thinking through strategies for holding the gains we'd made in minority recruitment while at the same time achieving the department's overall goals. In the beginning, our coworkers often tried to divide us. It didn't work. Our common concern was the welfare of our workers and of the administration. We also had a special dedication to the well-being of those who were the last hired and, all too often, the first fired.

I had learned early on that when you work in an agency, you are the voice of that agency. At the same time, I found that my previous involvement with the union—precisely the issue that had made Charlotte Carr hesitate in appointing me—was extremely useful. More than once it was valuable to be able to communicate directly with union leaders. When hearings resulted in dismissals, there was understandable disappointment. But the trauma was reduced, I believe, because throughout the welfare system people knew that every possible step had been taken to ensure a fair outcome.

Over time my white colleagues and I were able to increase the number of black men and women in the district offices as well as at the central office. It was clear that without a conscious and deliberate effort to place or promote workers of color, little or no progress would be made. Gradually, white colleagues came to understand that it was their responsibility to be constantly aware of the racial distribution among their staff and the racial factor in their work. I was gratified when they no longer turned to me every time the race issue came up.

Little by little, my coworkers reached the point where they felt comfortable discussing racial issues objectively. They accepted their responsibility to strive for equitable job distribution, and they could be honest about unqualified black candidates without fearing that they would be judged as prejudiced. At the same time, they learned that if they failed to raise the issues, I would. Often they made up their minds to beat me to it. I was very pleased when that happened.

On evenings when I didn't have to work, I sought out friends who were wrestling with even larger issues, like the nature of capitalism and the possibilities of other forms of government, or how to relate faith to social and political action. I was active in the United Christian Youth Movement, the Harlem Youth Council, the New York State Christian Youth Council, and the American Youth Congress. And after a while I realized that I enjoyed these extracurricular activities more than anything.

One day, when I was returning to New York City from a conference on "Christian Youth Building a New World," I told Amy Blanche Green about my dilemma. As the director for youth work at the Greater New York Federation of Churches, Amy had worked closely with us in the New York State Christian Youth Council. We had become real friends. I told her that I had a good job and I needed it, but that I had come to understand my life's work as more than a job. I felt that my interest in youth and Christian education and human service called for more than I could expect at the Welfare Administration. I was trying hard to put into practice some of the principles we had discussed in the United Christian Youth Movement.

A few days later Amy Green called to tell me she had an idea. I went right over to see her. When I arrived, she told me that she was anticipating giving up her position at the Federation of Churches and that she had recommended me to succeed her.

It felt like the answer to my prayers. Her proposal seemed especially portentous because just a few days before she had told the Youth Council that there would be a World Conference on Life and Work of the Churches meeting, focusing on life and work, in England that summer of 1937. It would draw church leaders from all over the world, and it would include thirty-five young people—ten of whom would represent the United States. I had been chosen to be one of the ten American delegates. It was like a dream.

Now, as I sat in Amy Blanche Green's office, letting her words sink in, I knew I was turning an exciting corner. It didn't take long for me to resign from the Welfare Administration and to accept the position at the Greater New York Federation of Churches.

Chapter Five

Building a New World

S HORTLY AFTER I concluded my studies at NYU, I was elected
an officer of the United Christian Youth Movement of North
America (UCYM), whose slogan, "Christian Youth Building a New
World," I took very seriously. By 1937, when I resigned from the
Welfare Administration, I was president of the New York State
Christian Youth Council and chair of the Harlem Youth Council,
and I represented UCYM in the American Youth Congress. More-
over, when A. Philip Randolph founded the National Negro Con-
gress to focus especially on the economic plight of Negro
Americans, I became an officer in its National Youth Congress.

In every one of these groups we grappled with tough issues. We
challenged each other from a wide range of political, social, and
religious convictions. In spirited discussion, we talked about whatever affected our lives, but always in the context of the larger
world, of our faith, and of changes geared toward action. Our

agenda ranged from boy-meets-girl issues to race, employment, and world peace.

Ever since childhood, I had been very curious about whatever was happening around me. My direct contact with people on welfare and the unemployed heightened my concern for the less fortunate. Amy Blanche Green, in her work as director of youth work of the Greater New York Federation of Churches, had greatly expanded my thinking. She was a remarkable person with a strong commitment to young people. Our New York youth group met with her regularly at a cooperative restaurant on Twenty-third Street. The agenda always included unconventional thinkers who challenged us to relate our faith to real-world problems. We were exposed to people like Larry Hosey of the Labor Temple, whose views on the economic system, work, and jobs were unlike any I'd ever heard. Concepts like the distribution of wealth and the unevenness of opportunity were new to me. I had never before thought about the collective responsibility we all bear for husbanding the treasures of the earth; what was in the mines near Rankin, for instance, did not belong to the mine owners but to all of us.

Although I had known and worked to help countless struggling individuals and families during the Depression, I had not recognized the fundamental flaws in our system, nor had I grasped the reasons why the enormous burden of our collapsed economy weighed so heavily on so many. Now I began to realize that although it was important, for example, to send Christmas baskets to the poor, as we had done at Emmanuel Baptist Church, it was not enough. I became conscious of the system and of its role, if it was working properly, in helping people to help themselves.

I remember especially the British political scientist Harold Laski. Famous for his savage polemics against capitalism, Laski also argued eloquently for political pluralism. "We owe no church or state a blind and unreasoning obedience," he said. "We owe it only the deepest insights of which our judgments are capable." I felt freed by those words and encouraged to question our own economic system. I was eager to examine issues like the distribution of wealth and opportunity, and I saw that there was nothing wrong with questioning—even criticizing—what government does.

The Harlem Youth Council also had a full agenda. Meeting at the Harlem YMCA once or twice a week, we took on problems of the community. Fortified with the help of eighty-eight other youth groups that cooperated when we needed massive social action, we tackled any form of discrimination we found. Together, Juanita Jackson of the NAACP and I organized the United Youth Committee Against Lynching. Whenever there was a lynching anywhere in the country, the NAACP headquarters at Fifth Avenue and Fourteenth Street downtown would hang out a black sign with white letters: "A Man Was Lynched Today." When that sign went up, we would call the member organizations, put on black armbands, take out our "Stop Lynching" buttons, and march around Forty-second Street and Times Square chanting "Stop the lynching."

The Harlem Youth Council brought together a remarkable group. In addition to Juanita Jackson—later Juanita Jackson Mitchell—we had Ethel James Williams, who later joined the faculty of the Howard University School of Social Work, and men like James Farmer, a student at Bishop College and later a founder of the Congress of Racial Equality (CORE). Kenneth Clark, then a student at City College, became the psychologist whose research helped persuade the U.S. Supreme Court to declare school segregation unconstitutional. Clinton Hoggard became a bishop in the AME Zion Church, and James Robinson, a student at Union Theological Seminary, went on to found and direct Operation Crossroads Africa and also served as John F. Kennedy's ambassador-at-large to Africa. Madison Jones later became an executive with Metropolitan Life. John Morsell became an NAACP executive.

These were the days of the United Front, when liberals, socialists, and Communists came together to fight fascism. We would gather to hear speakers like the great socialist leader Norman Thomas. There was no reason to fear meeting across political lines.

Because of the United Front, I got to know and work with Carl Ross, Henry Winston, Tony Morton, and other leaders of the Young Communist League. Communist and non-Communist, we were young people laboring together on issues about which we cared passionately.

It was an exhilarating time, a time to clarify just where I stood. A turning point for me was a meeting one evening in Greenwich Village. I don't remember what the subject was, but all of a sudden a young man turned to me and said, "Dorothy, I wish you would stop bringing in all that Christian stuff." Everyone stopped talking. Then he said, "Don't you know that I can fly in the face of your God?" I was stunned. Within the close-knit Christian family in which I came up, the suggestion that anyone could "fly in the face of" God was unconscionable. I thought about his charge for a moment, then asked, "Did it ever occur to you that my God gave you the capacity to learn to fly?"

After this exchange, I sat very still. It was the first time in my life I had to defend my faith, and it took my breath away. But in that brief exchange, I saw clearly how dialectical materialism and communism diverged from the values that are basic to my religious faith. I knew that my commitment to my faith and my work would never waver. I also understood a lot more than I had known before about how to operate in the midst of difference. It was a challenging moment of grace.

Though it was clear to me that I was not and never could be a Communist, I went to all kinds of Young Communist meetings after that. Many of us discovered among Communists new angles on ways to make our democracy work better. There was a remarkable vitality in the democratic experience as we lived it then. We knew it was more than a matter of majority rule or self-determination or multiparty systems. We were engaged in a serious struggle around the fundamental principles of a democratic society—how it could function fairly, remain true to its purpose, and serve all.

Among the Communists were some of the best minds that I had

ever come upon. The tactics I learned from them have something to do with my staying power today. I learned from the Communists that you have to listen, you have to be alert, and you have to watch what's going on. They had a philosophy, a program, and a passion.

The Young Communists also helped me understand the nature of militancy. Once they got the party line, they stuck to it and to each other in the best "communal" tradition. We Christians, on the other hand, celebrated our diversity and our democratic principles. I found this both a strength and a weakness. Christians often had the big theoretical picture, but it was a constant struggle to bring everyone together so that we could move forward on a given task. Communists would say, "Everybody has to have a job," but Christians would hem and haw and say, "Well...maybe some people can't work." Too often, people in Christian groups babbled on about how "all men are created equal" or "we're all children of God," but if you asked them what line they were going to pursue to make those ideas reality, their convictions seemed to crumble. "Oh, well," they'd say, "I think you're terrific, but my neighbors wouldn't understand having blacks come into our area to live." They'd always have some excuse for not taking direct action. Ever since those days, I cannot necessarily say that the actions of people who are "radical" or "militant" are wrong. I see their militancy as a way to attack a problem head-on rather than as a negative abstraction. At its best, direct action is indeed militant.

I learned in those United Front meetings that if you want to change somebody's mind about something, you must try to find out where he or she is coming from. What experience underlies this person's words? What hurt or fear is gnawing at his or her heart? If you understand these questions, you will know how to engage anyone constructively. I learned too that you must be open to new ideas. You need to know where you want to go, but if you don't look both to the left and to the right as you proceed, you will miss things that might help you on your way. Of course, you have to know yourself and where you stand.

Those years were a time of political involvement for young people more compelling, I believe, than any time since. We acted because we believed in something. Today young people want to know, "How can *I* advance?" Our question was, "How can *we* make sure that people everywhere move ahead?" We really believed, in those endless meetings, that we were building a new world. My early experience at the Emmanuel Baptist Church in Rankin had given me a foundation in the Bible and a sense of mission to be of service to the community, but it was in these youth group sessions in New York that I discovered the true spirit of social gospel.

Thanks to the national youth movements, I was actively engaged in helping to shape the agenda that set the goals for which I struggled for many years: laws to prevent lynching, the breakdown of segregation in the armed forces, free access to public accommodations, equal opportunity in education and employment, security for the aged and infirm, protection for children, reform of the criminal justice system, an end to bias and discrimination in housing, and recognition of women's rights. I was determined to make America worthy of her stated ideals.

The burdens of poverty, of widening gaps between rich and poor, of gangs, of children having children, of unspeakable neglect and abuse within families, of young people crushed in the tangled web of drugs and violence—these problems, alas, are still with us. I take every opportunity to share with young people what I have learned about the value of organizations. I urge them to join groups whose purposes challenge the best within them. I know from experience that more is accomplished together than one can do alone.

Not long after I became vice chairman of the United Christian Youth Movement in 1935, Oliver Powell, the chairman, and I spoke up to our national administrative body. The UCYM board was composed of highly respected, able people, but they were all over forty. We strongly recommended that young people should play a part. Not long after that, Oliver and I, an interracial team, became the first youth representatives on the UCYM board.

Soon afterward, Walter Howlett, treasurer of Riverside Church, told us that he wanted to try to get support for our youth work from the Colgate Corporation. He invited us to a luncheon to tell William Colgate, the president, what it meant to us to be part of the Christian youth movement.

We were delighted to have this opportunity, but when we discovered that the luncheon was to be held on Wall Street and that the board would be paying five dollars for each plate, Oliver and I said it was against our principles to have such an expensive luncheon in the midst of so much unemployment. We suggested instead that we meet at the cooperative restaurant on Twenty-third Street, where our youth group always met. Mr. Howlett smiled and said the hot dogs and baked beans would make Mr. Colgate "so uncomfortable he wouldn't give us a dime, even though he is a great Christian." So we reluctantly joined the men for lunch on Wall Street. Our message must have gotten through, and the sacrifice of our principles must have been worthwhile, because a week or so later Mr. Colgate made a generous contribution to the United Christian Youth Movement.

Oliver and I constantly reiterated our concern about the need for more youth representation on the board. Finally, Mr. Howlett took us aside and said, "Don't you two have any other message that you want to bring to this board? We want to hear what you think, not just your complaint that more youth should be here."

That incident taught me that even if you are a token, you have an important function to fulfill. Many times since, when I have been the only African American or the only woman in a situation, I have spoken up for greater representation. But I have always first made a point of contributing my thinking to the work at hand. The value of a group is that each member brings the benefit of his or her life experience. If you hold back, not only is the group deprived, but you have lost an opportunity to contribute.

In the summer of 1935 a Christian youth conference at Lakeside, Ohio, deepened my sense of what it meant to practice what I believe. On the very first day three thousand young people were called to test our faith in new ways as we listened to the keynote address. "How long will it be before you are thrown in jail?" Kirby Page, the speaker, challenged. "How long will it be before you are persecuted by those you love?" As he spoke, the life and work of Jesus and the principles by which He lived crackled with authenticity and power.

Not everyone at Lakeside was on the same track. There were those who felt that Christians should not be involved in political and social matters. Their principal concern was qualifying for passage into paradise. Others believed that if each of us could fundamentally change our hearts and minds, cleansing ourselves of our mortal sins, we would become true Christians and our problems would be solved. Some wanted to blur the distinctions among us and do away with denominations, while others wanted to convert everyone else to their own way of thinking. Wherever you stood, you had to join the fray. We talked far into the night, and no matter how or where we ended in the evening, the message the following morning always seemed to bring us back together.

Given the wide diversity of religious experience, there were often negative reactions to the worship services. But something extraordinary happened when Paul E. Deitz, the great musician and hymnist, introduced the hymn he had composed for the United Christian Youth Movement. He brought us all together through song.

I had volunteered for the conference choir, which Paul Deitz trained to lead the large group in learning the hymn, "We Would Be Building." For the first time I truly appreciated my father's insistence that all verses of a hymn should be sung.

In teaching the choir the hymn, Paul Deitz first read each verse and spoke of its meaning. Then he read the whole hymn, stressing its direction, its motion, and its action—how it called for our commitment, steadfastness, and participation in service. Each day one verse was the theme for worship and for discussion. "We would be building," the first verse, called forth our commitment to the higher purposes of the United Christian Youth Movement. "Teach us to build," in the second verse, challenged us always to seek to understand, to find meaning and the will of God in our lives. "O, keep us building, Master"—the third theme—was a reminder of the source of our strength in God's love for a lifetime of obedience and service. Whenever we gathered, we sang the song, which seemed to bring us closer, giving us energy to go on with our work:

We would be building; temples still undone,
O'er crumbling walls their crosses scarcely lift;
Waiting till love can raise the broken stone
And hearts creative bridge the human rift;
We would be building; Master, let thy plan
Reveal the life that God would give to man.

Teach us to build; upon the solid rock
We set the dream that hardens into deed
Ribbed with the steel that time and change doth mock,
Th'unfailing purpose of our noblest creed;
Teach us to build; O Master, lend us sight
To see the towers gleaming in the light.

O, keep us building, Master; may our hands
Ne'er falter when the dream is in our hearts,
When to our ears there come divine commands
And all the pride of sinful will departs;
We build with thee; O, grant enduring worth
Until the heavenly kingdom comes on earth.

My growing insights made me long to merge more completely the way I earned my living with what I was coming to see as my life's purpose—working toward a more just society. Almost every day at the Home Relief Bureau I had gained new understanding about the workings of the real world. In the evenings, when we gathered at the restaurant on Twenty-third Street, each of us would talk about our daily work. Through our shared stories and observations, we learned to scrutinize our society seriously, to see the way it functioned—its strengths, its weaknesses, when it worked well, when and why it failed. We were concerned about factory workers who had little to show for long hours of work. We studied management, labor relations, collective bargaining, and the trade union movement.

One evening someone quoted these lines: "Yesterday, I went shopping and I prided myself on my bargains. Today, I talked to a garment worker who had worked all day for fifty-nine cents. Tomorrow, I will look at my bargains to see whether they bear the trademark of death." The discussion of this quote, and the experiences I had as a student working in a garment factory, all came together. To this day I look for the union label.

I lived in the Harlem where A. Philip Randolph and Ashley Totten, founders and leaders of the Brotherhood of Sleeping Car Porters, were constantly speaking about the need for jobs with decent wages. There was no escape; the indignity of the culture of poverty was everywhere. Streets were filled with the unemployed and often strewn with the household goods of families who had been evicted because they could not pay their rent. Tenants waged protests and families fought back against overbearing marshals, but there was no mass organization. Harlem residents were exploited politically, merchants charged them more for food and clothing, and health and education facilities were woefully inadequate.

In the fall of 1936 Adam Clayton Powell Jr.—who went on to serve in the U.S. Congress from 1945 to 1971—took a survey and found that out of five thousand people who worked on 125th Street, only ninety-three were Negroes, all in menial jobs. This was a shocking statistic that struck at our core. That street was very special for Harlemites. Except when they went downtown to work or for some special shopping, they simply did not go below 125th. The street was a border. It was also absolutely central to the community. The merchants there richly benefited.

Early the following winter Adam Clayton Powell organized a campaign that he called the Coordinating Committee for Employment. He accepted the biblical truth that man cannot live by bread alone, but he also knew that man cannot live without bread. He taught the powerless people of Harlem that power is never given, it must be taken. He called for action. As an officer of the Harlem Christian Youth Council, I was one of the many whose first experience as a civil rights activist was on 125th Street under the Coordinating Committee for Employment.

To participate I had to attend classes on "informed action." Adam Powell led the discussions, bringing in leaders who reviewed the issues. We were prepared to walk down 125th Street in teams, picketing and interviewing shop owners. The campaign slogan was: "Don't Buy Where You Can't Work."

I was on the team assigned to Symphony Sam's Record Shop. Our message to Sam was that the people in the community bought his records, so he should hire some of them to sell the records. Sam, a middle-aged merchant whose business was lucrative, laughed and said, "Why come here? Why not go up to Spears' furniture store, up the street? You people can't take away furniture from that store, but you can easily steal my records. I would lose money if I hired you!" This made us furious. We immediately reported what Sam had said to the committee. Adam Clayton Powell assigned additional people to join us in picketing Symphony Sam's until he finally agreed to hire a Negro worker.

Many of the new programs designed to lift the country out of the Depression came under the National Recovery Act (NRA). But Adam Clayton Powell and others who were trying to find jobs or training—any kind of economic opportunity—for people in Harlem bitterly referred to the NRA as the "Negro Run Around." So many people went in and out of employment offices again and again. Carrying references, they were referred from one agency to another. Every place they went, they had to wait hours in line, only to find there was nothing for them. No matter how hard people of color tried, they kept finding the least desired jobs at the lowest pay.

I was deep in the struggle for economic change when the United Christian Youth Movement of North America selected me to attend the "World Conference on Life and Work of the Churches" at Oxford University in England. I was twenty-five years old, one of two young women and three blacks in a special ten-member American youth delegation. We would be joined by twenty-five young people from other countries in an ecumenical conference of clergy, theologians, officials, and scholars.

It was assumed that delegates who could not afford the trip would be sponsored by their denomination. I was not connected with a denomination. Even before I knew I had been selected, Dr. Harry Emerson Fosdick, pastor of Riverside Church, had sent a telegram to Amy Blanche Green: "If Dorothy Height is chosen as a delegate . . . you may count on a $100 contribution from Riverside Church." When Miss Green read the telegram to me, I hardly knew how to respond. At that time $100 was a lot of money, and this was not even my church!

Dr. Adam Clayton Powell Sr. got word of my selection and called immediately. "Dorothy, what is this I hear about your going to England?" he asked. "You had better come to church on Sunday night and tell them all about it. When Dr. Powell introduced me at the service, he said, "Dorothy is a smart girl. We're glad that she's going to the conference in England. But she can't walk on water, so let us do what we can to help her get there." The church collection gave me $200, and individual members later donated more. There is no way I could measure the value of these gifts, the spirit in which they were given. The journey to Oxford took on added significance.

My mother, sisters, and friends came to see me off aboard the

SS *Berengaria*. When the whistle blew and everyone went ashore to wave good-bye, I followed the advice of Mr. Dixon, the church custodian. He told me that from the pier, no one could really see whether you were on deck. So as the ship moved from the dock, I went to my cabin, lay flat on my bunk, and stayed there for a couple of hours until my body adjusted to the vibrations. I don't know whether Mr. Dixon's trick was responsible, but I never had a moment of seasickness, even though it was a rough crossing. On a number of occasions the ship's dining room was practically empty at meal times. But I was always there.

Dr. Benjamin Elijah Mays, dean of the School of Religion at Howard University, and his wife Sadie were the designated chaperones of the youth delegation. We had never met, but in our six-day crossing we got to know one another, as well as the official delegates and their families. We became like a big, forty-member family. It was Dr. Mays's idea that we visit the cathedral towns and Shakespeare country en route to the conference at Oxford.

At Southampton I faced a calamity. I could not find the keys to the beautiful new luggage I had been given for the trip. The ship's purser promised to search, and as we visited each cathedral town, a fellow delegate went with me to find a locksmith. But they had no keys that would fit the American lock.

Though I longed for a change of clothing, I was thrilled to be in England. The cathedrals were awesome. I reveled in learning about the history of the countryside and the details of the architecture. In one small town a huge crowd gathered as our group came out of the cathedral. They had seen us enter, and when we walked out into the sun, the women bowed as they looked toward me, whispering, "Ahh! There's the black Madonna." It was as if the people had never seen anything quite like this happy, curious procession, black and white, male and female, lay and clergy, young and old.

On the last day of the tour I was going through a small bag and felt something in a secret pocket. I suddenly recalled my mother saying, "Dorothy, I am going to put the keys to your luggage in this little bag." I was mortified. I had caused so much anxiety, and the "missing" keys had been right there with me all along. But we had become such a family that when I confessed, everyone simply felt relieved.

It was great to be in the care of Dr. Mays, who included me in some very special moments on that trip. I especially remember being part of a small group that visited Ethiopian Emperor Haile Selassie, who was living in exile in Bath. Great teacher that he was, Dr. Mays not only talked with us about the meeting itself, and its many ramifications, but gave all of us a lesson in the etiquette of meeting royalty. He made us put our feet flat on the floor and told us to remember not to cross them. He helped us to understand that we were not on a sightseeing trip. Whatever the political aspects of our visit, we were to strive to ensure that the emperor and his people felt that they had been host to a sincere gathering with people who cared about him, his country, and the world in which we lived.

During the conference I had the pleasure of living with Canon Cochin of Oxford University and his family. This was a special treat. The Cochins made me feel like a part of the family right away. They lived a beautiful, yet simple life. Often gathered in their living room, or around their dining room table, were many interesting and distinguished guests whom I could not have met otherwise.

Most of the youth delegates lived in the college dormitory. Each day at noon we came together for our meal at Magdalen College: boiled potatoes, Brussels sprouts, and mutton. We tried to be polite but grew very tired of eating the same thing every day. We were thankful when tea and scones arrived in the afternoon.

In a funny way, food brought us together. It was a great leveler. The Americans missed hot dogs and hamburgers, and others longed for their own national dishes. We all talked about what we missed. I felt especially fortunate to be able to look forward each evening to a good meal with the Cochin family.

The first days at Oxford, like those at most international gatherings, were dramatic and ceremonial. I could hardly believe that I was hearing firsthand greetings from the prime minister, a welcome from the queen, the special message from the archbishop of Canterbury. Then came the procession of theologians, scholars, and clergy from all parts of the world in their glorious robes. It was magnificent. Every day there was a worship service conducted by a leader from one of the great churches. By the end of the conference we had been enriched by messages from every branch of Christianity.

The need for a global conference was abundantly clear at that time of worldwide economic and social stress and concern about war. An ecumenical gathering to look at faith in terms of life and work was long overdue. Of course, we young people were not permitted to speak on the floor, but we were seated in a choice spot in the balcony choir loft, where we could follow every move. We were thrilled to be there.

The North American youth delegation carried our theme from home, "Christian Youth Building a New World," and the Oxford conference seemed to be the right place to get direction for our task. On the ship, on the road, during the conference, in prayer, and in our discussions and individual exchanges, we were always full of hope. This was something more than youthful idealism, I believe, because we never lost sight of reality. We knew that we had hard work ahead.

Each morning we joined the official conference delegates for the worship service, followed by an address by one of the world's great theologians. Then the youth conference moved into its own sessions chaired by Edwin Espy, an American Baptist. We were organized into five working groups. Each dealt with an issue of universal concern and was led by a distinguished scholar. I was one of seven in the "Economic Order" group led by the British economic historian Richard Henry Tawney, an ardent Christian and influential social critic.

I will always remember Professor Tawney for his extraordinary mind. But I was also fascinated by his massive eyebrows, almost two inches wide. He had a keen sense of humor, and he knew how to get a diverse group to think together. For two weeks he held us spellbound on the subject of equality in its deepest sense.

A young Welshman in our group, a Mr. Charles, constantly challenged Professor Tawney, arguing that his socialist theories could not possibly work. Toward the end of the two-week session, Mr. Charles said, "Professor Tawney, you say that all men are equal, but that surely cannot be the case. I work among Welsh miners. I see them every day, and I cannot believe that the Lord would consider Welsh miners to be my equal." A strange silence filled the room. Then Professor Tawney, peering intently from under his immense eyebrows and smiling sweetly, responded: "Mr. Charles," he said, "when I was your age, I too thought that the role of the Church of England was to see to it that at least one gentleman was placed in every village." That exchange and the meaning of equality dominated many a conversation among us young people from that afternoon on, and for many years thereafter.

John McMurray, another British economist, put us through different paces in his presentations on the inherent weaknesses in both capitalism and communism. "Whenever there are evils in a system," he warned, "it does not need to be destroyed from the outside. The system has only to keep working and it will destroy itself. You have to work to change the system."

On the last day John McMurray gave us some advice. "Be active! You cannot simply react to what is happening." But we had to be clear about our goals, or our energy would quickly dissipate, he cautioned. "There is no one so tired as a tired radical."

Richard Tawney and John McMurray taught me a great deal. They confirmed that people are born equal, but that society shapes opportunity and determines whether and how equality is realized for each of us. That revelation hit home when the Oxford evening paper headlined news about the ongoing trials of the Scottsboro boys, unjustly accused of rape, and their treatment by the Alabama "justice" system.

While in England, I had grown accustomed to queries from people who asked difficult questions about my status as a Negro in American society. Often, I was one of the first persons of color from the United States they had ever seen. They simply could not understand how it was that the United States advocated democracy so strongly and yet condoned such a plainly undemocratic practice as political, economic, and social discrimination against people of color.

Again and again I found myself saying, I am an American and I am proud of my country. But I also acknowledged the injustices. With the blazing headlines about the Scottsboro boys, this was no longer a discussion of theories. I did not try to be an expert; I could speak with authority only about my own experience. Occasionally I would describe the work of youth groups and other organizations to eliminate barriers to democracy. I was grateful when I could draw into the discussion some of the white American delegates I had met, especially Edith Larrigo, Winifred Wygal, and Rose Terlin of the YWCA, who shared my concerns about racism.

Every one of us in the youth delegation at Oxford was stretched and enriched beyond our imagination. While we respectfully accepted the fact that our voices had not been heard on the issues at hand, except in our youth sessions, we resolved that the time had come for a global conference of Christian youth.

That gathering—the World Conference of Christian Youth—finally took place in August 1939 in Amsterdam. By that time I had become a YWCA staff member and was chosen to be a member of the YWCA delegation led by Twyla Cavert. The theme of the conference was "Christus Victor!"

Our delegation was on the high seas when Adolph Hitler marched into Poland. World War II was inevitable. Uncertain about the dangers, the conference leaders appealed to Queen Wilhelmina of Holland. She urged the delegates to come on. "We need the gathering," she seemed to say. That spirit permeated the whole experience.

In Amsterdam delegates stayed in private homes. I lived with the family of the director of the Protestant Hospital. Because his wife was Jewish, there was constant concern in that family, a quiet fear about the direction of the war.

The organizing committee had asked me to chair the worship service to be presented by North Americans, and we developed the service with the help of a committee made up of members of youth groups across the country. All the services had to be approved by the main committee and translated into the five languages of the conference, so I sent a copy of our work to Holland well in advance.

Shortly after I got to Holland, I was called before the committee. The service could not be used, I was told, because it included music from the concert halls that was not sacred. "We Would Be Building," the hymn of the United Christian Youth Movement of North America, was written to the tune of "Finlandia" by Sibelius. I tried to interpret the meaning the hymns had for young people in North America, but there was a strong antisecular rebuttal. Another meeting was arranged.

This time I pointed out that the worship for each day was arranged and led by a different group based on its own experience. Our service truly represented the North Americans, I argued. I read the hymn as it had been taught to me in Lakeside, Ohio. Finally, reluctantly, the committee conceded, and our service took place as planned.

It turned out to be one of the great highlights of the conference. Along with "We Would Be Building," we had included in our service the Negro spiritual "Lord, I Want to Be a Christian." I simply cannot describe the reaction of the conference—the wholehearted participation and, in five languages, the unifying spiritual response. It was a joyous occasion.

Throughout my years in the youth movement, in fact, there were many joyous activities. Arts and crafts, music and poetry, services, rap sessions, great speakers, team sports, hikes, good food, quiet moments for reflection—all contributed to many memorable "mountaintop" experiences. I came to know the value of having higher goals that transcend the pettiness that we so often encounter in daily life. No one has to tell me that relationships are the key. I found that out early in life. And at the same time, I gained a deep, ingrained respect for persons who are different from me.

Chapter Six

Turning Points

NOT LONG AFTER I returned from Oxford at the end of the summer of 1937, I had a telephone call from Cecelia Cabaniss Saunders, executive director of the West 137th Street branch of the New York YWCA. She wanted to talk with me about coming to work as assistant executive director. I told Mrs. Saunders that before going to Oxford, I had signed a contract to become director of youth work for the Greater New York Federation of Churches. Even so, she made a very strong case for my coming to Harlem. She had been following my activities in the community for years.

After two soul-searching conversations with my friend Marion Cuthbert, a member of the YWCA national staff, I called Margaret Webster, who was both the executive director of the YWCA of the City of New York and chair of the personnel committee that had selected me for the Federation of Churches position. Miss Webster suggested that we talk to Dr. Robert Searle, head of the Federation of Churches and one of my mentors. He arranged a luncheon meeting and invited Mrs. Saunders and Lillian Alexander, chair of the Harlem YWCA's management committee, along with Miss Webster and Amy Blanche Green of the federation. This was a gathering of friends.

"We're here to discuss one *corpus delicti*, Miss Dorothy Height," Dr. Searle announced, a twinkle in his eye. And even though the night before I had not slept a wink, I jumped right into the discussion. I thanked them for the confidence in me that each had shown. I spoke of the special meaning of working with the guidance of Amy Blanche Green and of what an honor it would be to succeed her at the Federation of Churches. I also spoke of how I had discovered anew at Oxford what the YWCA was about, its commitment to equality and to the struggle to translate principles into practice. There were many issues in Harlem that were of concern to me, and I described how I could work on them from a base at the West 137th Street branch of the YWCA. After some discussion, Dr. Searle said he believed my commitment was clear to everyone, then added, "I want you to know that all of us will be with you, whatever position you choose."

In the end I chose to work for the YWCA. Dr. Searle and all the other Federation people were marvelously supportive. The only sadness came when I learned that Amy Blanche Green had resigned as youth director because she had terminal cancer. She had not said a word to me about it because she did not want her personal condition to cloud my career decision. And it was not long before Dr. Searle left the Federation as well. The organization had always considered him rather radical and, after a few years, dropped him. He took a job working with the family court on the Lower East Side of Manhattan.

Years later my phone rang, and a man asked, "Dorothy, do you remember Robert Searle?"

"How could I ever forget Robert Searle?" I said, smiling at his unmistakable voice.

"I have just read about what you are doing at the YWCA," he

said, "and I wish you could come down where I am now. I'm dealing with more black families than any other court. I remember that
as a young person you always had a capacity for caring. We need a
lot of that down here!"

The Harlem branch was outstanding in the YWCA movement.
Mrs. Saunders was a great institution builder. She won support
from the Julius Rosenwald Fund and also from John D. Rockefeller to fulfill her vision for the branch building, which spanned
the block from 137th to 138th Street. The building was well
equipped with administrative offices, program facilities, a gymnasium, swimming pool, auditorium, and cafeteria. The branch's
trade school specialized in training licensed practical nurses and
secretarial workers. Its employment department opened doors for
those seeking jobs. The residence, Emma Ransom House, had 260
rooms, a director's apartment, "beau parlors" for entertaining
guests, a beautiful reception hall, and all the modern conveniences.
Generally speaking, the Harlem branch was a favorite center for
community activities and social gatherings.

As assistant executive director, one of my principal assignments,
which later led to my appointment as residence director, was supervising the counselors assigned to the Emma Ransom House. During the 1939 World's Fair thousands of Negro girls came to New
York City in search of jobs. Emma Ransom House was one of the
very few places they could stay. At times the need became so great
that we converted a clubroom into an emergency dormitory. It was
hard to turn the girls away, so we often risked a night of overcrowding to help them get a start. Though the branch emergency dormitory charged only fifty cents a night, there were many girls who
could not pay even that amount. I heard countless stories of young
women on the streets, vulnerable and without recourse.

That is how I came to know of the Bronx slave market. Black
women, young and old, stood at designated street corners in

Harlem, and people who needed work done in their homes would drive down from the Bronx, look them over, select one, and drive her home to work. The women were mercilessly exploited and offered very low pay—and even that was often withheld. Many told of being paid for eight hours only to find, once they got outside, that they had actually worked twelve or more hours. The situation was outrageous.

Lionel Florant, a member of the Harlem Youth Council, was a brilliant student at City College. He had been studying this situation, and when he learned that I was working with so many exploited girls, he and I got together. I told him several stories, including one that especially touched me about a girl about sixteen—I will call her Sharon—who had come up from the South.

Sharon had found a job, but it didn't last. In desperation, she went to one of the designated corners, where she was picked up by a woman who took her to work in her house. When the woman left home, the man of the house took advantage of Sharon, then threatened to have her arrested if she told. Sharon was terrified. She came to us and told us the story, but she did not even know the address of the house, and there was really nothing we could do to right the injustice. We gave her a job as a substitute on the residence elevator. It was not long before we realized that she was pregnant and trying to hide the fact for fear of losing her job.

Stories like Sharon's inspired Lionel to join the movement to establish hiring halls where people in search of work could go and employers would be registered. When a hearing on the issue reached the New York City Council, Lionel asked me to testify. I told my office that I'd be back in a few hours and headed downtown for City Hall.

As soon as I arrived, I was called to speak. When I mentioned the Bronx slave market, the councilman from the Bronx interrupted: "You certainly don't mean to say *slave* market." The Brooklyn councilman intervened. "It doesn't exist in Brooklyn, does it?" It did, and I told them about that slave market too.

The Bronx councilman objected to my terminology. "You're just saying that people are hiring people without going to employment agencies," he argued. "It's not a slave market. That's a most unfortunate term."

I declared that it was indeed a slave market, that I had stood on those corners to observe what went on and had heard countless reports from girls and young women who were mercilessly exploited. A slave market was what it was, and that's what we called it.

The Bronx man began to get hot under the collar. "Well, you want to correct that, don't you?"

"No," I replied. "Maybe you don't know it, but when I say 'Bronx slave market,' everybody in Harlem knows exactly what I'm talking about, just as if I were to say 'Hi-de-hi-de-ho.'" That set the whole council laughing, because none of them expected me to quote Cab Calloway. But I got my message across.

Amazingly, the news of my testimony was picked up immediately all over the country—even as far away as England. By the time I got back to the YWCA, the phone was ringing off the hook! For a while the publicity sent the slave markets under cover. But they continued nonetheless, and the legislation to establish hiring halls was defeated.

On November 7, 1937, one month after I began working at the Harlem YWCA, I met Mary McLeod Bethune and Eleanor Roosevelt on the same day. Mrs. Bethune was hosting a meeting of the National Council of Negro Women (NCNW), which she had founded just two years before. Mrs. Roosevelt, America's first lady, was to speak. As the newest member of the YWCA staff, I was assigned to greet Mrs. Roosevelt and escort her to the meeting.

I alerted the receptionists at the two main doors to let me know immediately when Mrs. Roosevelt arrived. We were very excited, and each minute anticipating her arrival seemed an eternity. All of a sudden one of the janitors ran up. Mrs. Roosevelt had come in through the service entrance and was making her own way toward the auditorium.

I saw my little job going up in smoke. Greeting the first lady was my only assignment, and I had muffed it. Who would have thought that she would park her own car and come through the service entrance?

I intercepted her just before she reached the auditorium. I caught my breath, greeted her warmly, and escorted her inside.

Mrs. Roosevelt gave an exciting speech. As soon as it was over, she announced that she wanted to get to Hyde Park before dark, but Mrs. Bethune persuaded her to stay long enough for everyone to sing "Let Me Call You Sweetheart."

As Mrs. Roosevelt gathered her things, Mrs. Bethune turned to me.

"What is your name?" she asked.

"Dorothy Height," I whispered.

"I want to talk to you," she said. "We need you at the National Council of Negro Women."

I escorted Mrs. Roosevelt to her car—properly this time—and waved good-bye. By the time I returned, Mrs. Bethune had already appointed me to the resolutions committee of the National Council of Negro Women.

On that fall day the redoubtable Mary McLeod Bethune put her hand on me. She drew me into her dazzling orbit of people in power and people in poverty. I remember how she made her fingers into a fist to illustrate for the women the significance of working together to eliminate injustice.

"The freedom gates are half ajar," she said. "We must pry them fully open." I have been committed to the calling ever since.

People said that when Mary McLeod was born in 1875, the first free child in her home after fourteen born in slavery, her eyes were wide open. From the start she was different—lively and inquiring.

Early on she developed a vision of education and economic justice, and for the rest of her life she devoted herself to that vision with indefatigable energy and love. Before she was thirty she had fulfilled one of her cherished dreams, to create a school. In 1904, with five little girls, faith in God, and $1.50, she opened the doors of the Daytona Literary and Industrial School for Training Negro Girls in Daytona Beach, Florida. She is the only African American woman to have founded a four-year accredited college, Bethune-Cookman College in Daytona Beach.*

Then and throughout her life, Mary McLeod Bethune enlisted *anyone* she found worthy to join her. From the beginning she successfully appealed to white benefactors. Soon after she started her first school she had the mayor, prominent local businessmen, black ministers, and wealthy winter residents helping to plan its development. She believed strongly in interracial cooperation. And she was always task-oriented. We were dealing with important issues—education, child labor, the minimum wage, and substandard working conditions—and she meant business.

Mrs. Bethune fought as tenaciously for women's rights as she did for black education and freedom, and she came to believe that women were the key to change. Who knew the problems, the pain, and the cost better than they? Hadn't her grandmother and mother resisted and survived the horrors of slavery? "We shall find a way to do for our day what they did for theirs," seemed to be her motto. "Next to God," she once said, "we are indebted to women, first for life itself, and then for making it worth having." Everywhere Mrs. Bethune traveled, her ideas, her personality, and her achievements demonstrated what black women were capable of doing.

---

* Mrs. Bethune called Bethune-Cookman "the college built on prayer." She told of an early visit by her first major donor, James Gamble of Procter & Gamble. He surveyed her meager collection of supplies and asked, "Mrs. Bethune, where is your school?" She replied, "The school is in my mind and heart!" Today, it is an accredited coeducational institution, the sixth largest of the thirty-nine members of the United Negro College Fund. Under the leadership of Dr. Oswald P. Bronson, it is approaching its centennial year.

In 1935 she created the National Council of Negro Women to bring together the major black women's organizations to become a strong central voice for their eight hundred thousand members. That same year President Roosevelt had appointed Mrs. Bethune an adviser to the head of the National Youth Administration in Washington, D.C. In announcing her appointment, he said, "Mrs. Bethune is a great woman. I believe in her because she has her feet on the ground—not only on the ground but in the deep, plowed soil."

Soon thereafter she settled into a small apartment in Washington, D.C., and went to work, gathering around her many of the young people, black and white, who had flooded into the capital to help make the New Deal a success. They talked day and night, debating ideas for new projects and new approaches. They saw their work together as a once-in-a-lifetime opportunity to chart a new course for the future.

After our meeting in 1937 I joined that circle. I grew close to Mrs. Bethune, and she began to depend on me. It was always a treat to talk with her. She had so much wisdom to impart. She helped me feel that the philosophical and spiritual dimensions of our work mattered as much as its material impact. Her guiding principle was: "Make something of everything you have—head, heart, and hand are equally important. Learn to use them together."

As she gave us her support, her confidence, and her strength, we became like daughters and sons to her. She kept us involved. When she was in Washington and I was still in New York during the years after we met, she would call up and say, "Dorothy, there's a meeting going on up there about such and such. . . . Can you go over and sit in on that for me?" I could never say no to her.

Though only five feet, six inches tall, Mrs. Bethune was majestic. *Here I am!* she always seemed to be saying to the camera, *proud and beautiful.* Sometimes people found her overpowering, but no one disputed her ability to shake people out of their ruts and inspire them to do more than they thought they could. Prayer was an integral part of her work; when she felt the need for help, she gathered staff together and we got down on our knees. We marveled as her prayers were answered.

It bothered me that women would say mean things about Mrs. Bethune—that she was an Uncle Tom or a sell-out because she hobnobbed with white people in power. Most of those who talked like that weren't nearly so involved in social action as she was of course. Few had any idea of the reach of her work. But Mrs. Bethune just turned the petty charges around, transforming problems into opportunities. "Well, now," she would say, "Mrs. So-and-so [who had said something awful] is a lawyer, and we need a lawyer, don't we? Dorothy, let us get her on the phone and ask her to help us." It was not so much that she was getting her detractors off her back; she was simply letting them know that it was time for them to be something greater. She had a very kind but firm way of pressing people, causing them to reach beyond their own little worlds.

Everyone who knew Mrs. Bethune spoke of her with awe. They knew there was an iron fist in that velvet glove. She struck hard for what she believed in. She marched, she picketed, she boycotted, she signed petitions, she made speeches. She fought for laws to stop lynching, to end the poll tax, and to establish fair employment practices. Many people called her the "first lady of the struggle."

Perhaps it was because she had such a strong sense of self. She never asked for an appointment to see the president. She would call the first lady when there was a need or a problem and say simply, "Mrs. Roosevelt, the president needs to see me." And yet she had a great sense of humor. While there were those in the days of segregation who tried to belittle her, she would beat them at their game and laugh about it. On a train in the South the conductor asked, "Auntie, where is your ticket?" Mrs. Bethune looked up at this white man and asked, "Which of my sister's children are you?"

The very essence of Mrs. Bethune fortified me. She was a great champion of young people, especially of their right to assume responsibility in the world. She did not try to speak for us. She pressed us hard, making us think our ideas through, and she expected us to be responsible for whatever action we took. And yet at the same time she gave me a sense of release—a sense that you didn't need to worry about whether your ideas were the best in the world, just as long as you kept working on them. One time, after we had worked together for a while, she said one of the reasons she had been trying to get the YWCA to lend me to come work with her "officially" at the National Council of Negro Women was "because you and I are on the same wavelength—we think alike." I believe that she saw in me all that I could be and decided that she would help me along the way.

In 1938 I was one of ten young people privileged to work with Mrs. Roosevelt in preparing for the World Conference of Youth at Vassar College in Poughkeepsie, New York. With war clouds over Europe, we wanted to bring together more than six hundred young people from fifty-four countries, representing a multitude of races, religions, and points of view, to demonstrate our desire for peace and international justice. Many adults scoffed at our "incorrigible optimism" and "starry-eyed idealism," but we didn't mind. We believed that the hard-boiled world around us, teeming with violence and lawlessness, could use a little more optimism and idealism.

Mrs. Roosevelt agreed, and several months before the conference she called the ten of us to Hyde Park to spend a day at Val Kyl Cottage with her, hammering out what the conference would be about, what our objectives were, and how they could best be achieved. We talked with great intensity and, I am sure, immense innocence matched only by our tremendous sense of our own vital importance to the future of world peace. As we talked about saving the world, Eleanor Roosevelt served us hot dogs and ice cream on her porch.

When we asked for help, she would listen carefully, ask a few questions, then offer what help she felt she could provide. A major problem with the Vassar conference was how to finance it, as money for such activities was very scarce. When we raised this issue, Mrs. Roosevelt pressed us about the arrangements that were to be made with Vassar College, about the scheduling of our own work, about all the other details related to financing. Once we sorted them through and developed a sound plan, she helped open doors to people who would support us. But she always made us do the thinking.

Each of us who worked with Mrs. Roosevelt felt that she knew and cared about who we were. She talked to each of us personally, not generically to "young people." She was talking to me, Dorothy Height, and she knew that she and I had common concerns. She worried about the problems we were grappling with, and she wanted to find solutions just as much as we did.

Not surprisingly, Mrs. Bethune and Mrs. Roosevelt developed a strong friendship. Mrs. Roosevelt came to believe in everything Mrs. Bethune stood for. And yet it was not as if she had always appreciated the indignity of racial injustice. A long-standing member of the Daughters of the American Revolution, she had felt no difficulty in her affiliation until the bitter day the DAR voted against allowing Marian Anderson to sing in Constitution Hall. Mrs. Bethune appealed to Mrs. Roosevelt, who immediately resigned from the DAR and called upon the secretary of the Interior, Harold Ickes, to intervene. He arranged for Miss Anderson to hold her concert on the steps of the Lincoln Memorial. On Easter Sunday, 1939, Marian Anderson sang to an audience of some seventy-five thousand. The first words she sang were, "My Country, 'tis of Thee!" The crowd went wild!

*

By 1939 Mrs. Roosevelt had a remarkable grasp of the problem of racism, and her commitment to racial equality was clear. She never faltered. With Mrs. Roosevelt's support, Mrs. Bethune was able to extend her influence far beyond her position as adviser to the National Youth Administration. Just as she had brought black women together, she united nineteen black men—all advisers to federal agencies—in what she called the Federal Council on Negro Affairs, a group that soon became known as Roosevelt's "Black Cabinet." The only woman member of the council, Mrs. Bethune held weekly meetings at her Washington home, encouraging each member to attack discrimination in government facilities and, when possible, to open opportunities for blacks in government jobs.

When the University of North Carolina Press asked Mrs. Bethune to write a chapter in the book *What the Negro Wants*, she had me arrange a meeting with some of the key men to help her write the chapter. In her small apartment on Ninth Street she served tea and pound cake and listened for two and a half hours as they presented their responses to the question. Mrs. Bethune thanked them profusely, and then she said, "I hear you. I know what the Negro wants. He wants what everyone else wants." There was great laughter, and all departed knowing they had experienced vintage Bethune!

Mrs. Bethune was especially concerned about housing, and she thought President Roosevelt should name an African American to the Office of Housing. She asked Mrs. Roosevelt to encourage the president to move in that direction. A few days later Mrs. Roosevelt responded by letter. "Mrs. Bethune," she wrote, "my husband feels, and I am inclined to agree with him, that it would be better to appoint a white person who understands your problems and would be able to do more to help you than a Negro could do in that position." Soon after she received the letter, Mrs. Bethune called the first lady. "Mrs. Roosevelt," she said, "I do not believe there is anyone who can speak for me better than I can speak for myself." Within a matter of weeks the White House announced that Frank Horne had been appointed to a senior position in the housing agency, the first person of color to fill such a high position.

The integrity and forthrightness of the collaboration of these two women were striking. One time Mrs. Bethune asked Mrs. Roosevelt's help in raising funds to support a favorite project of hers at the National Council of Negro Women. The first lady thought carefully about it, then asked, "Mary, how many women do you say you represent?"

"Eight hundred fifty thousand," Mrs. Bethune replied.

"Well," said Mrs. Roosevelt, "if each one of those women gave a dollar, you'd have more than enough money to meet your needs!" Mrs. Bethune agreed. Such a simple, straightforward approach was just right to meet the requirements of the project at hand.

These two remarkable women spoke frankly and respected each other all the more when they did. They were involved in big, complex issues, but they cared about little things that mattered as well. Here's one example. When Mrs. Roosevelt was still in the White House, she regularly invited members of the National Council of Negro Women to visit. Now, this was a fabulous new thing, going to the White House to visit the first lady. After the first visit, women in the group exclaimed as they emerged from the East Wing, "Look! I have a napkin," or some other small thing. This greatly distressed Mrs. Bethune. Before each subsequent visit, she lined everybody up. Then she said, "Now, I do not want anyone coming out of there with napkins or food or anything. If you want souvenirs, you can go to the ten-cent store downtown and buy them." I loved that.

One of my favorite recollections of Mrs. Roosevelt happened many years later, in the fifties. She had just made a speech to a group I was leading of women from Asian countries. She was ready to leave when a woman from Taiwan spoke up: "Mrs. Roosevelt, before you go, may I ask you a personal question?" She nodded and sat down on the edge of a table to hear the question. "How did you get to be such a wonderful person?"

Mrs. Roosevelt smiled. "I was married to a wonderful man," she replied. And then she told a story. "When he was the governor of the State of New York, my husband would send me out on different missions because he could not travel himself. He wanted to know what was happening to people. On one of these early assignments, I visited an orphanage. When I returned, my husband asked, 'Eleanor, what did you find?' I gave him a glowing account of how wonderful everything was, how good the food was, how clean it was. He looked me straight in the eye and said, 'Eleanor, surely you don't think it's like that all the time. Surely you know that it was like that today because the governor's wife was there! It doesn't do any good if you are just going to let them show you what they want you to see. You have to decide what you want to see. The next time you go to a place like that, don't look only at the food they offer you, but ask them to show you the menus for the last two weeks. Ask them to let you see their pantries and kitchens. Look at the children. Do they look healthy and well fed? Ask the children what they are doing, how they feel. The children will tell you the truth!'

"Later, when he was president and I went on trips abroad, he would say, 'When you go to a foreign city, they will want to take you down certain streets and you must go wherever they take you. But you can also find out before you go where the worst neighborhoods are, and if your hosts don't take you there, you must ask to see those streets too. Even on the streets they want to show you, look beyond what they want you to see. Look at the clotheslines—they will tell you a lot. Look at the condition of people's clothes. Then you will know whether they are doing well or if they are poor. It's the little things you have to look at.'

"Because of his advice," Mrs. Roosevelt concluded, "when I went out to Asia and I saw people dusting the streets with little short brooms, I realized why they had so much tuberculosis! I suggested that if they tried long-handled brooms, perhaps they wouldn't get so sick. I never would have thought of anything like that if it hadn't been for my husband."

Twenty years later the woman who had asked Mrs. Roosevelt

the question turned up at a meeting I was attending in Taiwan. She reminded me of Mrs. Roosevelt's answer and told me how much it had meant to her.

In December 1961, President John F. Kennedy appointed me to the President's Commission on the Status of Women, and once again I had the opportunity to work closely with Mrs. Roosevelt. The commission's brief was to assess the position of women and the functions they performed in the home, in the economy, and in society. It looked carefully into where women were in the federal establishment and in the private sector. It explored the portrayal of women by the mass media and considered the special problems of Negro women.

On June 15, 1962, Mrs. Roosevelt hosted members of the commission at Hyde Park. It was an unforgettable day. At one point she said to us, "Because I anticipate success in achieving full employment and full use of America's magnificent potential, I feel confident that in the years ahead many of the remaining outmoded barriers to women's aspirations will disappear. Within a rapidly growing economy, with appropriate manpower planning, all Americans will have a better chance to develop their individual capacities, to earn a good livelihood, and to strengthen family life."

American Women, the report of the commission, was presented to President Kennedy on October 11, 1963, the first anniversary of Mrs. Roosevelt's death. I was designated to represent the commission on that day at the Roosevelt family observance at her graveside at Hyde Park.

When Mrs. Roosevelt died in 1962, I joined hundreds of mourners at her memorial service at St. John the Divine in New York. It was a cold, drizzling November day, and as I came out of the service, I bumped into Georgia Turner, whom I had first met many years before when she had worked in the Roosevelts' home. We greeted one another, then stood on the corner in the rain and talked.

Mrs. Turner had been with President Roosevelt at Warm Springs. She had lifted him, served him meals, and taken care of him. In later years she had developed a heart condition, and when she could no longer work, Mrs. Roosevelt provided for her in a nursing home in Baltimore. Many years later Mrs. Roosevelt called the Emma Ransom House, where Mrs. Turner was then living, and invited her to come to tea. "And so I did," said Mrs. Turner, beaming. "We sat and talked, and Mrs. Roosevelt said to me, 'Georgia, you have really done such great things in your life.'" Mrs. Turner looked at me radiantly. "Can you imagine?" she asked. "This woman telling me I've done great things! I went back to that old YWCA in Harlem where I was staying and sat in my room and felt like a queen, like I was sitting in a palace because I had just had tea with Mrs. Roosevelt."

As the rain dripped from our hats, Mrs. Turner continued. In her last few weeks Mrs. Roosevelt had sent for her. She beamed again. "Of all the people in the world, I'm one of those she invited to be there with her at the end." One day the week before, Mrs. Turner recounted, she had gone into Mrs. Roosevelt's room. "She had been on one side and wanted to turn to the other, but she just couldn't do it by herself. She said she needed to turn, so I put my arms under her, as I had done so many times with Mr. Roosevelt, and started to try to lift her up. But she called out, as spent herself as she was, she called out, 'Georgia, your heart! Please call the nurse to help you. Remember, the doctor told you not to lift anything heavy.' Can you imagine her remembering then that I had a bad heart?"

I loved listening to Mrs. Turner remember the way Mrs. Roosevelt cared about people, right up to her very last moment. When we finally moved to go, Georgia Turner grabbed my sleeve. "You know, Miss Height," she said, "when Mrs. Roosevelt called out for me not to lift her, I would have done it, even if it killed me. I would have done anything if it would have made her live."

It was a privilege to know Mrs. Roosevelt and Mrs. Bethune, two extraordinary women. I never thought of them in terms of veneration or devotion. They were both too human for that. You got involved in what they cared about, and they helped you see what special contribution you alone could make, whatever the cause. Both knew that each small effort, each tiny gift of time or treasure or talent, was essential to the whole. They graciously appreciated whatever people did, reserving their discontent for bigger things—the injustice, unfairness, and poverty they saw around them. They never wasted time on trivia. They got right to the point because their work was urgent. Their energy seemed incandescent. It galvanized thousands of women.

Mrs. Bethune and Mrs. Roosevelt made me and countless others want to be like them. They represented a rare breed of true leaders, at once heroic and humble. Their integrity and commitment to the causes for which they fought were unassailable. Their kind was rare in their time and seems even rarer today.

If you want to keep rare people like these with you always, the best you can do is be yourself when they are alive and you are with them. If you are yourself, you can draw tremendous strength from such wise elders, in part because you know that they are not going to be there forever. Then, when they go, you discover that their strength has become part of you. When the moment of separation comes, you discover how your own inner resources have been nurtured and strengthened because you lived so fully in the relationship. You feel blessed and challenged to prove worthy of their trust.

At Mrs. Bethune's funeral after her sudden death in 1955, the great African American philosopher and preacher Howard Thurman spoke of the uncanny way she had of turning hardship, disappointment, and frustration into shafts of light. Her radiance still gleams, illuminating my life as it shone throughout her own.

Chapter Seven

Wartime Washington

THE 1939 YWCA National Convention, held in Columbus, Ohio, was my first, and it proved quite an experience. One of the local hotels, the Neil House, refused to serve an interracial group of student delegates. That led to a protest that was loud and clear. It brought the desired results.

Then there was a special meeting called by Cordella Wynn and her sister, Eva Bowles. They had been instrumental in recruiting and training Negro women for executive positions in the YWCA, and their agenda was focused on getting acquainted, sharing experiences, and finding ways to make participation in the YWCA movement more rewarding for Negro women. Two of those who attended, Mrs. Kelly Miller and Mrs. Lettie Calloway, had come to the convention in search of an executive director for the Phyllis Wheatley YWCA in Washington, D.C. They later told me that I had stood out in their minds because I was the only young woman in the room who was not smoking! During and after the convention they pursued me, and the personnel office of the national board of the YWCA urged me to take the job.

It was not an easy decision. I loved Harlem. My family and friends were in New York. My family had finally moved to town—to an apartment on Morningside Avenue.

I was devoted to my work as well. Cecelia Cabaniss Saunders had talked me into becoming director of the Emma Ransom House, the YWCA residence for Negro women and girls. I had moved into the director's suite and soon found I was always on call, since so much seemed to happen late at night.

As a result, I was not surprised one spring night when my phone rang very late. But for once it was not about an Emma Ransom House resident. It was my sister-in-law, Fay Briggs, who was calling to say that my mother had fallen at her bedside earlier that night. It had become clear during the course of the evening that she was hurt more seriously than she at first thought, and Fay had called for an ambulance. It arrived after midnight. The elevator had stopped running by then, and the attendants said they could not get Mother down the six flights of stairs.

Frantic, I rushed to the apartment. We were able to reach the building custodian, who restored elevator service, and my mother was taken to Harlem Hospital. There the doctors determined that she had suffered a slight stroke and that she had fractured her hip. While the hip was healing, she contracted pneumonia. At 2:00 A.M. on April 6, 1939, with several other family members and me waiting at the hospital, she died.

Earlier that evening, after combing Momma's soft gray hair, cousin Ethel Sayles had asked, "Aunt Fannie, what else do you want me to do?" My mother's answer was, "Fry my Dorothy some chicken and make her a sweet potato pie." For the rest of her life Ethel remembered those words. Whenever I turned up anywhere near her Texas home, Ethel Sayles made sure that I had fried chicken and sweet potato pie.

My mother's sudden, untimely death was a great shock to me. I will always regret that she who had invested so much in me did not live to see some of my achievements or to share some of the honors bestowed upon me.

But after her death I felt less tied to New York and more open to considering some of the opportunities I was being offered. Ultimately I accepted the position at the Phyllis Wheatley YWCA in Washington, D.C.

There was one possible complication: I was scheduled to be a delegate to the World Conference of Christian Youth in Amsterdam that August. Happily, Carolyn Bond Day, the retiring executive of the Phyllis Wheatley YWCA, and the board of directors, chaired by Julia West Hamilton, were ready to accommodate my schedule. An interim executive was appointed, and I was to begin work on October 1. At a briefing session with association leaders, Mrs. Day gave me some personal advice. After all, at twenty-seven, I would be the youngest executive in the movement. She said I should know that Washington was deeply divided between the masses and the classes. Her broad pronunciation of the letter *a* made her statement sound dramatic. I had to think about where I would live in Washington, she said, because if I lived among the masses, I would never be accepted by the classes. I quickly replied that I would live at the YWCA.

When I moved to Washington that fall of 1939, the city was completely segregated. There was not a toilet downtown that a black person could use. Union Station was the only place a black person could go to get a sandwich.

Given that segregation, the history of the Phyllis Wheatley YWCA was particularly interesting. It had been founded in May 1905 by members of Washington's Negro aristocracy. Mostly fair-skinned and highly educated, the founders had organized a book club that grew into the YWCA. Later a group of white women decided to organize a separate YWCA. They learned that in several other cities there was a "central" YWCA, serving white women, and a Negro "branch." So the white YWCA organizers wrote to the

Phyllis Wheatley women, asking if they would like to become a branch of the new organization. The Phyllis Wheatley women, represented by Frances Boyce, responded directly. "Since we were organized first," Mrs. Boyce wrote, "we think it would be very good if you would become our branch." The white women were not prepared to follow that suggestion, and so Washington became the only city in the United States to have two autonomous YWCAs, one on Rhode Island Avenue, organized by black women, and another at the corner of 17th and K Streets, organized by white women.

The Washington school system was similarly segregated. Divisions one to nine were white, and ten through thirteen were colored. A full assistant superintendent was in charge of each division. Teachers—black and white—heard distinguished educators speak, but they heard them separately. Each speech was given twice—once for the white teachers and again for the blacks. All teachers, regardless of color, received the same salary. If there was any place in the country where "separate but equal" actually worked, it was in the Washington schools. Some of the black schools, in fact, were superior. As the seat of Howard University, Washington, D.C., had the highest concentration of highly educated blacks of any city in the world. This presented some interesting challenges for the Phyllis Wheatley YWCA.

After the attack on Pearl Harbor in December 1941, Washington became a beehive of war activities. It was almost like a repeat of my Harlem experience. I had been at the YWCA there when the World's Fair drew to New York so many young women who needed help. With the advent of the war, young women poured into Washington and, once again, looked to the YWCA for support.

Soon the YWCA was open twenty-four hours a day. Early on we discovered that the United Service Organization (USO), set up to entertain the troops, was for white soldiers only, so we set up USO activities for black service men and women. We trained hundreds of girls as hostesses to serve army camps. We also offered language classes. You could take Spanish at seven o'clock in the evening or seven o'clock in the morning—whatever your work schedule would allow.

The young black women who streamed into the capital from the South were emboldened by telegrams they had received from the government telling them to "report in seventy-two hours" to one department or another. Many were skilled and hoped they'd get jobs as secretaries. But usually they were stuck in a clerical pool with few if any assignments. Whenever there was a top job, the managers almost always selected a white woman. Worse still, there was hardly any housing available to young black women in the Washington of the early forties.

I knew that new housing facilities had been built for white girls, and when I asked why no provisions had been made for young women of color, I was told, "The blacks always look after their own." I was outraged. These girls had left home, many of them for the first time in their lives and some having given up pretty good jobs, to respond to the summons to contribute to the war effort, only to find themselves unwelcomed by the very government that had called them.

When we began to investigate, we found that our young women were renting rooms wherever they could find them and often were being exploited mercilessly by landlords. There were landlords charging four girls in a room fifteen dollars a week each, thus making sixty dollars from a room that might have one dresser with only three drawers. People tucked them in anywhere, just to collect their money. And as the girls were being brought in so fast by the federal government, they had to put up with whatever terrible and terrifying conditions they found.

In the government housing agency, I found one black official, Robert Taylor of Chicago, and was horrified to discover that even he had bought the story that black families could always make room for a few more. When I told him about the exploitation of these young women, he said it couldn't be that bad. I pressed him, and finally he agreed that if we could document what was happening, he would see that the message got to the proper authorities. It was a Thursday afternoon. He said he would come to the YWCA the following Monday for a presentation of our findings.

Skilled young volunteers from many agencies poured into our office over the weekend, happy to fulfill Mr. Taylor's request for documentation. By midday Saturday we had developed a questionnaire, and young women from several agencies were circulating it through the neighborhoods where young women were staying four to a room. The statements from the young women were thorough: "I am Mary Smith, and I live at such and such a place. I came to Washington on such and such a date. I had a telegram saying for me to report in so and so many hours. I was to be classified as such and such, and I understood I was to earn thus and so. I live at such and such a place." Then they would tell what rent they were paying, what services they had (or didn't have), how many were in the same room, what they needed, and what it had cost them to come to Washington.

We collected several hundred completed questionnaires, and when Mr. Taylor arrived on Monday afternoon, three hundred young women were on hand to receive him. He was more than a little surprised. He told those present what the government was doing and what kinds of allowances they were going to try to make for them. The girls very politely let him finish, but when he opened for questions, they were not shy about letting him know exactly what their circumstances were. By the end of the evening Mr. Taylor confessed that he'd "had no idea that anything like this was going on." Not too long after that the government appropriated funds to develop the Lucy Diggs Slowe Hall, named after the legendary dean of women at Howard University. Midway and Wake Halls followed, and the pressure to find adequate housing for young black women in Washington was at last relieved.

During the war years women faced some unusual challenges in the U.S. armed forces. Even though every branch had women members, everything was designed for men. As army chief of staff during the Second World War, General George C. Marshall recognized the problem. During the Korean War, when he became secretary of defense, he recommended Anna Rosenberg, who had served the Roosevelt administration in many capacities, to serve as assistant secretary of defense for manpower. Soon after her appointment, she recommended the creation of the Defense Advisory Committee on Women in the Services, which came to be known as DACOWITS. I was honored to be appointed to it and sworn in by General Marshall himself on his last day of duty.

Our assignment was to get acquainted with the needs and concerns of women in the armed services. Early on we learned that if we were to be useful we had to operate as if we were inside the defense establishment, and yet at the same time we had to act as ordinary citizens. On one of our first briefing expeditions, General Bedell Smith of army intelligence took us to Camp Lejeune in North Carolina. He showed us the kinds of new aircraft and equipment with which women in the services would be involved. As we concluded the tour, he said, "You have to see this and have this information so that you will understand the critical nature of your assignment. You must move about and act as if you have knowledge of all of this, but you can never speak of it to anyone."

In the course of our work we visited all kinds of installations, then made recommendations for changes in policy or practice on behalf of women. I was on a subcommittee assigned to housing along with Mary Pillsbury Lord and Mary Rockefeller. Another subcommittee considered diets and nutrition, since so many women were complaining that the army hardly ever served salads of any kind and its offerings were heavy on meats.

Imagine our surprise when we found that most of our subcommittee "draft" recommendations were put into action as soon as they reached the Defense Department—even before DACOWITS members had had a chance to discuss them in our full committee! "You recommend it and we promulgate it," the brass explained.

Everywhere we went we stayed in the barracks so that we could experience what life was really like for women in the services. Inevitably I observed and was called to investigate racial situations too, as there were any number of reports of discrimination from or concerning women of color.

DACOWITS was a wonderfully interesting experience for me. As we moved from one installation or camp to another, we saw a whole side of American life that I hadn't realized existed, and certainly there was a kind of glamour about the defense service that you don't generally find in social welfare. But the work was disheartening too. All of us confronted constant resistance to women in the services. We kept having to point out that women really were quite capable and could perform many of the same roles as men. I'm not sure that notion has been fully accepted even now. DACOWITS made a difference in the social welfare of women in the services, and what they did made life better for men, too.

In January 1941, I was in a terrible accident. It was a bitterly cold day, and I was driving back to Washington with two friends after making a speech at St. James Presbyterian Church in New York. We were very tired. And because it was so cold, we closed the windows, unaware that the exhaust was faulty. As carbon monoxide seeped inside, all of us fell asleep. The car crashed into a telephone pole on Sixteenth Street. When the police arrived, we were bleeding profusely. I realized that my leg was broken. As we waited for an ambulance, a policeman covered me with his jacket.

We were rushed to Emergency Hospital. Almost immediately an intern began stitching up my face. He whistled softly as he worked, and even though I was in shock, I recognized the tune. It was "Finlandia," the melody of the United Christian Youth Movement hymn. As if singing along with him, I repeated in my mind the words I had learned in Lakeside, Ohio, and later used in the worship at Amsterdam:

We would be building; temples still undone,
O'er crumbling walls their crosses scarcely lift;
Waiting till love can raise the broken stone
And hearts creative bridge the human rift;
We would be building; Master, let thy plan
Reveal the life that God would give to man.

Overcome by an inexpressible awareness of grace, I felt I'd already begun to heal. There, in the tender care of a stranger whose hands were stitching my body back together and whose music I shared, my faith was reaffirmed. I felt I received all the strength I needed to survive. In the days that followed the hospital allowed me no visitors. Because I had lost so much blood, they sent out a call for blood donors. Yet from the moment I heard the intern's song, I knew that I was safe in God's hands.

By all odds, I could have died. When my status was upgraded from "critical" to "serious," I learned that the glove compartment had flown open and slashed my face as I fell forward. The rim of my left eye had been cut, my nose was pushed down flat like a squashed tin can, and one cheekbone was gone completely, giving my face a most peculiar contour. The gash started below my right ear and went up across my face to above my left eye. Sixty-seven stitches were required to repair the wound. It was so horrible that they wouldn't allow me to look in a mirror for many days. Sadly, my friend Lila Scott lost one eye.

But as it turned out, I am blessed with some kind of miraculous healing power. My blood supply replenished itself so rapidly that I was able to donate the contributions that came in for me to the hospital's general blood bank. And though an eminent plastic surgeon volunteered to reconstruct my face, my cartilage rebuilt itself so well that I never needed surgery. My broken leg healed so fast that it was a little crooked and they had to break it again to get a straighter new growth. I was in a cast up to my hip, then in one up to the knee, and through it all I had to be in bed, in a traction device. I was in the hospital for eighty-nine days.

Emergency Hospital was thoroughly segregated. The superintendent of nurses was the sister of New York Representative Hamilton Fish, and through her word of my accident quickly reached Eleanor Roosevelt. A few days later three dozen red carnations arrived, accompanied by a card from the White House. There were so many beautiful flowers that I asked the nurses who were taking care of me to distribute them to all the beds in the ward, which brightened up our segregated area considerably!

One day I had drifted off to sleep when a nurse said, "Dorothy, there's someone here to see you." There was dear Mrs. Roosevelt, standing by my bed. When I opened my one good eye to look up at her, she said, "I always remember you had a very pleasant smile, Miss Height, and I know that you'll be smiling again soon." Mrs. Roosevelt's visit was so comforting, and it touched me that she called me Miss Height. The hospital workers, who hardly knew me, called me Dorothy. I mentioned this to my nurse, who explained that they'd been told not to call colored patients by their last names. I let her know what I thought of that: "Don't you think it is a little preposterous for the first lady of the nation to say, 'I'm glad to see you, Miss Height,' and for you to awaken me calling me 'Dorothy'?"

Several days later I learned that some of the hospital workers had not been so pleased with the first lady's visit. When word came that she was on her way to the hospital, the orderlies had been directed to clear away the dishes from the meal they were serving—probably because they didn't want her to see what sort of food we were given. After Mrs. Roosevelt left, one of the orderlies stood in the middle of the floor and stomped her feet. "What's wrong with these people, making us go through all of that just because she was coming?" she snorted. "After all, who is she anyway? She's just a woman like I am." My own nurse was upset by the orderly's behavior. When she told me about it, I noted that there probably was no other country in the world where you would hear a hospital worker speak like that about the wife of the head of the country.

What the orderly resented, no doubt, was that the president's wife had visited me. Had she gone in to see someone on the other side, where the patients were all white, I suppose it would have been all right. She couldn't understand why Mrs. Roosevelt was coming to visit a young black woman.

My nurse was wonderful. During those long weeks that I was immobilized, she taught me how to knit. I couldn't read because they were trying to preserve my eye, so the nurse read to me. Among other things, she read all the cards people sent, and as she did I memorized what each one said. It was a way to keep my mind working.

People in the hospital kept asking who I was. Was I a movie star? A dancer? A singer? They just couldn't understand why so many people were sending good wishes to a young black woman they'd never heard of. That people from all over the country, including some whose names I hardly recognized, sent heartwarming messages gave me great strength. When I came out of the hospital, I had more than a thousand thank-you notes to write!

In 1943, after I had recovered from my accident, the student division of the national board of the YWCA offered me a position working with the student movement in the South. I accepted an invitation to travel to Nashville, Tennessee, to be interviewed. I took the overnight Pullman down from Washington, having been advised that I would be met by Dr. Celestine Smith, whom I was to succeed, and Augusta Roberts, with whom I would be working. When I got to Nashville the next morning, I saw Augusta Roberts through the window of the section for whites only. Dr. Smith and I proceeded to the small dingy room for colored people to get a bite to eat. We sat at a small table.

Dr. Smith beckoned to an old man behind the counter. He brought two cups and a pot that looked as though it had not been washed in several days. He poured out a dark substance—more chicory than anything else. Dr. Smith opened a shoe box offering boiled eggs, fried chicken, bread and butter, a piece of fruit, and a small can of juice. As she took a can opener out of her bag to open the juice, I felt a strange wave of discomfort. I simply could not eat.

After a while, Dr. Smith indicated that it was time to connect with Augusta Roberts, and the three of us proceeded to the Seventh Day Adventist College—one of the few local places that would allow an interracial meeting and the site of the YWCA student conference. From the first moment of the opening meditation, the enthusiasm and spirit among the black and white students was high. At lunch I was disappointed to find that everything had been made of soybeans—not my favorite food. Seventh Day Adventists, I discovered, do not eat meat.

Throughout the day I was involved and challenged. I have never had better responses than in the discussion I led with the whole group—a wide-ranging exploration of the students' concerns and frustrations about discrimination on campus and in community life. Yet at the end of the day my beleaguered body and burdened soul conspired to let me know that I was not ready to undertake the student YWCA work across the South. Although I was committed to tackling racism and segregation, I honestly did not think that I was prepared to give my best in a situation where I would confront blatant segregation every single day.

The following evening we met at the Negro branch of the YWCA with Dean Hilda Davis of Talladega College, chair of the YWCA's personnel committee. For the first time in my life I was unable to imagine how I could make change happen. Even in Washington, D.C., the most segregated place I had ever lived, I was not confronted daily with "White Only" and "Colored Only" signs or the need to negotiate every move, manipulating the system simply in order to function. I thanked Dean Davis for considering me for the position and for what, despite it all, had been a rich experience. I told her that for personal reasons I could not accept. I would remain at the Phyllis Wheatley YWCA.

Many years later I realized how important my Nashville experience had been. No one ever had to tell me about the impact of racism. I could not get out of my mind the sense of hope and determination of those young students who had come together across racial lines. Deep down I resolved that whatever else I did, I would give myself to the struggle for justice and equality.

In 1944 Helen Wilkins, who had been secretary for interracial education of the national board of the YWCA in New York, resigned to get married and move to Michigan. When I was invited to succeed her, I was delighted. I could see clearly how, in that position, I could make a contribution to the national effort to end racism and segregation. At the same time I could return to my beloved New York.

Before I could leave Washington, there was one last assignment I wanted to complete: desegregating the system of giving money to community organizations. What is now the United Way was then called the Community Chest. Whites gave according to where they lived; there was a Rock Creek section, a Capitol Hill section, and a Georgetown section, for example. But the black contribution—no matter where an individual donor lived—was called the "Capitol Division." Black agencies had to organize their own campaign, with black teams that canvassed only black homes all over the District to solicit contributions.

In 1944 Howard Long, assistant superintendent for black public schools, was invited to chair the Capitol Division Community Chest drive. Seeing this as an opportunity to change the system, Dr. Long accepted the invitation on two conditions. First, he insisted that Capitol Division volunteers be integrated with the whole Volunteer Corps and that this be the last year of the Capitol

Division's existence. Second, he wanted me to serve with him as the agency executive.

The board of the Community Chest agreed to the conditions. Volunteers in the Capitol Division were reassigned. If you were a member of a team that went to Fourteenth Street, you would talk to all the blacks and all the whites who lived on the street. After taking great pains to prepare people for the change, we were surprised by their response: whites just took the change in stride, but blacks didn't like it at first—probably because they feared hostility among the old-timers. But ever since, giving in Washington has been integrated.

At the end of October 1944 I returned to New York. I was lucky to find an apartment one flight up in a building on 152nd Street. It had a balcony in the front, and across the street was a rare private house with a stone marker in the yard that read, "1769—Nine Miles to New York." This honest-to-goodness milestone had been there nearly two hundred years.

By the time I returned to Harlem most whites had left the area, but there were still a few, including some who lived next door to me. Our building was small, so most of the families knew each other. Even if you came to live there as a complete stranger, you'd soon get acquainted. People visited from one apartment to another, and there were several older people in the neighborhood with whom I developed warm relationships. I used to make Christmas wreaths and decorations for them. I remember Mrs. Thompson especially well. Christmas didn't arrive at Mrs. Thompson's house until I put the wreath on her door or brought her a little tree. I loved the neighborliness.

I had never lost touch with Harlem, and when I came back, I noticed that people on 152nd Street treated me with some awe. When a story appeared in the newspaper or word got around about my activities, the neighbors were proud. I was also a political presence in the neighborhood, an active participant on the streets and in the community.

I had walked the streets with Adam Clayton Powell Jr. and had tried to quell the fury in the neighborhood during the riots in 1935. I never stopped caring about this place where my roots were so deep. I was proud of Harlem—it was my community. And to my great delight, I discovered that Harlem was proud of me.

Chapter Eight

Step by Step

DURING THE YEARS I spent at the Phyllis Wheatley YWCA in Washington, D.C., the national organization began a process of soul-searching and self-examination that was to transform it completely.

Before World War II, women from the racial branches traditionally gathered in special conferences of their own—a practice established in 1913 by Cordella Wynn and her sister, Eva Bowles, the first Negro national staff member to work with community-based associations.* I participated in the 1940 YWCA Negro Leadership Conference at West Virginia State University. There was a warm climate of fellowship at the conference. The women present— mostly branch executives and branch committee officers—freely

---

* The YWCA of the USA established the first Negro branch in 1895 in Dayton, Ohio. In so doing, it became the first national organization whose leadership was drawn from the majority population that included an administrative unit under the leadership of Negro women.

shared their concerns. A recurring complaint was that the leaders spent most of their time discussing people who were not there—that is, the "white leadership."

Some of us were convinced that more could be accomplished on behalf of both the branches and the association as a whole if the black and white leadership came together. I stayed up most of one night with a small group discussing this issue. By morning we had drafted a resolution recommending that the 1940 Negro Leadership Conference be dissolved. We proposed to seek every opportunity to participate fully in all aspects of YWCA life.

This was a hard-won decision; the Negro Leadership Conference had become a great source of fellowship and strength for everyone. There was fear that without it we might lose what pioneering Negro women leaders had contributed. These women were trailblazers. They had built institutions, showing what the YWCA could be in the community. All agreed that their names—Cecelia Cabaniss Saunders of New York, May Belcher of Indianapolis, Lucy Thurman of Detroit—should go down in history.

In the end, through cheers and tears, the resolution passed. The separate Negro Leadership Conference became a historical footnote. We resolved that whatever goals the association adopted, black and white women would have to work together to achieve them.

That same year, at the fifteenth national YWCA convention, the National Student Assembly challenged the YWCA to make an intensive study to determine the impact of racial segregation on association and community life. Soon after, the national board asked Helen Wilkins, who was black, and Juliet Bell, who was white, to take on the task, aided by a commission of YWCA leaders from around the country. Their report, *Interracial Practices in Community YWCAs*, was published in 1944, shortly before I succeeded Helen Wilkins on the national staff. It included thirty-five recommendations for action. First and foremost among them was "the inclusion of Negro women and girls in the main stream of association life...as a conscious goal."

The recommendations were the first call to close a particularly glaring gap between the YWCA's purpose and its achievement by moving away from the branch system toward full
integration. It seemed to me that the message was clear: even
though the larger society continued to allow itself to be
demeaned by the practice of segregation, it should no longer pre-
vail within the association.

Community associations had been given a two-year "trial"
period before the recommendations would be adopted as official
national policy. During that time association leaders across the
country reported their reactions, sought help on practical problems,
and interpreted the needs of their communities. As Helen
Wilkins's successor as secretary for interracial education, my job
was to facilitate this process by working with associations and their
branches and helping people to appreciate and respect their differences and to work together. Women of all races and creeds were
attracted to the organization, and its mission challenged us to help
one another overcome whatever old prejudices and fears still
divided us.

The YWCA's national president at the time was Mary S. Ingraham, a devout Quaker and one of the women I have cherished
most in my life. Shortly after I arrived, I requested a meeting with
Mrs. Ingraham to get her signature on a letter I had drafted in support of a bill before Congress to establish the Fair Employment
Practices Commission. She read the letter carefully, then said, "You
know, Miss Height, I do not believe that we can bring about this
kind of change with laws." She spoke passionately of her concern,
then added, "I therefore don't see how I can sign this letter,
because I know it will not come through law." I told her that I
understood how she felt and knew that if it were up to her personally, she would bring about fair employment practices without legislation. But the national board, I argued, had to work through
existing legal structures. It was our obligation to lead others to

make the system work for fairness and equality.* Mrs. Ingraham thought for several long moments, in the silent Quaker manner. It felt like forever as she reflected, and I was almost afraid of what she might say. When she lifted her head, her blue eyes were sparkling. She said, "There is an understanding between thee and me." Then Mrs. Ingraham signed the letter, as president of the YWCA of the USA.

Many people agreed in principle with the concept of racial equality but floundered when it came to practice. Not long after I joined the national staff, there was a call for a primer on how to organize and work with interracial groups—and the task of preparing it fell to me.

I struggled with the very concept; there was something about a primer that I didn't like. Why was it so hard for people to understand how to get along with one another? What on earth would a primer on human relations look like?

One day I was talking about this problem with my friend Polly Cochran, who was a member of the national staff of the Girl Scouts. Polly and I worked together at the Harlem branch of the YWCA and had been friends ever since. We were in touch every day. I told Polly that I did not want to call this a "primer" on human relations, and a few days later she called me early one morning and said, "You are always talking about the process and the steps involved. Why don't you call it 'Step by Step'? For some it will be a primer, and for others it may seem elementary, but it will give everyone a chance to learn together and help each other." It was just the push I needed.

---

* I had felt strongly about fair employment practices since the 1930s. I had been very active in the union of the Home Relief Bureau in New York, and when I was working at the Harlem YWCA, I was very interested in efforts by the national staff to organize a union among professional YWCA workers. After I became a member of the national staff, I joined the Community and Social Agency Employees Union. I still cherish the perspective on organized labor the union experience gave me.

I tried to set forth in the booklet the kinds of situations that would be favorable to interracial understanding and what was actually important in that "understanding." There was, for instance, a section called "Little Things That Make a Difference." Now, in these sophisticated times, it may be hard to realize that basic matters, like how people were addressed, were so little understood. But back then there were simple principles of courtesy that people had to learn. Across most of the South, for instance, a woman of color was addressed as "girl" and a man was called "boy." People freely used all sorts of derogatory terms; "nigra," for instance, was a word that white people may have thought was a dressed-up version of "nigger," but it was deeply resented by women of color. I gathered a lot of material from colleagues and friends about little ways in which people pulled themselves apart even while they were trying to get together, often raising barriers where none had existed before.

The "Step by Step" booklet tried to help each reader examine her own anxieties, fears, and frustrations. Beyond prescribing a set of techniques, it encouraged readers simply to be aware of how others felt and to be sensitive in situations fraught with potential for misunderstanding. Too often when we tried to meet fear of interracial experience on a rational level, we failed because that kind of fear is nearly always irrational. Many have assumed that the pattern of segregation exists because of prejudice. Quite the contrary, it seems to me that people are prejudiced because they have been estranged by segregation. They don't know one another, and they fear the unknown. Tasks and meaningful activities undertaken together help people find each other around common goals.

In 1946 the YWCA held its seventeenth national convention in Atlantic City, New Jersey. On the agenda was a document called the Interracial Charter, which had grown out of the Wilkins-Bell report of 1944. Among other things, it declared: "Wherever there is injustice on the basis of race, whether in the community, the nation or the world, our protest must be clear and our labor for its removal vigorous and steady. And what we urge on others, we are constrained to practice ourselves."

Several weeks before the convention more than two hundred YWCAs, most of them in the South, had been stirred up by a letter declaring that if the charter were accepted, the YWCA would cease to exist. The letter, circulated by the executive of the Nashville YWCA and signed by several others, called on community associations to come to the convention prepared to vote against the charter.

In Atlantic City, Mrs. Ingraham met with all the dissenting associations. Though she wanted to hear their concerns, she also wanted to help them understand why adopting the charter was central to the mission of the YWCA. Mrs. Ingraham's message and the theme for the convention, "One God, One Nation Indivisible," were brilliantly illuminated by the keynote address delivered by Dr. Benjamin Elijah Mays, president of Morehouse College.

As Dr. Mays spoke of the evils of segregation and described how it diminished all of us, black and white alike, the audience was very attentive. He said, "I realize what you have before you, what you are trying to do, and . . . most likely all across the country you will hear people saying, 'The time is not ripe.'" There were nods of agreement in the audience. Then he said, "In the Christian ethic, the time is always ripe to do justice. Given your honorable purpose as the Young Women's Christian Association, if the time is not ripe, then it is your job to ripen the time!"

When the time came to vote on the Interracial Charter, some delegates walked out, saying that if they were on the floor during the vote they would not be able to return to their communities. But they were far fewer than the numbers who had arrived in protest. After several days of hard work, discussions, soul-searching, and tears, the Interracial Charter was finally adopted.

When she announced the results of the vote, Mrs. Ingraham stood tall, and her sense of gratification was clear. "The Interracial

Charter has been adopted," she declared, "as a *conscious goal* for the YWCA of the United States of America." Then she put a question to the two thousand association members in the hall. "Do you think it will be easy to implement this charter?" she asked. A muffled roar—"*No*"—came from the assembled. But it was a different kind of no from the one we had heard from the protesters. It was an acceptance—of both the charter and the challenge it presented.

It was a great moment for me. I felt part of a movement that had not only been embraced by the YWCA but also seemed to be gathering steam across the United States. In that huge hall in Atlantic City, women of every creed and color looked the race issue in the eye and agreed: no matter how hard it will be, we are committed to bringing our daily activity truly into line with our ideals.

At that moment I was prouder than ever to be part of the history of this courageous organization. Of course, the YWCA realized that its program would never be a panacea for the evils of racism in the world. But the convention action in 1946 committed every community YWCA to a sincere effort to work toward its goal of inclusiveness.

Shortly after the Interracial Charter was adopted, I visited a newly integrated group of girls at a community YWCA. They told me that their group previously had been much larger, but in the months since the adoption of the charter it had been shrinking. When I asked why, they said, "Now all we do is race-relate, but we'd much rather work together on a community project. We want to do something!"

This was a good tip, and it inspired me to include in the "Step by Step" booklet ideas for bringing people together around productive activities that moved them beyond the introspective, often painful discussions of how to relate to one another. Looking back now, it all seems so simple. But then we knew little about how to help people transcend their fears. We had little experience of working interracially to accomplish something that was larger than any one of us could do alone. We understood that desegregation would not be easy or rapid, that it would be disturbing on both sides of the color line. Bitterness, hostility, and the desire for self-preservation had deepened fears and prejudice within many people of color. Doubting the sincerity of national efforts toward desegregation, many African Americans moved into newly integrated situations with, at best, suspended judgment and, at worst, an inability to be themselves.

Not long after I had begun serving as secretary for interracial education, one of my colleagues, Grace Martins, said, with frustration in her voice, "Dorothy, you always bring up race no matter what we are talking about!" I told her that in my experience there usually was a racial dimension to almost anything we discussed. "I hope that someday others will understand that, so I don't have to be the one who speaks to it all the time," I added. "I hope one day everyone will be conscious that race is not just an interesting subject. What matters is how our life experiences may be truly different from one another. Who we are and what we stand for are what's interesting. When you feel free enough to bring up race yourself, then I will know that I have done my job."

Grace smiled at me, and from that moment I could always count on her. She and I had a special understanding that would last a very long time.

My first major assignment after the 1946 convention was to help YWCAs think about how they were going to implement the recommendations in the Interracial Charter. It did not get off to a good start.

Dallas, Texas, was my first stop. The executive of the association called me at the hotel. "They tell me that you are a Negro," she said. "I didn't ask for any Negro to come here." She made it clear that I would not be welcome at her office. I decided not to argue with her and called Myra Smith, who was in charge of my department in New York, to report my predicament. Myra said she would talk to the Dallas people and sent me on to Chattanooga, Tennessee. I got the same chilly reception there that I'd received in Dallas. I decided I'd better return to headquarters to regroup.

I knew that ordinarily a national staff member would be received by the executive of the central association and have the leverage to convene the officers of both the white central and the black branch in each city she visited. I knew that in many cities such a meeting would be the first time the two groups had ever gathered around the same table—except for when the black women of the branch presented their annual budget proposal and the white women of the central association decided whether they'd accept it. I also knew that such gatherings would tell me a lot about why so many communities were having difficulty putting the Interracial Charter into practice.

Exactly one year after the Interracial Charter was adopted, it was agreed that we should study the seventeen southern YWCAs that had made notable progress, especially in having all members vote for the board of directors. Dothory Sabiston and I were designated the interracial team to do the study. Dothory came from a small town in North Carolina, and she frequently explained, "My people were so backward, when they thought they were naming me Dorothy, they couldn't even spell it right, so my name came out D-o-t-h-o-r-y." Poor dear, people would always try to correct her spelling, and then she would have to correct theirs.

One of the cities that seemed to have made terrific progress was Fort Worth, Texas. When it was time to elect their board, the executive mailed a ballot to everyone on the roster—both central and branch members. The idea was to break the old pattern in which white women elected the board and black women elected the branch committee.

When Dothory and I got to Fort Worth, we congratulated the central leadership. We were in for a surprise. That executive, several leaders said, had overstepped her bounds. She did not have widespread support. Indeed, she had resigned shortly before our

visit, and her successor seemed to have little interest in the goals of
the Interracial Charter. Fort Worth hadn't made such great progress
after all.

Soon we got an even more telling sense of the distance Fort
Worth still had to go. Customarily on our trips Dothory would stay
in a hotel and, because hotels in the South were segregated, I
would be housed with a black family. Usually my hosts prepared
breakfast for me and I'd be out for dinner. But the locally prominent family with whom I stayed in Fort Worth did not consider a
YWCA staff member worthy of their high station. When I awakened, no one offered me so much as a cup of the coffee I could
smell. I was directed to a tiny restaurant that wasn't even open during the day.

When I got to the YWCA, we went straight into a meeting. Neither coffee nor Danish was offered. At noon sandwiches were
brought in, and then at about four o'clock we had a cookie and
some punch. That evening Dothory kindly suggested that I go
with her to her hotel so that she could bring a sandwich out to me
for supper. The following morning, again without breakfast, I
asked if we could have morning coffee at the YWCA. We did, and
again, there were sandwiches at lunchtime.

At the end of the afternoon the board member responsible for
financial matters—one who had most heartily disagreed with the
erstwhile executive's attempt to make the board election more
inclusive—told Dothory that she wanted to "go over some things."
Brandishing a folder of receipts, she said angrily, "Look at these
expenses—coffee, sandwiches, drinks in the afternoon! We don't
need all of this." Dothory began to explain, but the board member
interrupted, saying that I should leave the room.

Dothory said, "But we're a team, we work together."

"We don't need two of you to do this," the woman snapped.
"Y'all have just come down here to cause trouble." Her tone was
bitter.

Perhaps it was my empty stomach, or maybe it was my heavy

heart, but I couldn't hold back. I drew myself up and said, "You're part of the YWCA of the United States of America. We represent the national board, and our job is to be supportive." We had come to Fort Worth, I explained, to express appreciation for the association's work and to learn from what they had done. "Apparently you haven't liked the process in which we are involved, or what the Young Women's Christian Association is all about," I said. "Perhaps you should know that it hasn't been easy for Miss Sabiston and me to work together with you either. We have not said anything about this community—it is your community—but as a member of a woman's movement concerned about people and community, you might be interested to know that I have been in this town for three days and I have not had one hot meal. I have been treated as a roomer without privileges. I would have thought, knowing something of southern hospitality, that any person coming to Fort Worth as a visitor should be able to expect to have at least one hot meal. But I have not. And yet I have worked through these days with you, I have tried to be supportive and to be of help."

Those experiences in the field often were painful, but they were valuable to me and to the association. I learned that efforts toward desegregation rested heavily on experiences that gave people the courage to be themselves. I learned to disagree without being disagreeable. And I learned that when opportunities were created for people to get acquainted, to cooperate in stimulating common tasks, and to increase their mutual understanding, their attitudes changed and opened. We also discovered that if we waited for attitudes to be changed just through hopeful encouragement, we'd be waiting forever.

One of the toughest jobs in the days of segregation was finding a meeting place that would welcome persons of different races on equal terms. Since 1922 the YWCA had had a policy of holding national meetings only in places where members of all races were accepted. In 1947 the YWCA planned a gathering at Camp Merrie-Woode in the Black Mountains of North Carolina. The camp was owned by a recently retired white army officer who understood what we were about and supported us—a rare find in those days.

But even there we sometimes ran into trouble. One of our earliest gatherings at Merrie-Woode had gone quietly enough, but when we went to the train station to go home on a hot August day, a guard told me I could not stand on the open-air platform with my white coworkers. I was to go into the colored waiting room, a tiny, airless spot. When I refused to move, a black station attendant told me the guard had called the police, and sure enough, a policeman on a motorcycle suddenly zoomed onto the platform. He shouted, "You go in that colored waiting room!" A young black girl from the conference grabbed my arm and pleaded, "Oh, please, let's go in the colored waiting room. They told my brother the same thing in Louisville, and then they shot him in the arm when he didn't go."

Just then our train arrived. The cop followed me as we moved toward the segregated car at the front. He yelled again for me to go in the colored waiting room. "This is my train," I called, starting to run, and he growled, "Don't you go straight on that train or I'll blow your brains out." At that moment my white colleagues came up beside me and escorted me to the front car. We just kept moving forward, no matter what the cop said. As the young girl and I squeezed into the crowded segregated car and the train chugged away, the cop stood watching us with as mean a look as I'd ever seen. As the train pulled off, the girl had a hemorrhage and had to be hospitalized. I reported this incident to Roy Wilkins, executive director of the National Association for the Advancement of Colored People. He said, "Dorothy, had you been a black man, you would have been dead."

The following summer, when it came time to choose a site for an interracial conference of young industrial workers, I recalled this incident, confessing that the Merrie-Woode camp was not my favorite conference site. The problem was that we had no other.

When we arrived, a YWCA and YMCA interracial student meeting had just ended. We were met by two very concerned coworkers. The week before, when students had taken film to be developed at the local pharmacy, the druggist had blown up one of the photographs and hung it in his window with a sign: "See how the YWCA is mixing the races!" The whole town was stirred up, and there had been threats against the camp owner.

We had to decide immediately whether to go ahead with our conference of three hundred young women from all over the South, many of whom were already on their way. The camp owner offered to appeal to the mayor and others in the community who he thought might help. Brooks Creedy, the project director, went with him, but the two were received with unresponsive chilliness.

The camp owner was shaken. My YWCA colleagues wanted to hold firm, but I was the only black person in the advance group, and the owner said it was not safe for me to be there. He made arrangements for me to stay at the home of the principal of the local colored school. My white colleagues went to a nearby motel, taking with them our international guests for the conference, young YWCA workers from China and Lebanon.

When I arrived at the principal's home, my nervous hostess suggested that I hide upstairs in the attic. Assaulted by swirls of dust and dog hairs in the small, airless space, my asthmatic bronchi nearly closed. I wondered whether it mattered whether I died there in the attic or in an assault by rednecks on the campground. After an hour I was willing to risk the latter. I climbed down from the attic and told the principal that I had heard of a regional NAACP president who might be able to help. I persuaded her to let her ten-year-old daughter take me to his home. It was a long, painful walk. As the afternoon turned into dusk, every bush that could do so made a sound, and every sound suggested danger.

When finally I met the NAACP president, I told him about the meeting the YWCA planned to convene. He looked at me pensively. Then he said, "I am fifty-nine years old, and I have never talked to a white man about anything except a job he wanted me to do or a job I was looking for." When I told him about the camp owner's meetings with the mayor and the sheriff, he offered to intervene. He could handle those two officials, he said, because neither of them could have been elected had he not rallied the black vote for them. I felt better.

Before dawn the next morning, Brooks Creedy, my coworker, came out to the principal's house to let me know that earlier some three hundred Klansmen had marched on the camp. Armed with bats and pipes, they had ransacked every corner of the grounds. They didn't find the interracial group they were looking for, and the owner told them that we were a peaceful group, that we wouldn't make any trouble. When they left, the camp owner felt that we could proceed as planned.

Meanwhile, we made contact with Constance Anderson, the national president of the YWCA. The organization appealed to the governor of North Carolina, who promised protection by the state police. Then, shortly after 10:00 A.M., the NAACP president drove up. His confident air of the evening before had vanished. "I am very sorry," he said, "but the mayor said he wasn't certain that you all should have these meetings. You know how it is down here. The sheriff has already left town."

But we decided to proceed. After our young workers arrived, we told them what had happened. But their delight at being together was greater than their misgivings. Even when Klan members rode nightly through the grounds, pointing blinding searchlights and hurling racial slurs through our windows, the women seemed fearless. They even went into town to shop, although no one took film to be processed at the pharmacy.

Our international guests, Edma Bayuth of Lebanon and Hin Sin of China, found the situation more difficult. Both came near to hysteria before the conference ended. They were especially perplexed that they could be accepted at the motel but I could not, when we all had about the same skin color. Years later, when I was visiting

Beirut, Edma Bayuth introduced me and told the story of her visit to North Carolina—a challenging introduction, as I was planning to speak about recent progress in race relations in the United States.

After the conference, when I got back to New York, I visited the YWCA doctor, who examined a rash that had developed on the back of my neck. She laughed as she told me that at New York Hospital they called this form of herpes zoster "The Great White Ailment," because its only cause was stress and she had never seen a person of color present that rash. When I told her about those six days in North Carolina, she chuckled and said, "No wonder! We always pay a price."

In 1949 the citywide YWCAs in Grand Rapids, Michigan, and Princeton, New Jersey, both elected a Negro woman as president. The same year the national convention pledged, as a participating member of the World YWCA, "to seek deeper insight into the international implications of the Interracial Charter and to exert greater effort to realize its religious and ethical goals on a world-wide scale." Slowly, we were making progress.

Then, in 1954, the U.S. Supreme Court struck a fatal blow to the legal basis for racial segregation. In the landmark case of *Brown vs. the Board of Education*, the court declared desegregation in the public schools unconstitutional, outlawing the "separate but equal" doctrine. At YWCA headquarters we produced a booklet, "Our Schools and Our Democracy," to encourage associations to participate fully in helping desegregate the schools. We also convened a southern regional conference in Atlanta to discuss the problems and opportunities of desegregation. A series of foundation grants enabled the National Student YWCA to work specifically on issues of race and human relations. I worked with the student leadership to develop simple things that people could do, such as escorting a child to school when it was first integrated.

Even so, the road to full racial integration throughout the

YWCA remained long and rocky. As a national voluntary organization dependent on the goodwill—and the contributions—of the community, we had to call up a special fund of courage to take unpopular steps. But we were acutely aware of our shortcomings and our moral obligation to practice the democracy we preached.

In 1963, as the push toward full equality picked up momentum across the nation, I invited civil rights leaders to meet with the national board of the YWCA. That meeting inspired the board to allocate funds for "a bold assault" on racial injustice—a two-year action program to achieve integration throughout YWCA programs, membership, and leadership. The weightiness of the commitment was lightened for a moment when, during the discussion of the bold assault, one board member who was hard of hearing earnestly asked, "I understand why we're all concerned about achieving full integration, but why do we have to do it with a 'bowl of salt'?"

Florence Harris, a white southerner, and I were asked to take responsibility for the bold assault. In appearance, she and I were opposites. I am tall and dark, and Florence was quite short and fair, and several of our colleagues dubbed us Mutt and Jeff. To begin, we decided to assess how well associations across the country were doing. The board urged us to visit places where the associations had been slow to change, to see what we could do to help. Several times, when we sent word that we would be coming, community associations wired back, "You don't have to come, we have just done such and such." Then they enumerated what they had done—that very week!—to remove barriers to racial integration.

Discouraged after our first round of visits, Florence Harris and I decided to take a long and careful look at public policy as it affected racial segregation, discrimination, and integration—abroad in the land as well as internally within the YWCA.

We put together some tough questions. We asked how the pattern of segregation had affected us in our lives and in our association. We looked closely at how institutional racism affected the YWCA's own policy, practice, leadership roles, and distribution of resources. We decided to take a formal internal audit. What was the composition of our board? Did we have diversity in our decision-making process? What was the composition of our membership, and how did the membership of each community association relate to the demographics of the larger community?

When we reported on our work at the next annual convention, an irritated national board member came up to me and said, "Really, Miss Height, we have done so well. I hate to hear you talk about things like institutional racism. We've had such good relations, why spoil it all with that kind of talk?" I replied that she was right—we had made progress in building bridges of understanding. But now we had to look at why the bridges needed to be built. "It is not personal prejudice," I told her. "It is simply the way that racial inequality and discrimination are built into our systems."

In 1965 the YWCA established the Office of Racial Justice. I was named director, charged with leading a massive campaign to eradicate discrimination in the YWCA and in society. I knew that we wouldn't change overnight, but I decided to encourage a new direction—to move from solving problems to changing systems, from liberalism to liberation, from simply "giving equal opportunity" to creating an equitable society.

The range of reactions to this aggressive agenda was interesting. Some of our white sisters feared that the concern for the empowerment of minorities rendered them useless, with no place in the struggle for justice. Integration was on trial because the token presence of one or two from a minority group had too easily become sufficient, and to some that trial seemed to deprecate their personal efforts. Soon after the Office of Racial Justice was created, we gathered women in groups according to racial background. We wanted them to talk and to listen to one another—to hear how people felt, what and whom they feared, and what obstacles were in the way of their acting together to resolve issues that were tearing their communities apart.

In 1966 President Johnson announced a White House conference, "To Fulfill These Rights," that would consider the status of minorities in education, employment, housing, and the justice system. YWCAs across the country met on these issues and submitted recommendations, and I served on the advisory committee for the conference itself. Ben Heineman of Chicago, the chair, was bothered by the fact that I was knitting through the meetings. He expressed his concern to Carl Holman of the U.S. Commission on Human Rights, who advised him not to worry. After a break, I raised a question that redirected the discussion. Mr. Heineman turned to Carl Holman and with great good humor said, "I see what you mean."

In 1967 the national YWCA elected Helen Wilkins Claytor as its first black president and adopted a constitutional amendment: any association not "fully integrated in policy and practice and thereby living up to the Statement of Purpose" would be disaffiliated. The following year, under the direction of my office, community and student YWCAs continued to examine the subtleties of racism in America. The national board adopted YWCA Project Equality, pledging to purchase goods and services from equal opportunity employers, to review its own employment practices, and to recruit women leaders from minority groups. Associations around the country worked on Operation Breadbasket, supported the Farm Workers Union's grape boycott, and supported black businesses and university divestiture from South Africa. Beginning at headquarters and then around the country, we held racial justice institutes and black economic development seminars. It was gratifying to see women grappling with the real issues.

There was excitement and enthusiasm about our work, and yet, at the same time, I began to sense growing unease, particularly among black members. Many of these women had been part of the YWCA since the days when they were not always treated so well. They had stayed because they believed in the organization's stated commitment to its purpose. As the tumultuous sixties were coming to a close, I felt it was time for the black women of the YWCA to gather together once again to take stock.

We began with a small planning session. Some women expressed concern about an all-black meeting. "This is not about being separate," I replied. "It's about how as black women we make our contribution to the whole and how the whole receives our contribution." Ellen Dammond, one of the most skeptical women there, told me that her husband had said she had better attend if Dorothy Height called a meeting. "I'm so glad I came," she said, "because we are not talking about the white women, we are talking about ourselves, asking, What do we have to bring to the organization?"

Ultimately we announced a national conference of black women members of the YWCA in Houston, Texas, just prior to the 1970 national convention. Immediately people in the larger associations started talking. We heard things like, "Why are you calling for segregation?" I worried that such widespread misunderstanding about our motives might mean we had taken too radical a step.

Mary Ingraham was no longer active with the YWCA, but her wisdom was still a source of strength for me. I sent her material about the conference, and when we met, I described what I hoped to accomplish. As always, she listened thoughtfully and then pointed out that black women were examining their role in the YWCA and that was very useful. We should have the conference in Houston. Her reassurance convinced me that we were doing the right thing.

In the spring of 1970, five hundred black women and girls from thirty-eight states arrived in Houston. The main agenda item for the national convention was a list of seven imperatives the national board was recommending to focus the YWCA on the issues of the day. In addition to "combating racial injustice," the imperatives had to do with world peace, environmental quality, the elimination of poverty, and encouraging youth and women to aspire to greater leadership roles in society.

At the meeting of black members, one woman pointed out that there was "a racial dimension" to each of these imperatives. "What we need," she said, "is *one* imperative: to eliminate racism." After hours of debate we produced wording for the "One Imperative": "to thrust our collective power toward the...elimination of racism wherever it exists and by any means necessary." We agreed that we should go into the convention not as a caucus or a protest group but as a part contributing to the whole. At the proper time we would bring our recommendation to the floor. It would not be revealed before then.

Ultimately the Twenty-fifth National YWCA Convention—2,709 women representing 329 community associations, 41 student associations, and two registered clubs—went on record:

> That the YWCA thrust its collective power toward the one issue inherent in all of the imperatives stated in the 1970 convention Work Book, and that imperative is the elimination of racism wherever it exists and by any means necessary.

The whole convention seemed uplifted by the One Imperative. In part that was because the vote was the culmination of all the workshops, roundtables, institutes, and neighborhood work that we had done from Maine to California. Power shifts were under way. Women and students, blacks and browns, were moving from words to acts.

Following the convention, we developed a national program to attack racism. Once the broad outlines were defined, we held separate conferences with white women, Asian women, and Native American women. We explored how institutional racism operates like a web: where you live influences where you go to school, which influences where you get a job, who you know, and what you believe.

I knew that people need a handle to take hold. They do best when there are activities and tasks that help them learn and act. To that end, I worked with a team to design an "Action Audit for Change." Each association was to study itself and recommend ways to encourage racial justice throughout the surrounding community. We also examined the national board and staff. How representative were they? Did our institutional structure hinder or encourage the elimination of racism?

In June 1972 the national board called a National Convocation on Racial Justice. I was honored that Ruth Bunche and Mary F. Rockefeller chaired the planning committee. Mrs. Rockefeller's only question was, "Why would we call a meeting on racial justice rather than on race relations?" But once I discussed the need to move beyond interpersonal relations to the underlying issues in racism, she understood.

Representatives of more than one hundred cooperating national organizations from five continents and forty-four states came together in what we hoped would be a renewal of the fight for racial justice. McGeorge Bundy, president of the Ford Foundation, set the keynote: "The fundamental obstacle, not only to the advancement of black people and other minorities but to the establishment of a general and accepted sense of social justice in our country, is, in fact, racism."

The outstanding presentations on key issues and the statements developed by each of the five racial groups made for an enlightening and inspiring convocation. The recommendations from the convocations were sent to the platform committees of both the Republican and the Democratic National Conventions.

The meeting took on a special quality when fourteen Native Americans representing twelve tribes protested the Wooden Indian—a bar in the Americana hotel. Not only was the stereotype of the "drunken Indian" in the bar's name, but many items in its decor violated Native American religion.

When a delegation of Native Americans and the YWCA leadership met with the executive management of the hotel, there was a real meeting of minds. Pat Bellinger of the American Indian Movement expressed in the *American Indian Community House* newsletter appreciation "for the powerful moral support given by the National YWCA Convocation" and the understanding of hotel managers "when, for the first time, they really realized the deep meaning of the situation."

As we labored to discharge our pledge during those years I often thought of Mrs. Roosevelt's words before the United Nations in 1958:

> Where, after all, do universal human rights begin? In small places, close to home—so close and so small that they cannot be seen on any map of the world. Yet they are the world of the individual person: the neighborhood he lives in; the school or college he attends; the factory, farm or office where he works. Such are the places where every man, woman, and child seeks equal justice, equal opportunity, equal dignity without discrimination. Unless these rights have meaning there, they have little meaning anywhere. Without concerted citizen action to uphold them close to home, we shall look in vain for progress in the larger world.

In 1937 I chose the YWCA, and I have been glad ever since. It gave base and meaning for my life's work. I was humbled and thankful to have been made an honorary member of the national board in 1977. And I was honored in April 2000, when the YWCA established a Dorothy I. Height Racial Justice Award, which Alexine Jackson, the national president, presented to President William Jefferson Clinton. It is heartening to me to know that the mission of the YWCA for the immediate future is "to empower women and girls, and eliminate racism."

Chapter Nine

The Land of the Free

WHEN I WAS a little girl, there was a black actor named Canada Lee who was famous for belting out the last lines of "America"—the ones about the "land of the free and the home of the brave." I presumed the words meant that each of us has the right to say, "This is my country—this is where I belong." It was many years before I realized that when Negroes talked about the "mainstream," we really meant white people. We had to remind ourselves again and again that since slaves were first brought here, blacks have been a part of whatever stream there was. We have not been in the mainstream of opportunity, but we have always been Americans.

An incident in Europe when I was twenty-five seared my consciousness about race in this country. After the Oxford conference in 1937, I took a side trip to Germany. The day after I arrived I was boarding the hotel van to go into town when the only other passenger, a white American, objected to my getting on. In deference to her, the hotel doorman called me back. I protested. He muttered, "If you were in your own country, wouldn't you be lynched for getting in a car like that?" That hit me hard, and I fought back. I told him Americans of all races were working against lynching. "We are free to work against it, and we do," I said, feeling proud of my country.

Later that night I found myself wondering why I had so strongly defended this land that I knew was not free for many of the brave who called it home. If I had been traveling with a white American, I wondered, would she have defended me? In the end my sense of belonging to America proved stronger than my fears about the possible truth of the German doorman's harsh words. I pulled myself up and chastised myself out loud: "Why are you even asking such a question? You are an American!" But I resolved that when I got home, I'd find out whether my confidence was justified. For many months thereafter, whenever I spoke before a group, I'd ask, "Who here is ready to fight to see that a person like me is not lynched and that lynching is abolished? Who among you is ready to join hands to bring justice for all?"

A few years later, during the war, I was seated on a train from New York to Washington next to Elizabeth Dillinger, an outspoken Communist. Throughout the ride down this woman kept asking me, "Why do you people fight? Why are black men willing to risk their lives overseas for the United States?" I didn't respond, but I understood why she was hounding me.

The truth is that black people have fought for this country from the beginning. The first blood shed in the American Revolution was that of a runaway slave, Crispus Attucks, in the Boston Massacre. Blacks have always been in the army, even when they were mistreated. Certainly some protested from time to time, and a few have asked, "Why should I go overseas and fight for democracy when there isn't any for me here?" But I doubt that any history of blacks producing a traitor could be found.

There has always been within the black community a sense that this is our country. We haven't really been able to say, "My country cherishes me, and that is why I do this for my country," but we still say, "This is my country." We have a heritage here. We are African American. We belong here just as any other Americans belong here. Negro Americans always have felt a strong sense of patriotism that calls us to fulfill our obligation to our country while we continue the fight for the right to be free.

I've often thought that young whites generally are denied the opportunity to think seriously about what it means to be a citizen, much less a patriot. They're deprived because they're not confronted by the question in the way that a black person is every day. Many whites take for granted the benefits of democracy, assuming that the rights of citizenship are "guaranteed" to everybody. They've never been forced to understand the true meaning of the privileges of democracy, nor do they realize that many people of color still don't have them.

Yet when someone less privileged challenges the system because it isn't working as it should for everyone, whites are inclined to respond by grabbing hold of what they think they have—and fear they might lose. All too few are ready to say, "Let's listen. Maybe there is something to what these people are saying." Instead, they say, "You are better off here than you would be anywhere else. Don't you see how well you are being treated?"

It is as if full democracy belongs exclusively to them, as if their citizenship has greater worth than ours, just because our skins are dark and theirs are not. They seem to fear that if we gain, they will lose, that freedom is finite and there's not enough to go around. It saddens me that civil rights issues so often are used to polarize people rather than to move us all ahead. Few seem to understand how much we lose as a polity when the potential of so many is diminished by the tyranny of second-class citizenship.

It troubles me when whites, without any real knowledge of the black experience, mistakenly attribute African Americans' enthusiasm for a strong federal system to our "dependency" on government. There is a good reason why protection promised by federal laws based on democratic principles always has meant more to black people than to whites: it was the only hope we had! After the Emancipation there were no civil rights laws enacted until 1957. Progress came through the courts.

In the darkest days of segregation, when each state adopted and strictly enforced its own segregation laws, if you were an African American who moved from one place to another, your rights were defined by the particular state you were in. I know no one who wants to be "dependent" on the government, but when the constitutionally protected civil rights of certain citizens are blatantly abrogated by states, what more important or proper role is there for the federal government than to uphold the Constitution in defense of those citizens' rights? When I hear candidates for public office today who proudly run *against* government, I wonder if they would take that position so glibly had they walked with us through the streets of Selma or Jackson in the early sixties.

Some would say that the struggle for civil rights got a jump-start in 1942, when A. Philip Randolph threatened to call a march on Washington to protest racial discrimination. In response, President Franklin Roosevelt issued Executive Order 8802, which banned discrimination in government and defense industry hiring and established the Fair Employment Practices Commission. Six years later President Harry Truman's order to desegregate the armed forces was the first major step toward the dissolution of segregationist policy at the national level. In those days it was only through executive order or, on occasion, the federal courts that progress toward full enfranchisement for Negroes happened. The Civil Rights Act of 1957, which weakened restrictions on black voter registration, was the first piece of civil rights legislation to be passed by Congress since the Emancipation Proclamation.*

---

* In 1950 A. Philip Randolph, Roy Wilkins of the NAACP, and Arnold Aronson, a Jewish leader, organized the Leadership Conference on Civil Rights (LCCR) to focus on civil rights legislation. The LCCR has coordinated activities on every major civil rights law since 1957. In 1994 I was asked to succeed Benjamin L. Hooks as chair of the LCCR, having been a member since the first meeting in 1950. It is a challenging role. Today the LCCR consists of 180 organizations representing persons of color, women, children, people with disabilities, gays and lesbians, older Americans, labor unions, and religious, civil liberties, and human rights groups.

If you tried to make progress through legislation in those early years, you ran up against people who'd say, "You can't legislate what's in people's hearts." Whenever I heard that, I'd remember the words of the Anglican theologian William Temple, later archbishop of Canterbury, at the 1937 Oxford conference. In answer to the charge that laws do not make people honest, he said, "But you can put the burglars in jail." Laws are in place to help people live civilized lives. Laws also can help society restructure relationships, as we learned after public accommodation statutes changed in the 1960s. When restaurants started serving black people, they soon were full of white people too, many of whom had said they'd never sit in the same room with a person of color. Once the laws changed, people began to behave differently.

For many the push for comprehensive civil rights for black Americans didn't really begin until the Supreme Court decided in *Brown v. Board of Education* that school segregation was unconstitutional. Few of us who were living at the time will ever forget May 17, 1954, the day the decision came down. People recall it as vividly as the day war broke out, or the day President Kennedy was assassinated—except this was a day for celebration. I was at a meeting at the YWCA when the word came. We immediately adjourned. We felt like declaring a holiday! People even made jokes, like one man who went into a restaurant and asked if they had black-eyed peas or chitterlings. When the waiter said no, the man said, "Well then, y'all are not ready!"

That the court's determination was unanimous gave me more hope than I had felt in a long while. At last the doctrine of "separate but equal," established in the *Plessy v. Ferguson* decision of 1886, was dead. The new ruling said that if you make people separate, you are saying that they are not equal. It was breathtaking to think that in this country, with its deeply ingrained racist doctrine, you could get such a clear-cut decision.

Of course, there were immediate efforts to circumvent the ruling. Mississippi passed a state law that said schooling was no longer required—just did away with compulsory education entirely with the stroke of a pen! The most dramatic response was in Prince Edward County, Virginia. There they closed the schools rather than obey the Supreme Court ruling. Sixteen hundred white and seventeen hundred Negro children were denied any possibility of decent public education. The chant of county officials was resolute: "There'll be no racial mixin' in schools down here."

Makeshift classrooms were hastily organized to school white children, using private funding. Under the leadership of the Reverend L. Francis Griffin, black parents organized the Prince Edward County Christian Association (PECCA), which proposed to establish ten educational and recreational centers to "counter the harmful and deteriorating effects of forced idleness on Negro children." PECCA made clear that these centers were not to be interpreted as a substitution for public schools but merely as an interim accommodation for black students. When PECCA appealed to the National Council of Negro Women (NCNW) for support, we were happy to help. A corps of volunteers rang doorbells across the county to raise funds and tell the story. Ethel Payne, the journalist, created the theme, "Knock on every door!"

The problems were by no means limited to the South. When the reality of school desegregation hit New York and Chicago and Boston, people in those cities realized that they had problems too, and they didn't know how to cope with them. In many places in the North the push for full integration caught people off guard.

And of course, even as the South moved haltingly toward desegregating schools, segregation in every other part of life held fast. For years after the Supreme Court decision, any African American traveling below the Mason-Dixon Line was immediately caught up in a web of discriminatory practices.

In the early sixties this began to change. When the "Freedom Riders" tried in 1962 to integrate "Whites Only" or "Colored Only" waiting rooms and eateries in bus stations throughout the

South, they were testing a new Interstate Commerce Commission (ICC) law that promised federal protection against segregation to interstate travelers. Many were carted off to jail for "disobeying" local law enforcement agents. But despite its failure to take hold immediately, the new federal law to protect state-to-state travelers against segregation kept alive the black community's faith that democracy could work one day at the national level.

Stephen Currier, the president of the philanthropic Taconic Foundation, was known for his deep personal interest in civil and human rights. In 1960, eager to find ways to encourage other philanthropists to get more involved, Currier asked a group of like-minded Americans to meet regularly with him and the Taconic Foundation staff. To make it work, he designed some rules for a new kind of partnership. The group would meet monthly, if possible. Participation was limited to the heads of organizations—no surrogates allowed. And the chairmanship would rotate among the members.

The group included Whitney Young of the National Urban League, and A. Philip Randolph, leader of the Brotherhood of Sleeping Car Porters and vice president of the AFL-CIO. There was Roy Wilkins, head of the NAACP, and Jack Greenberg of the NAACP Legal Defense Fund. The group was rounded out with James Farmer, head of the Congress of Racial Equality (CORE), C. Eric Lincoln, a student of the Black Muslim movement, and me—and of course, Martin Luther King Jr. of the Southern Christian Leadership Conference (SCLC).

I had first met Dr. King just after World War II, when I was heading a YWCA training team in Atlanta and was a house guest of Dr. and Mrs. Benjamin Mays, my chaperones and mentors at the Oxford conference in 1937. Dr. Mays had since become president of Morehouse College in Atlanta, and Martin Luther King, who was then only fifteen years old, had been admitted to Morehouse as a gifted student. He quickly became one of Dr. Mays's favorites. At dinner Dr. Mays asked whether Martin had made up his mind about what he wanted to do with his life. It was fascinating to hear this extraordinary young man talk. He was considering law, medicine, and the ministry, and he spoke about his choices with a special kind of youthful maturity, a seriousness that shone through. Just ten years later that precocious young man emerged as a preeminent figure in the civil rights movement, and by the early 1960s he was our undisputed leader. His very presence commanded respect.

The task of the group Stephen Currier had assembled was to examine specific areas of concern and produce a study that could be of use to potential donors. The areas we chose to consider were law and the criminal justice system, housing, the role of social agencies, employment, health services, business, and education. Each of us agreed to be the resource person for one of these areas and to bring together a small advisory group to contribute to the study. I elected to work on the role of social agencies.

As we began our work there was a quickening of nonviolent civil disobedience in the South. In April 1963, Dr. King was jailed in Birmingham for demonstrating without a permit. During his eleven-day incarceration he wrote the famed "Letter from a Birmingham Jail." But although the protests were peaceful, some in the South reacted to the growing calls for racial justice with brutal violence. On June 12, 1963, Medgar Evers, the Mississippi field secretary of the NAACP, was assassinated in front of his home in Jackson—shot in the back.

After Medgar's death, Stephen Currier hurriedly called our group together. Concerted action was needed more than ever we agreed.

Stephen agreed to solicit support among his friends and associates in the philanthropic community. He dispatched telegrams to one hundred eminent people, inviting them to an early breakfast a few days later. When he got no responses, he became suspicious and discovered that not one of the telegrams had been delivered by Western Union. Stephen took the issue to the highest levels, then re-sent his invitations. This time the telegrams went out immediately.

The day Medgar Evers was buried in Arlington Cemetery, ninety people came to breakfast at the Carlyle Hotel in New York. Special arrangements were made for Roy Wilkins to speak first so that he could leave for the burial ceremony. All of us were asked to speak from our particular vantage point about the civil rights struggle. I talked about conditions affecting children and youth and their treatment at the hands of law enforcement officers. At the end of the discussion Whitney Young made it plain that all of us knew more about what needed to be done and how to do it than our resources would allow. "We are all hurting," he declared.

The response was amazing. Within an hour that gathering contributed nearly $1 million to advance civil rights. While most of the contributions were designated for tax-exempt purposes, more than one-third were not, and many who gave at that breakfast in 1963 have remained steadfast supporters over the years.

A few days after our meeting at the Carlyle the five participating organizations established the Council for United Civil Rights Leadership (CUCRL) as a tax-exempt corporation. The CUCRL gave us a structure for collective planning and allocation of funds. Under its banner, we set to work with rekindled faith.

I have often felt that it was the hand of God that had brought us all together many months before. Because we had established relationships and a sense of common purpose, we offered a unified response when it was most needed.

Dr. King tried to keep us centered on our common goals, and he especially appreciated the role women played in the civil rights struggle. On September 15, 1963, four little girls died in Birmingham, Alabama, when a bomb was thrown into the Sixteenth Street Baptist Church. That atrocity caught the attention of the nation. Dr. King asked me to bring some women to meet with the mothers of Birmingham, who were understandably deeply distressed. Fourteen women leaders agreed to accompany me to Mississippi the following weekend. When we were just about to leave, we got word that the motel where we planned to stay had been bombed.

Even so, every one of those women was determined to make the trip—and the mothers of Birmingham welcomed us with open arms. We talked with them for hours, gratified to realize that even black people who had long accepted segregation were now awakening. We returned home with a new sense of commitment.

Though I was the only woman in the leadership group, I was treated as a peer. Years later a historian pointed out that each of the men was employed by his agency—I was the one volunteer! Although sometimes the men had trouble seeing why I was always linking desegregation with hunger and children and other social welfare issues, we had as strong a male-female peer relationship as people could at that time in history.* There were times when the men disagreed with each other and I could bridge the gap.

Especially in the early days there was considerable jockeying for position among the men. Ever since the 1955–56 bus boycott in Montgomery, Alabama, Martin Luther King Jr.—who had led the boycott, along with the Reverend Ralph Abernathy—had been like a magnet to the press. Inevitably, other leaders of long-established organizations were somewhat envious. But the group never squabbled—it was far too sophisticated for that. Roy Wilkins, the senior member and head of the oldest civil rights organization, the NAACP, was chosen as chair. He was witty, brilliant, and very secure. Usually quite diplomatic, he did not hesitate to lash out at the tactics of groups he felt were undermining what the NAACP had achieved working through the courts.

---

* Once, when the civil-rights group was meeting with President Johnson, Roger Wilkins of the Justice Department and Clifford Alexander, an Assistant to the President, took me aside. It was hard, they said, to find a picture of me in meetings with the President. I tended to sit on the Vice President's side of the table, while the men sat on the President's side—where the photographers focused. To correct that, the two walked me into the room in advance and placed me at the chair to the President's left. But when my friends and colleagues entered, Roy Wilkins eased into his usual place, moving me down the line without a chair. Roger Wilkins added an extra. When the LBJ Library opened in Texas, the picture taken that day was hung in a prominent place. Sure enough, there I was at the end of the table.

I smile when I recall the meeting at which I suggested including the Student Nonviolent Coordinating Committee (SNCC) in the civil rights leadership. The youthful members of SNCC, full of revolutionary zeal, were using tactics some saw as counterproductive. But I was concerned that the young people were not at the table. Whatever our differences, we needed our young people with us—we needed to support each other. I was very pleased when my colleagues agreed to admit SNCC to the Council for United Civil Rights Leadership. Within SNCC, the national chairman and the executive director shared power, so either chair James Forman or executive John L. Lewis—but not both—could attend any given CUCRL meeting.

As time went along we came to understand that it was unity, not uniformity, that was important. When there was controversy over his marches in the South, Dr. King jokingly said that at least he had made the NAACP, which worked through the courts, look more respectable. Whitney Young often chuckled that when SNCC or CORE kicked over the traces, it opened the way for the National Urban League to negotiate. We wasted no time evaluating or criticizing the different tactics of our groups, and in the end we developed a kind of mutual appreciation and respect, an uncommon meeting of minds.

In one meeting Jane Lee Eddy of the Taconic Foundation asked whether we wanted help from volunteers. Roy Wilkins, who was presiding, quickly said we all had lots of volunteers. After the meeting I told Jane Lee that I would be interested. She gave me information about several women, and at the next meeting I said I was especially interested in the one who had written a piece entitled "Sunrise at Campobello," because I felt that if I had been in the same situation, I would have wanted to cover it in the same way. "That is Polly Cowan," she said.

Jane Lee Eddy contacted Polly Cowan, who was on Martha's Vineyard, and Polly called me right back. She said that she could come to New York the next day. As promised, she came to the hotel where I was attending a convention, and we got acquainted. I told her that A. Philip Randolph had once again called for a march on Washington and that the National Council of Negro Women wanted to lead a meeting after the march. I wanted her help in the planning. She mentioned a friend, Trude Lash, who was also on the Vineyard, and said the two of them would work on it as soon as she got back.

In June 1963, at a meeting at the White House, President Kennedy had told a civil rights group that "Bull" Connor—the Alabama police chief who'd been seen on television and on newspapers with his foot on the neck of a black woman—might prove to be the best friend of the civil rights effort. It was true that many people who were not worried about subtler forms of discrimination came to their senses when they saw the blatant inhumanity of Bull Connor, the youths being washed away with fire hoses in Georgia, or black women being poked with cattle prods as they tried to register to vote in Louisiana. A tempest of violence against black people throughout the South had aroused a profound sense of national disgust.

The idea for harnessing the growing indignation in a march on Washington originated with A. Philip Randolph. It was clear to all of us that conditions were growing worse, and he felt strongly that it was time to rally for jobs and freedom. His idea was not immediately embraced. Some thought he was simply resurrecting his old plan from the 1940s—the march to protest the exclusion of black workers from defense industry jobs, which he had called off after President Roosevelt, feeling the pressure, banned such discrimination. Others doubted that there would be enough support in 1963 for such a march to make much of an impression.

But Mr. Randolph did not back down. He made his vision clear. It was time to face up to the grievous economic situation of African Americans. With the momentum gained from the public outcry against Medgar Evers's assassination, and as atrocities across the South filled the nightly news, it was impossible to turn down an idea that promised to bring people of many backgrounds together in support of equal treatment for all.

To plan the march, Mr. Randolph invited cooperating partners to join the black leadership: Mathew Ahmann of the National Catholic Conference, Eugene Carson Blake of the National Council of Churches, Rabbi Joachim Prinz of the American Jewish Congress, and Walter Reuther of the United Auto Workers. Mr. Randolph's able assistant Bayard Rustin served as coordinator. In fewer than sixty days he brought people from every corner of the country into a process that crystallized the nation's indignation about racial inequality.

In anticipation of the march, there was fear of violence in the streets. In a preparatory meeting Roy Wilkins of the NAACP asked the chief of the District Police whether he had any message for the civil rights leadership that could be sent out to people before they left home. The chief quickly replied, "Tell them do not put any mayonnaise on their sandwiches." There was great laughter and relief.

In the end a quarter of a million people answered the call. They came to Washington from all walks of life, all races, all income levels, all creeds. Busloads by the hundreds, carrying blacks and browns and whites, liberals and laborers, rich and poor, Christians, Muslims, and Jews, men, women, and children, converged on the nation's capital.

August 28, 1963, was a glorious day—clear and bright. It seemed to have been made especially for the march. There was great excitement in the air. The crowd began to assemble early in the morning—several hundred women set out from the headquarters of the National Council of Negro Women—and it continued to build during the course of the day.

During the planning for the march there had been much discussion of time limits for those who were going to address the crowd.

Some thought all speakers should have equal time; others argued that Martin Luther King should be allowed more than the rest. I felt strongly that there should be no time limit on Dr. King. In the end there was a consensus that in any case, Dr. King should be the last speaker. I do not think there was anyone who really would have wanted to follow him! And as history has recorded, the matter of time turned out to be irrelevant.

I was seated on the platform a little more than an arm's length from where Dr. King spoke. As I looked out at that huge audience on the Washington Mall, I found it inspiring almost beyond words. There were so many people between the reflecting pool and the base of the Lincoln Memorial that you couldn't see the grass. People crammed into the space, eager to hear every word and get a glimpse of every speaker. And all who spoke did so with passion and eloquence.

When it was time for the last speech, A. Philip Randolph's grand, deep voice introduced, with a flourish, "Martin Luther King *Junior!*" Then Dr. King stood on the steps of the Lincoln Memorial and, reciting from the patriotic song, declared, "From every mountainside, let freedom ring." It was a riveting sermon that struck the conscience of America and instantly took its place as one of the most famous speeches in human history. "This sweltering summer of the Negro's legitimate discontent will not pass until there is an invigorating autumn of freedom and equality," he said. "I have a dream today!" A moment of grace, of transcendence, touched the thousands who were there and the millions more who watched from afar on television.

Even on the morning of the march there had been appeals to include a woman speaker. But Bayard Rustin held fast, insisting that women were part of all the groups—the churches, the synagogues, labor—represented on the podium. In the end Mahalia Jackson, who sang the national anthem, was the only female voice. That moment was vital to awakening the women's movement. Mr. Rustin's stance showed us that men honestly didn't see their position as patriarchal or patronizing. They were happy to include women in the human family, but there was no question as to who headed the household!

Because of the concern about security, Washington-based organizations had been asked not to hold any auxiliary meetings around the march so that our 250,000 visitors could get out of the city as quickly as possible. But as the sole woman in the civil rights leadership group, I was determined to bring wise women together to learn and gather strength from the experience. Quietly, on August 29, we assembled at our NCNW offices and at the Shoreham Hotel. "After the March—What?" was the theme.

I was concerned that many women's organizations had rather narrowly focused on discriminatory practices. There were equally important civil rights issues that affected women and children more broadly: decent housing, child care, schooling, and employment. When we came together, many of our members agreed. They called for greater attention to the urgent everyday needs of women and children. Paulie Murray, a brilliant lawyer and clergy, presented a paper in response to the exclusion of women in the March on Washington. She built on the implications of Dr. King's speech and made clear the need to work against sexism as well as racism.*

The March on Washington had been a defining moment. One could feel expectations rising. But the euphoria was short-lived. When Congress passed the Civil Rights Act of 1964, the long-

---

* Mary Church Terrell, a charter member of the NCNW, used to speak of "the double handicap of race and sex." The women's movement gained strength through the civil rights movement, yet much tension was engendered by different perspectives. Many black women were reluctant to work wholeheartedly with the women's movement because they felt all their efforts should be focused against racism. It took a while for women's movement leaders to understand that some of the issues in which they were most focused had less appeal to black women, who were caught up in bread-and-butter issues.

sought opening of places of public accommodation held little meaning for many African Americans. Young people who had gone to jail singing "We Shall Overcome," who had worked so hard to get the bill passed, realized that neither they nor their parents had the economic wherewithal to pay the check at places newly opened up to them.

Then, in 1967, we had a "hot summer." In Watts and eighty-five other cities, there was rioting. Urban communities, too long neglected, simply exploded. Along with A. Philip Randolph, Andrew Heiskel, president of Time Inc., called together corporate, business, union, and religious leaders to develop strategies not only to deal with the unrest but to rebuild urban strength. John Gardner, a former secretary of the Department of Health, Education, and Welfare (HEW), became president of what eventually became the National Urban Coalition. I was one of the first women invited to serve on the board.

Martin Luther King knew that the deprivation he had seen in rural communities across the South was ravaging black neighborhoods in northern cities as well. In the last few years of his life, he devoted himself to the Poor People's Campaign. Through television, newspapers, and magazines, he brought before the nation striking pictures of poverty in rural and urban communities. He believed these images would do for economic mobilization what marches had done to marshal support for civil rights legislation. Dr. King was determined to pull people out of the economic quagmire in which so many had become trapped.

But he was unable to complete his work. On the fourth of April in 1968, as he was planning a Poor People's March on Washington, a gunman snuffed out his life.

I was in Aurora, Illinois, at a YWCA training session when the news came of Martin Luther King's death. Someone interrupted the session, sending in a note to let us know that he had been shot. The announcement brought an audible gasp from every part of the room. Black and white together, we had to drop what we were doing. We needed to find out what was happening. And as the word got out we began to hear reports of disturbances in the streets.

I soon got a call from Lee White, an assistant to President Lyndon Johnson, summoning me to the White House for an emergency meeting. My YWCA colleagues helped me get back to Washington quickly, and there the remaining members of the CUCRL group and a handful of other black leaders met with President Johnson, congressional leaders, and cabinet members.

The president, visibly shaken, told us that he had been on the phone throughout the night with Negro and white community leaders across the country, asking for their guidance and strength. He had asked HEW Secretary John Gardner to engage the National Urban Coalition in getting Negro and white leaders together in every city where it operated. The president had good reason to be concerned. Our nonviolent leader had met the ultimate violence, and there was a deep sense of loss in that room as we struggled to find ways to discourage further turmoil. Together we discussed how we could make sure it was understood that someone might have killed the dreamer, but that person hadn't killed the dream.

In a statement to the nation later that afternoon, President Johnson tried to console and bring people together, "to deny violence its victory." But his best efforts were not enough to quell the fury of inconsolable rioters in Chicago, Detroit, New York, Boston, Memphis, and just blocks away from the White House itself in the nation's capital. Before nightfall the army and the National Guard had to be called out to restore the peace.

After the assassination of Dr. King, when more than four hundred cities were burning, President Johnson appointed the Kerner Commission to study the disturbances in the streets. At bottom, the commission declared in its report, the problem was white racism. The cause of the violence in the streets lay in the violence in people's lives—hunger, malnutrition, poor education, unemployment, poor housing, discrimination. The Kerner Commission concluded that this nation was fast becoming two—one white, one black, separate and unequal.

In sending copies of the report to associations, I called for dialogue groups—and to answer those who wanted action and not "just talk," I drew upon the teachings of a British theologian who taught that dialogue *is* action. It is through dialogue that people gain the understanding needed to move into responsible, significant action. There can be no concerted action without dialogue. Across the country dialogue groups quickened the readiness for action.

Our Council for United Civil Rights Leadership was not, of course, the only focal point for the fight against racial injustice. By 1963, for instance, the ranks of the Nation of Islam—adherents of Elijah Muhammad, a militant advocate of black separatism—had swollen to thirty thousand. One of their most visible spokesmen was Malcolm X, who finally broke away from the Nation of Islam in 1964 and founded the Muslim Mosque. That same year, after a transforming trip to Mecca, Malcolm X put out the word through Ossie Davis and Ruby Dee, artists extremely active in the civil rights movement, that he wanted to meet with other black leaders. It would be an all-day meeting at the home of the actor Sidney Poitier in Pleasantville, New York. Sidney himself picked me up and drove me out.

Malcolm X was a very complex person. He cared deeply about his people and the injustices heaped upon them, and he told hard truths in a strong voice. But he was also very gentle and kind. I wish that many who quote him or his teachings knew the man I had the privilege to know.

We listened as Malcolm X spoke of his new vision of how we should work together. Too much time and energy had been focused on the white man, he said. More progress would be made if we did not allow the press and others to divide us. His spirited message stressed the importance of talking *to* each other, not *at* or *about* each other, in the best interest of black people.

Lorraine Hansberry, the author, was lying on a couch. She followed up on Malcolm's charge of talking with each other, asking him, "How do you think I felt when I was in the hospital, watching you on television criticizing me for marrying a white man? You don't know anything about him or why I married him. You never asked me anything about it." Whereupon this strong, dynamic man replied in the gentlest tone, "Sister, you are right." What an unforgettable moment!

Meanwhile, the Black Power movement was growing increasingly more vocal—and more important. At CORE, Floyd McKissick replaced James Farmer, bringing a much stronger separatist line. Mr. McKissick, in turn, was replaced by Roy Innis, whose views were even more radical. A separatist and Black Nationalist, Innis considered the rest of us integrationists, a position he could not support.

The essential message of some in the Black Power movement, as I understood it, was that we elders in the struggle for civil rights were leaving a legacy of dependency to the next generation. It was true that, by 1966, not only had the problems of black people not been overcome, but they seemed to be evenly distributed all over the country. In the South as well as the North the axioms of racism were the same: poor education, substandard housing, lack of jobs, inadequate health care. The perception that the economic system was as crushing a force as racial discrimination convinced young proponents of Black Power that only when black people themselves organized and led the revolution might we even begin to imagine a decent society.

This was a troubling message, and there were times when even the best of us had difficulty answering the new generation's question: "What makes you think your way is going to solve our problems?" When young people ask such questions, they often tend to do so in the manner of all emancipating adolescents—rudely and thoughtlessly. This has nothing to do with race. It is the nature of the young.

The young people who pushed Black Power resented the involvement of any white people in the civil rights movement. "No one who has not suffered as we have has the right to dictate to us the form of our struggle," James Forman intoned at the 1967 National Conference for a New Politics in Chicago. Like many of their ancestors before them, the leaders of the Black Power movement saw little more in whites than their whiteness. Whites weren't persons. That was an approach, of course, that white America itself had patterned as it became accustomed to treating Negroes as "coloreds," not as full-fledged human beings. Young African Americans coming up in the sixties had witnessed the most concentrated and publicized spate of white violence against blacks our country had seen since slavery. So it was a natural development that they would treat everything white as evil.

However inevitable a step on the road toward racial justice, their crusade took its toll. Suddenly many of the most sympathetic white supporters of the civil rights struggle no longer felt appreciated or needed. Years later, my dear friend and steadfast supporter Polly Cowan, who had more than once put her life in harm's way for the cause, confided, "It took a whole summer, and you, to get me out of that feeling of being blown away. I felt as if I'd just been discarded."

It was also hard for us when our youngsters talked of going back to Africa or tried to become Africans in the United States, repudiating any identification with their immediate past. It was not easy for those of us who had become symbols of the struggle for equality to see our children raising their fists in defiant contradiction of all we had fought for. I remember a young SNCC activist named Ralph Featherstone who came to a meeting of the leadership group. He looked around the table at us elder statesmen and said, "We have our problems because you have been buffers. You are too understanding. You identify with the white liberal and understand his position. If you didn't, it would be easier to attack the enemy. As it is, you are delaying the day when we will have our freedom."

I have thought often about those words, and as I look back at that period now, I can see that for all the quiet work that was done, it took direct action through the marches and the Selmas and the more militant attacks on the problem to bring about real changes. At the height of the Black Power movement I suggested that the young militants find a more constructive rallying call. But it didn't take long to realize that simply talking about bettering race relations—without fundamentally changing the power relationships—would not get us very far. We had been treating symptoms rather than causes. There were still major roadblocks to full equality, and a more direct approach was urgently needed.

I was not the only person who recognized that fact. While he lay in a hospital shortly before his death, Stokely Carmichael, one of the recipients of the NCNW scholarships for students who interrupted their education to be active in civil rights, gave me a call. He wanted to meet. He wanted to see us all get together, young and old, to chart a new course. He felt that despite their differences, people would respond to my call. He had a new realization that we cannot afford a generation gap!

By the early seventies economic conditions among African Americans had not improved very much. The opening of opportunities after the civil rights legislation of the sixties had shown the world just how grim real life was for the majority of black Americans—how few were equipped to seize the day, to make the laws come alive with their full participation as first-class citizens. It was startling how few among the leadership, other than A. Philip Randolph, Martin Luther King Jr., and Whitney Young, seemed to have recognized the desperate economic conditions of the black community. Even among the most thoughtful supporters of civil rights there was little awareness of the long-term devastation being wrought by poverty within our community.

It was not just an issue of people not having money; it was no longer just a matter of creating jobs. For too long far too many had so few of the necessities of life that they weren't just unemployed, they had become unemployable. We were engulfed by a large and growing community of people whose only inheritance was welfare. Many had long since given up looking for work, and most people living in poverty felt totally powerless to change their lot. Legislative triumphs in Washington only deepened the disillusion among these hard-core poor as they, and the rest of the nation, mistakenly assumed that passage of civil rights laws would set things right.

Impatience about the lack of change was as keen among the privileged as it was among the poor. The difference, of course, was that those who were well off freely raised their angry voices to blame the victims. "Now they have the laws. What more do they want?" they'd ask in exasperation. A young lad I knew in Harlem told me that one day he'd gone downtown and talked with some white fellows who challenged him in just that fashion. My young friend replied simply, "I want what you all got."

When Whitney Young was teaching at Westchester College, he used to tell a story about his commute by train every day north out of New York City through Harlem. Other faculty at the college took the same trip, he said, but never looked out the window—or if they did, never saw what he saw. They would always see it only as block after block of blight. They would never know the real strengths and weaknesses of people in Harlem—the way they struggled to survive and coped in spite of the horrendous odds against them.

In fact, the "victim blamers" may have done us a service: they gave us an important insight for our next major piece of work. We saw that as we focused on economic development in the black community, we needed to look beyond our own perimeter for guidance. Collectively African Americans make up close to a $3 billion market. We had to stop taking our business out into the white community, and we had to boycott white-owned stores in our own community that did not hire blacks. "Don't Buy Where You Can't Work" again became our rallying cry, and little by little our purchasing power began to be felt.

Faced with recurring questions as to whether the civil rights movement was dead, especially after the death of Martin Luther King Jr., I realized how little was understood about how far we had to go to eliminate deeply embedded racism.* The climate of righteous indignation that prevailed after the March on Washington was replaced with a kind of self-righteous indifference. We needed a new movement, one that would empower African Americans to improve their own lives and to expand their opportunities to participate fully in American social, economic, and political life.

---

* Ten years after Dr. King's death, Vernon Jordan, then president of the National Urban League, took a much-needed initiative. Urged on by Carl Holman of the National Urban Coalition, he brought together representatives of the organizations that had been central to the civil rights movement. Out of that grew the Black Leadership Forum, of which I was a founding member. Its mission is to promote creative and coordinated black leadership.

Chapter Ten

"Women Are the Shock Absorbers"

IN 1977 I RETIRED after thirty-three years on the national YWCA staff. I did not have ten minutes of unused leave. While carrying a full-time job at the YWCA, I had also spent forty years volunteering untold hours at the National Council of Negro Women. Since 1958 I had been its elected president, devoting almost all my "free" time to NCNW business.

From the moment I met Mary McLeod Bethune at the Harlem branch of the YWCA in 1937, I was pleased to do whatever I could do to help her cause. She had founded the NCNW in 1935, and until 1944 its business was conducted where Mrs. Bethune lived, in a small rented apartment in Washington, D.C. During the first seven years there was no paid staff. Mrs. Bethune simultaneously administered the National Council of Negro Women, the Bethune-Cookman College in Florida, and the Division of Negro Affairs of the National Youth Administration, and she was the acknowledged leader of Franklin Roosevelt's "Black Cabinet." In spite of these demanding responsibilities, during the fourteen years that Mrs. Bethune served as president she established NCNW as a major player working for child labor laws, public housing, the minimum wage, and quality desegregated education.

From 1939 to 1944, when I was employed by the Phyllis Wheatley YWCA, I would work at my regular job during the day and for the NCNW most evenings and many weekends. Perhaps my greatest contribution was to help Mrs. Bethune see that she needed a full-time NCNW staff. With her blessing and board support, we recruited our first executive director, Jeanetta Welch Brown, who had been national public affairs director for Alpha Kappa Alpha Sorority. Mrs. Bethune made me chair of the personnel committee to develop policies and help with board-staff relations, and I continued to serve her successors, Dorothy Boulding Ferebee and Vivian Carter Mason, as president.

I wish I could have been president of the NCNW while Mrs. Bethune was alive, even for just one year. If that had been possible, I believe some of the things that have been so difficult to accomplish could have been done much more easily. Mrs. Bethune was a dreamer, but she was a realist too. Though a great deal of her vision had been expressed, she knew when she died in 1955 that very little of it had been realized.

When I was elected president of the NCNW in 1958, three years after her death, we had two full-time staff members and one part-timer, and we faced a major financial challenge. Mrs. Bethune had depended heavily on members of means and a few wealthy white donors to tide the organization over during times of financial crisis. On my first day in office I received a certified letter calling for immediate payment of a $7,500 loan from the Industrial Bank of Washington. I quickly realized that we had a problem and called my cousin, Campbell C. Johnson, who was on the bank's board. He interceded, and the bank kindly allowed us to pay off the loan in installments.

There was good reason to get our financial house in order: our work was more urgent than ever. In the early sixties the momentum of the war on poverty and the civil rights movement thrust the NCNW into a position of leadership. Our unique involvement in the struggle for freedom in the South began in early October 1963, when I received calls from James Forman, then executive secretary of the Student Nonviolent Coordinating Committee, and Prathea Hall, a young SNCC staff person in Selma, Alabama. Both alerted me to the serious mistreatment by the Dallas County police of young people involved in a voter registration drive.

At the time only a handful of black adults in Dallas County were registered. In Selma, the county seat, young people had taken it upon themselves to do whatever they could to get their parents and other adults registered to vote. Within a few days after their drive began, three hundred children and youth had been arrested. Miss Hall reported horrifying stories of police brutality and threats of violence against these young people. Their parents were frantic. There was no jail in Selma big enough to hold that many people, and no one knew where they were. Miss Hall asked if the National Council of Negro Women could help.

On October 4, 1963, an interracial team of two white and two black women—Shirley Smith, executive director of the recently formed National Women's Committee for Civil Rights, Polly Cowan of the NCNW and the New York Citizens Committee for Children, Dr. Ferebee, who had become director of health services at Howard University, and I—flew to Atlanta on our way to Selma. I invited these three to join me because we already had been working closely together on civil rights issues. We knew and respected each other.

When we arrived in Atlanta, we tried to reach our contacts in Selma, both white and black, but we couldn't get a phone call through. We were met at the Selma airport by James Forman, who briefed us on the situation and strongly advised that we split up— that white women and black go separately into town. It was our plan that Shirley Smith and Polly Cowan would meet with white women who were said to be sympathetic to the voter registration drive, and Dorothy Ferebee and I would seek out Negro women and families whose children had been detained. But the car that was to drive Dorothy and me into town failed to materialize, and we saw no alternative but to pile into the backseat of the rental car Shirley and Polly were driving.

Two white women and two black women in the same car was a dangerous way to operate in Selma in 1963, but the two of us in the backseat said we'd claim to be the hired help if the police stopped us, and we all laughed. Our laughter ceased moments later. As we left the airport two suspicious-looking cars careened out behind us. From that point on those cars followed us wherever we went.

In spite of this ominous escort, we drove straight to the Negro church, where sixty-five teenagers and their parents had gathered to talk with Dr. Ferebee and me to tell us what had happened to the three hundred who had been detained. When Shirley Smith and Polly Cowan saw the eager crowd, they decided to stay with us to hear the firsthand accounts. The children confirmed reports of police brutality and hideous jail conditions. The cells had been so overcrowded, they told us, that no one could sit or lie down. There was little food—and that was stretched with sawdust—hardly any drinking water, and the coffee had been served with salt instead of sugar. There were no blankets, and no privacy in the toilet facilities. The girls were constantly threatened with sexual assault by the officers assigned to guard them.

One mother introduced her eleven-year-old daughter. The child was skin and bones. The mother said that her daughter had a rare stomach condition and needed special food, which she had taken to her every day, once she found out where she was being detained. A week or so later, when the children were released, she went to collect her child and found her totally emaciated. All the food the mother had brought was sitting in a corner, rotting, filled with maggots and vermin. Her daughter had never received it.

Other children said they had been fed "boll weevil gravy."

Young girls reported huddling together at night, taking turns staying awake to keep watch in case the guards came in to harass them. As they told one horror story after another, we were stunned by the bravery of these young people. In spite of all they'd been through, they were determined to keep fighting for their parents' right to vote.

After we had heard all their stories, I looked at one little boy who couldn't seem to stop talking, and I said, "You talk about these white people as if they were all terrible. Don't you think there are some good white people in Selma?" He thought for a moment and then, very tentatively, he said, "Well, I guess there must be some." The wariness in his voice made you know that it was hard for him to believe it. He seriously questioned whether any good white people existed anywhere.

The children also explained why so few blacks had registered to vote. In Dallas County, when a Negro went to register, the lines usually went around the block. Those in charge took one person at a time and kept her for an hour or so while she completed a long form containing all sorts of obscure questions about the Constitution of the United States. Very few of the hopeful registrants ever passed this "test." After calling two or at most three people during the morning hours, the registrars closed for lunch. After lunch they might take one more. Then they closed for the day.

All the people who waited in line knew that their employers or others who had power over them surveyed the line to see who was on it. Then they'd take pictures. One day all the women who worked in one of the hospitals, some of whom had worked there for years, were pushed out of the line with cattle prods, sent back to work, and then fired for having taken the time to stand in line to register.

In spite of such intimidation, the young people refused to give up their campaign. The evening we arrived they held a huge rally to get people ready for a big "Freedom to Vote" registration push the following day. Dorothy Ferebee and I were included on the program, and Polly Cowan was asked to speak. Not long after we arrived in the hall we noticed that two white men from the press were sitting in the audience and two white policemen were recording the evening's proceedings.

At the end of the rally a white photographer from out of state made his way up to the platform and urged us to leave as quickly as possible. All the way out of the church people thanked us for coming. As we got to the door we saw that the building was surrounded by a sea of state troopers wearing yellow helmets with Confederate flags painted on them. Each trooper carried what seemed to be standard equipment: club, pistol, carbine, riot gun, submachine gun, tear gas bomb, and electric cattle prod. It was an armed camp.

Instinctively we four women knew we should not acknowledge one another as we walked out. Dorothy Ferebee and I moved in one direction and Shirley Smith and Polly Cowan in another as we headed for our accommodations on opposite sides of town. Dr. Ferebee and I went to the home of Amelia Boynton, a leader in the movement. The conversation at our dinner was lively. The children were passionate: if they could get their parents into the "responsible electorate," their lives would be better and their job done.

The next day, when I returned to New York, I was advised that a subpoena for my arrest had been issued in Selma. I was charged with "contributing to the delinquency of minors." I never returned to Selma.

After I left Polly Cowan and Shirley Smith met with two white women whose names they had received through a mutual friend. It was a difficult meeting. Even though the two Selma women had taken steps to ease some of the tensions in the community, their fears had been raised by rumors that the voter registration drive was inspired by Communists and that the young people were being paid to go to jail. The women said their religious convictions had motivated them to call the mayor's office to protest the arrests of the young people, but the mayor had told them to stay home and lock their doors because "nothing was going to change in Selma."

Finally, the Selma women agreed to meet with a local woman leader in the Negro community and with Dorothy Tilly. Mrs. Tilly was a remarkable southern white woman who had been working quietly and courageously for years to unmask the Ku Klux Klan in Atlanta. Her commitment to racial justice inspired us all. In the midst of KKK violence, Mrs. Tilly organized a "Fellowship of the Concerned," a group of similarly spirited women, white and black, who joined in an informal coalition across the South. Whenever there was a lynching or people were thrown in jail for civil rights activities, members of the fellowship would mobilize to get help or publicize the wrongdoing. Mrs. Tilly also organized groups of women to go into the courts to witness the justice system at work. When someone asked their business, they would reply, "We're just listening." And that's just what they did. Soon their presence was making a visible difference. Everyone in the courtrooms seemed more mindful of what was going on, and white judges were increasingly reluctant to play fast and loose with jurisprudence when Mrs. Tilly's ladies were on the scene.*

We hoped that Mrs. Tilly could help encourage communication between the white and Negro women of Selma, given their common concern about racial tensions and the welfare of their young people. But two days later, when Mrs. Tilly arrived in Selma, no one was at the airport to meet her. One of the white women had agreed to be there, but when Mrs. Tilly phoned her, she said there would be no meeting. The day before the Selma newspaper had published a full report of our team's participation in the rally. "Mrs.

---

* As word spread about Mrs. Tilly's quiet work, she became vulnerable to taunts and threats from people who opposed her. In her later years, alone after her husband died, she often received threatening phone calls. Gently, she'd say, "Just one moment, please...." Then she'd put the phone down next to her record player and turn it on. Whoever was there, ugly and menacing on the other end of the line, heard the hymn "Abide with Me," loud and clear.

Cowan and Miss Smith have deceived us," the woman told Mrs. Tilly. "They told us they came because they were interested in this community, but how could they care about us when they went to be with those people [the protesters]?" Even Mrs. Tilly's remarkable powers of persuasion could not change the mind of this woman who believed that she had been betrayed.

The Selma experience taught us a useful lesson. Having generated heat where we had hoped to bring light, we learned that if we wanted to be helpful, we had to be sensitive to the perspectives of people on both sides of the issue. We would have to go into tension-filled communities quietly, anonymously, and—even when our most deeply cherished principles were violated in the process—with respect for local custom. But we had to make our purpose clear.

My report of our Selma experience to the national board of the YWCA inspired immediate action. Board members enlisted the help of the National Council of Catholic Women, the National Council of Jewish Women, and Church Women United. The heads of all of these organizations had been present with me, as president of the National Council of Negro Women, at a White House meeting three months before. President John F. Kennedy had challenged us to act for social change—to find the way to end domestic inequality, racism, and poverty. Many who attended that meeting already were working for open housing, voter registration, equal educational opportunity, and civil rights legislation. Upon hearing the Selma report, my colleagues in these four major women's organizations agreed that it was time to turn their attention—and their considerable clout—to the South.

In March 1964, the National Council of Negro Women, the YWCA, the National Council of Catholic Women, the National Council of Jewish Women, and Church Women United convened an off-the-record meeting in Atlanta to discuss police brutality and the treatment of women and girls who had been arrested for civil disobedience in the seven most troubled southern cities. In preparation, each of the five sponsoring organizations invited leading members from the seven cities to visit local jails and courts to see what conditions really were and how laws were being administered so that they could bring firsthand reports to Atlanta.

It was interesting to me that many of the white women we spoke with around the South did not understand how young people could be so involved in the civil rights movement. They expressed concern that somehow the youth were being used. Why was it that teenagers and children were put in the streets to fight what they considered to be an adult battle? Certainly it couldn't be good for children to be out there doing whatever it was they were doing!

This concern demonstrated how distant the white women's reality was from the front lines of the civil rights struggle raging around them. It also raised the much larger concern, particularly among my colleagues on the national board of the YWCA, as to how women from different parts of the country—of different races and different religious beliefs—could actually collaborate in support of this embattled quest for racial justice. At best, we decided, the Atlanta meeting would be a brave experiment.

We made every effort to avoid publicity because the women who came to Atlanta did so at great risk. In our effort to protect them, we puzzled about such simple things as the sort of notice we should put up in the hotel lobby to let the participants know where the meeting was being held. We had no official name—neither for the organizing group nor for the conference. We were just a patchwork of women, drawn together to try to solve a problem that was tearing our communities apart. Then Ethlyn Christiansen of the YWCA had an idea. "Why don't we call it the Women's Interorganizational Committee?" she suggested. "That's truthful and harmless." So that's what we did. Not only was the title innocuous and nonthreatening, but there also was nothing else like it on the hotel bulletin board. None of our women had any trouble finding the meeting room.

It was an extraordinary gathering. Women came from Albany and Atlanta, Georgia, from Montgomery and Selma, Alabama, from Jackson, Mississippi, Charleston, South Carolina, and Danville, Virginia. Margaret Mealey, president of the National Council of Catholic Women, later observed that the poor knew one another and the rich had met on occasion. But seldom before had southern middle-class women come together across racial lines as they did in Atlanta.

The meeting was agonizing, joyful, and tense all at once. We heard from prison personnel and police officers and from experts on penal standards and prison reform. We heard firsthand the stories of young women, black and white, who had suffered unspeakable indignities in prison. Students at nearby Spelman College spoke of their determination to desegregate restaurants and department store lunch counters downtown. Before our meeting we had been told by city officials that Atlanta had already opened up and long since integrated its eating places. We quickly discovered that this was merely pretense. We found little evidence of integration of public accommodations anywhere in Atlanta, including our own hotel. In fact, ours was the first gathering at the American Hotel at which white people and people of color had ever broken bread together. Our meeting quietly brought down the color barrier there.

Still, tension permeated the air. On the second day, when a camera flashed during one of our discussions, it almost started a riot. A Jewish woman from Alabama nearly had a stroke. "I'll never be able to go back to Montgomery if you take pictures," she cried. Nearly all the southern women there, black and white alike, were frightened, fearful of nameless reprisals when they returned home because they had come to such a "radical" interracial gathering.

At luncheon on the final day I was asked to chair the discussion. I invited all the women to sit together by community, as it was clear that most of those from the same cities had not met before. Certainly, before this meeting, none had ever met across color

Rankin High School Graduation Day (1929)

With my niece, Jean Randolph, in Harlem, NY (1932)

My mother and her three sisters in New York City: Aunt Sally White, Mother, Aunt Molly Sayles, Aunt Susie Christian (1938)

As volunteer Executive Director of the National Council of Negro Women with my mentor, Mary McLeod Bethune (1942)

With my three sisters: Anthanette Aldridge, me, Josephine Ryals, Jessie Randolph (1959)

Mrs. Eleanor Roosevelt, Mrs. Katherine Ellickson, Mrs. Helen Hill Miller (standing), Dr. Marguerite Rawalt, and me at Mrs. Roosevelt's Val-Kill Cottage (1962)

Watching as President Kennedy signs the Equal Pay Act (1963)

I join the crowd on the platform at the March on Washington for Martin Luther King Jr.'s historic "I Have a Dream" speech (Aug. 28, 1963)

Attorney General Robert Kennedy joins Civil Rights leaders: Martin Luther King Jr., me, Roy Wilkins, Whitney Young, and A. Philip Randolph

The one woman in the crowd: Roy Wilkins (NAACP), Floyd McKissick (Congress of Racial Equality), me, A. Philip Randolph (Brotherhood of Sleeping Car Porters), Whitney Young (National Urban League), and Martin Luther King Jr. (Southern Christian Leadership Conference)

A meeting with President Lyndon Johnson in the Oval Office

President Ronald Reagan holds a White House reception to honor the 50th anniversary of the NCNW

At the White House: Mayor Coleman Young of Detroit, Louis Martin (Presidential Advisor), Vernon Jordan (National Urban League), Roslyn Carter, me, President Jimmy Carter, Benjamin Hooks (NAACP), Coretta Scott King, Jesse Jackson (P.U.S.H.), Clarence Mitchell (NAACP)

A briefing at Blair House: President Ronald Reagan, Vice President George Bush, Arthur Fletcher, Vernon Jordan, me, and M. Carl Holman

A NCNW meeting with President George Bush at the White House

President Bill Clinton presents me with the Presidential Medal of Freedom at the White House

Black Family Reunion Celebration (1993)

The National Council of Negro Women's new headquarters at 633 Pennsylvania Avenue, midway between the Capitol and the White House

All decked out (1992)

lines. When everyone was seated, I asked a question. "We hear a lot about how national civil rights activists, many of whom are considered 'northern intruders,' only make conditions worse in your communities," I said. "As the struggle for civil rights becomes more and more intense and intrusive in your lives, do you, as local leaders, see any value in belonging to a national organization that is concerned and committed to the civil rights struggle?"

There were many interesting responses, but none so compelling as that of the table from Jackson, Mississippi. The Jackson women had selected our NCNW representative, Clarie Harvey, as their spokeswoman. "Here we are," said Mrs. Harvey, gesturing toward the four white women from Jackson. "We have never met before, we have never sat together before, and we have decided today that we will never be separated again. We have too much work to do! Yes, there is value to each of us in being part of a national organization, because you can help us. You can be like a long-handled spoon, reaching down and stirring us up, bringing us together in ways that we could never do by ourselves. We've discovered that all of us have been working with the Freedom Riders or with other groups in our community, but none of us knew the others were there. Now we know, and from now on we're going to stick together."

Mrs. Harvey paused, took a deep breath, and added, "We know that we are going to have a long, hot summer. In a few months students will be coming to Mississippi from all over the country to set up freedom schools and voter registration drives. Police and sheriffs across the state already are armed to the teeth, eagerly preparing to harass and hurt the students. We are going to need your help. If northern women could visit us regularly during the summer, to act as a quieting influence by going into areas that are racially tense, to try to build bridges of communication between us, between our black and white communities, to be a ministry of presence among us, it would be of tremendous help to us."

There was a hush in the room as people absorbed what Clarie

Harvey had said. As those of us at the head table looked at the women around the room and then at each other, we realized that the concerns Clarie had expressed were shared by women in all seven of the cities represented. Then, all of a sudden, we felt a sense of strength gathering, a collective desire among the women to stay by one another—and gratitude that the larger organizations to which they belonged supported their struggle.

After a few moments a woman from Charleston stood up. "As we go back, we know things are bad and very dark, but we must remember that we are the Women's Interorganizational Committee," she said, repeating what Ethlyn Christiansen had made up for the bulletin board. "That says W-I-C, and that's what each of us needs to be—like the wick on a candle, a light in the darkness. If each of us does what we can, right where we are, we will do a lot. If we continue to work together, we will make a difference."

Dorothy Tilly added her own wisdom, drawn from her years of experience protesting injustice in our host city. "Women's power is neither financial nor political," she reminded us. "Women are the shock absorbers. That has always been our role."

There was immense vitality in the room that afternoon. A sense of courage and solidarity infused us. The cautiousness of the early hours of the meeting had largely vanished. All of us knew that something important had happened in Atlanta. None of us would ever be the same.

Chapter Eleven

Behind the "Cotton Curtain"

WITHIN WEEKS of the Atlanta meeting plans were announced for what came to be known as the Great Mississippi Project. Bob Moses, head of the Council of Federated Organizations (COFO), together with James Forman and the Student Nonviolent Coordinating Committee, had visited dozens of northern colleges to recruit young people—black and white—to spend the summer in Mississippi. These volunteers would live in rural communities across the state, establishing "freedom schools" and running voter registration campaigns.

Meanwhile, the white establishment was gearing up to meet the COFO offensive. Denouncing the northern youths who would soon "invade" Mississippi as Communist-inspired "outside agitators," the White Citizens Council equipped the mayor of Jackson with an ice cream truck refitted as an armed tank. The state legislature enacted laws curtailing constitutionally protected rights to public assembly and free speech. Out in the rural areas, law enforcement officers—both official and self-appointed—erected stop signs in places they'd never been before to confuse and ambush the out-of-staters. Booby traps were laid everywhere.

Polly Cowan, traveling with her husband on a plane to England, wrote me a note. She was concerned about the attitude toward the students volunteering to help in the freedom schools. Her own children planned to be there.

Polly had an idea. She suggested that we organize teams from what she called the "Cadillac crowd"—black and white women whose prominence could have a quieting influence. The women would go into Mississippi in interracial teams each week throughout the summer. They would bring outside resources into the state—including their own skills and talents to enrich the freedom schools—and take home firsthand reports of what was going on. They would meet with local women as well as with visiting "freedom" young people. They would, as Clarie Harvey had requested, stir up people and build bridges between black and white women.

We felt it was important to talk again with the white Jackson women to be sure that they still wanted women from the outside to come into Mississippi. In May, Polly Cowan and Shirley Smith went to Jackson to discuss the question. The atmosphere already was tense. *Anyone* from the outside was suspect, and many of the women were dubious about the idea. But not one said, "Don't come." Many said, "Please try it. Try anything."

With the green light from Jackson, our planning proceeded. I don't think any U.S. president ever had more drafts of a speech than we had drafts of plans for how we'd get biracial, interfaith teams of distinguished women into and out of Mississippi once a week, every week. We decided that the trips would begin on Tuesdays and end on Thursdays in Jackson; the intervening Wednesdays would be spent visiting COFO projects in places like Hattiesburg, Canton, Meridian, Vicksburg, and Ruleville. We called the project Wednesdays in Mississippi (WIMS). It was sponsored by the National Council of Negro Women, with participation by the YWCA, United

Church Women, the National Council of Catholic Women, the National Council of Jewish Women, the League of Women Voters, and the American Association of University Women.

Our next step was to appoint a biracial staff to work on the ground in Mississippi. We recruited Doris Wilson, a Tuskegee graduate who had two master's degrees and twelve years of experience with the YWCA, and Susan Goodwillie, who had joined the NCNW staff as my special assistant in 1963, two months after graduating from Stanford University. Because of Susan Goodwillie's youth and her vulnerability as a white outsider, we were delighted when her Stanford roommate, Diane Vivell, agreed to join her. Then we began recruiting influential women from northern cities to make up the visiting teams.

In Mississippi in 1964 it was very difficult to know who in the white community was a potential friend. In the end we were blessed with a handful of angels, black and white Mississippi women who worked with us 100 percent as we set out to demonstrate that women of goodwill, white and black, northern and southern, Christian and Jewish, could come together to quell violence, ease tensions, and inspire tolerance in racially torn communities. Without the courage and support of our Mississippi women friends, we never could have begun, much less sustained, the Wednesdays in Mississippi project.

A June memorandum to WIMS participants stated our official mission: "We believe it is important that private citizens of stature and influence make it known that they support the aspirations of the citizens of Mississippi for full citizenship, that they deplore violence, and that they will place themselves in tension-filled situations to try to initiate both understanding and reconciliation." The specific goals of the project were to establish lines of communication among women of goodwill across regional and racial lines, to observe the COFO student projects and discuss them with local Mississippi women, and to lend a "ministry of presence" as witnesses to encourage compassion and reconciliation.

With the memory of our experience in Selma still fresh, we decided to conform, where necessary, to local practices in race relations. That meant that our Negro and white staff and visiting team members had to be housed separately. This was hardest on the white women. Doris Wilson and other black team members were warmly welcomed into homes in the Negro community. But white team members had to stay at the Sun 'n' Sands Motel, and Susan Goodwillie and Diane Vivell lived in an apartment in Magnolia Towers, a complex owned by stalwarts of the White Citizens Council. Monthly rent payments, issued on an NCNW check, had to be laundered through the bank account of Ann Hewitt, one of our local angels.

Another problem was finding a place where Doris, Susan, and Diane could meet to plan each week's team visit. Unless she carried a basket of laundry through the service entrance, Doris might have been arrested if she had tried to enter Magnolia Towers. And Susan and Diane could not get to Doris's house. No white taxi would go there, and no black taxi would take them. Finally Lilly Belle Jones, the director of the branch YWCA, took a deep breath and said they could meet in her back room. The meetings would have to be brief, she cautioned, and Susan and Diane would have to be extremely careful.

Outside Jackson, our biracial team members traveled together. This was not without risk, to be sure, and often they were followed by angry-looking white men with weapons prominently displayed in their gun racks.

We took every possible precaution to protect our staff and team members. Our staff was briefed by the U.S. Department of Justice, the President's Lawyers' Committee, the American Civil Liberties Union, and the Lawyers' Committee for Civil Rights Under Law. Plans for the WIMS project were communicated by letter directly to President Lyndon B. Johnson, Attorney General Robert F. Kennedy, and Governor Paul B. Johnson of Mississippi. It was also agreed that our staff in Mississippi would maintain weekly contact with John Doar, the Justice Department's agent in Jackson.

In late June our three staff members attended the weeklong training session sponsored by COFO for northern student volunteers at Miami University in Oxford, Ohio. There they learned the principles of nonviolent disobedience—how to go limp if arrested, how to exercise their legal rights when under fire in a racist society. They became acquainted with many of the COFO volunteers, including a young man from New York, Andrew Goodman, who went on to Mississippi before the training ended. Our staff and many of the COFO volunteers were still in Ohio when the news came that Goodman and two others—James Chaney and Michael Schwerner—had been arrested and released, then had mysteriously disappeared. It was widely presumed that they had been murdered by Mississippi law officers.

Polly Cowan and I were part of the first WIMS team to go into Mississippi. We arrived a day or two after the Civil Rights Act of 1964—which, among other things, outlawed discrimination in public accommodations—had gone into effect. Even so, when we got to the airport, the white members of the team were directed through one door and we women of color had to go through another. It was hard for many of the team members to understand at first why these precautions were necessary. But all of us learned that behaving according to the unwritten rules of the Mississippi "system" was deadly serious.

Our first night in Jackson we went straight to a rally organized by Martin Luther King Jr. After the rally Clarie Harvey invited me and my black teammate, Marion Logan, to have supper with her at the most convenient location for us all, the Sun 'n' Sands Motel restaurant. We noticed that the hostess was very cool to us. Speaking barely above a whisper, Clarie reminded us that the Civil Rights Act had just become law on July 1. Our presence in this heretofore lily-white establishment, she assured us, was "strictly legal."

A few moments later the owner of the motel swaggered up to our table. "What are you girls doing here?" he snarled. "You must be from out of town." Clarie Harvey spoke right up: "I'm from Jackson, Mississippi." "If you're from Jackson," the man sneered, "you must know how dangerous it is for you to be in here. You know that your people aren't supposed to be comin' in here."

Most of the other patrons, all white, walked out of the dining room. No one else entered, except for several white men in uniforms with odd-looking badges who began to close in around us. We ordered our meal. All three of us chose fruit salad. After we had given our order, we saw that several black kitchen workers were peering at us through the glass in the swinging door, their eyes wide in disbelief. For some reason that reminded us of our commitment, as WIMS team members, not to go anywhere without telling our staff where we were. I had helped write that rule and now, having failed to pay attention to it, I was surrounded in enemy territory. Clarie slipped away to find a phone.

Then black employees began to move slowly through the dining room, cleaning ashtrays that had already been emptied and straightening place mats already neatly laid. Their proximity was small comfort, but we knew they meant well. After what seemed an eternity, our meal was served by a young black waitress. We gaped at the most luscious fruit salads we had ever seen—most likely, the most magnificent the Sun 'n' Sands kitchen crew had ever made. But as we gazed at the plates so lovingly prepared our hunger seemed to evaporate. We realized that we'd better get out of there.

As we moved toward the cash register, one of the uniformed men planted himself in front of us. "You know you're not supposed to be here," he growled menacingly. We paid our checks and said nothing. As we left the building we were surrounded by the black kitchen staff. They had lined up like an honor guard to protect us as we made our way into the parking lot. As we proceeded through this friendly phalanx, a young man stepped forward. "I just want you all to know that if they bother any of our women here tonight, they will never forget it," he said. "We have heard what they are saying and what they plan to do, but it's not going to happen here." We nodded a silent thanks. A moment later we were in Clarie's car, driving across the city. Though we traveled only a few miles, it seemed like forever before we would be safe again in our own part of town.

The next day we went to Hattiesburg, a town of a few thousand in the southeast corner of the state. We found our way to the Morning Star Church, where we were glad to be reunited with our white teammates. The first to greet us was Arthur Reese of Detroit, who with his wife was directing the Hattiesburg freedom school system. He told us that the response of the children to COFO's makeshift freedom schools had been amazing. Though their exposure to classroom education had been limited, their curiosity had not been dulled. In fact, said Arthur, they were the most exciting students he had ever taught. Arthur told us about older students too, who came to evening classes. In one class the youngest pupil was sixty! And those who had come south to help, said Arthur, were learning almost as much as their students. "We thought we were broadminded, but we've been shown our own prejudices," he explained. "Surrounded—and equally threatened—by this poisonous system, white and Negro are closer here than we have ever been in the North. Here we need each other."

As Arthur spoke, several northern college students gathered around with their young local charges, who wanted to give us a tour of the church. We had just started to walk away from the entry with the children when a peculiar hissing sound sputtered behind us in the vestibule. The college students rushed toward it, gesturing us all to stay back.

A Molotov cocktail had been thrown into the church. Miraculously, it had fizzled and failed to do its dirty work. When the allclear signal went up, one of the northern students, a music major from Oberlin College in Ohio, strode over to the pipe organ and struck the opening chords of the "Hallelujah Chorus" of Handel's *Messiah*. We joined him with our voices, clasping hands in a circle as each one sent up a private prayer of thanks that no one had been hurt and no major damage done. We were a group of strangers united in a common crusade for which, each of us knew, all were prepared to die. Amazing grace.

From the Morning Star Church we went on to the community center, stopping along the way at a small white house. In the yard there were four or five children playing, Negro and white together. A young white woman stood at the door of the house. She was the wife of the Reverend Bob Beech, who headed the ecumenical Ministers' Project that had done much of the groundwork to ensure the success of the COFO summer project in Hattiesburg. Bob Beech was our guide for most of that day.

The community center was a brown shingled structure, and when we entered, we were invited to sit on rough benches. There were tables of the same sort, a broken-down piano, and the remains of a crib on a tiny stage at the far end of the room. The walls and ceiling were cardboard, and several panes of glass were missing from the windows. In the middle of the room a lively young Negro girl told us how the center served its people through arts projects, theater, and music. She worried about what would happen to it in the fall, when all the volunteer college students would leave to go back up North.

As we were leaving for Jackson, we were told that we would have a police escort out of town. This had been arranged by young people in the local COFO office, who felt it was necessary because we had been riding around town all day interracially. We didn't know whether to feel relieved or apprehensive to be in such close company with the notorious Mississippi state police.

That evening Clarie Harvey invited us all to dinner at her home, where we reviewed the day's highlights. Marion Logan told about a little boy who interviewed her for the *Freedom School Press*. The interview consisted primarily of his expounding on his own life and thoughts. He mentioned a time when he and another boy were having a tussle and were stopped by their teacher, who said,

"You boys mustn't fight among yourselves, you must be friends so that you can fight against the white people." "Isn't that right?" he asked Mrs. Logan. She thought for a moment and then told the boy, no, she really didn't think so. You must not fight against a race, she told him, you must fight against a system. There are many freedom-loving people all over the world, of all races and all colors, who are fighting that fight with you. Marion had pointed to the two white COFO teachers whom the students loved. "They are your friends, aren't they?" she asked. "You wouldn't want to fight against them, would you?" "Oh, no," the boy replied. "but they're different." Because these white people were kind, they had been excused, in the mind of that ten-year-old reporter, from the white race.

Another team member, Jean Benjamin, a community activist whose husband was the president of United Artists, also had been interviewed. She had been given the same sort of spiel by another male reporter for the *Freedom School Press*. But then an eleven-year-old girl asked if she might interview Mrs. Benjamin too. The boy protested that she didn't work for the newspaper. "No," said the girl, "but I am writing a book." With that, the young reporter withdrew and the girl started her own interview. And, said Mrs. Benjamin, "a *New York Times* reporter could not have been more perceptive. She asked who I was and what was I doing here. She asked if I liked Mississippi and if I liked the people here. Did I think all white people were bad? What had I thought about the three civil rights workers who had disappeared? Wasn't I fearful of coming down?" Mrs. Benjamin glowed as she told this story.

At ten o'clock that evening, we went to a meeting of Woman Power Unlimited, a group of Negro women who had come together to express their concerns through action. Among other things, they had been responsible for seeing that the COFO workers had places to stay, furniture, bedding, and food, which they provided for those who could take the Freedom Riders into their homes. Mostly these were white women providing supplies to Negro women. They asked eagerly for our impressions of what we had seen. When each team member had spoken, I said, "We all know that our country is in the midst of a revolution, and we must not lose sight of the quiet revolution that women are involved in. That, in the long run, will make the difference. Each of us now can put faces on the freedom schools; we have met some personalities. We know now what it means for women like you to see that these schools are taken care of, and we would like to support and reinforce you in any way that we can."

As we were leaving the gathering, we learned that the Reverend Bob Beech, our guide in Hattiesburg, had been thrown in jail less than an hour after we left. We drove directly to the Jackson COFO office to get more facts. Polly Cowan was especially concerned and offered to call Attorney General Robert Kennedy at home. The COFO staff assured us that if we could be helpful in any way, they would let us know in the morning. The charge against Reverend Beech ostensibly involved an overdrawn account at the local bank. But most feared that his arrest more likely had to do with his kindness to us and with our interracial presence at many of his projects. He was a victim of tactics used to intimidate in the name of the law.

Wherever we went, we were impressed by the dedication of the young people, both black and white, who had come south to work as volunteers. The locals invented hundreds of ways to torment the outsiders, and yet the volunteers seemed unbreakable and responded politely to rude taunts and ugly threats. Mississippi that summer was a nightmarish place, a lawless society in which any white man could appoint himself an enforcer of the "rules"—an ugly, surreal situation in which outsiders were in constant peril.

None of us who were part of WIMS that summer returned home unchanged. What all of us saw of life behind the "cotton curtain" shocked and outraged us. I remember especially one report from a highly successful Negro woman from New York. She wrote:

The thing that touched me the most was the utter lack of communication between the [local] whites and Negroes. I found it stunning. From the time we walked down the ramp until we were back on the plane we had no communication, not even by looks. Their eyes were simply dead. Now I understand why people who have lived in the South have a difficult time adjusting when they come to the North. They have been treated as nothing, and there is nothing so deadly or so chilling as to have a man look at you and not see anything.

Our staff on the ground worked tirelessly to arrange our teams' trips to cities and towns around the state, setting up meetings with local women. The staff's excellent groundwork made it possible for us to do at least six days' work in three. On the four days between team visits each week, staff members attended teas and coffees and church services, ever expanding their circle of acquaintances in Jackson and always hoping to find one more "angel." At first it was mostly black women who would welcome an entire team; only a few white women would dare to meet even the white team members. By the end of the summer forty-eight women from six northern cities had met and talked with some three hundred southern women, nearly half of whom were white.

Fear of reprisals against their husbands—or of what their husbands would think—were constant themes among the white Mississippi women. Several months before our visits began the League of Women Voters in Jackson had invited a speaker from the United Nations to a meeting, and a few weeks later the husband of every woman who had attended received a letter telling him to get his wife out of the league or suffer the consequences. That sort of wholesale intimidation was commonplace. "My husband told me he would divorce me if I got involved with civil rights," said a trembling young wife to white WIMS team members at a gathering in her neighbor's living room.

And yet, as the summer progressed, an amazing number of local white women came forward, quietly and often apprehensively, to join our project. They said they decided to do so because they didn't want to rear their children in such a climate of hate; or because they knew integration was inevitable and they wanted to help make the transition as smooth as possible; or because they simply could no longer stand by, simply watching, as innocent people were harassed or even killed because they dared to try to register to vote. One white woman who had invited a prominent white member of one of our later teams to stay with her family had to withdraw the invitation at the last minute because she felt threatened by disapproval among members of her church. She and her husband, a distinguished surgeon, were deeply disturbed by the incident. "We don't even ask you to forgive us," she said. She hesitated. Then, with sudden understanding, she said, "This is a terrible way to live, isn't it? We're not free, are we?"

By the end of the summer, as they encountered whites in the community who were willing to step forward to work for the cause, black women could begin to see the prospect of change. For their part, the northern women returned home eager to marshal badly needed material support for the COFO projects they had visited. They also were impatient to tell their families, friends, and the media what they had seen: a ragtag army of students and courageous local women and men and young people trying to bring about change. Many of our northern women looked at their own neighborhoods with a fresh perspective. They saw that major work needed to be done in their own backyards if the bright promise of the Civil Rights Act was to be realized.

Just after Labor Day 1964, the *New York Times* ran a front-page story about the Wednesdays in Mississippi. The headline announced: "Women Tear Down the Cotton Curtain." Several weeks later we invited northern and southern women who had participated in the summer project to help us evaluate the results of our work. At the time of the meeting no decision had been made about the future of the project. But by its end the women from

Mississippi had tipped the scales. They said that WIMS started something invaluable. The northern visitors helped them understand what was really going on in race relations in their communities, and they saw a great potential for expansion of our work. They begged us to continue the program. With extended civil rights activity expected in Mississippi during the summer of 1965, they persuaded us that the presence of an "eminently respectable" group of persons who could not be branded "troublemakers" would be needed more than ever. By acclamation, the National Council of Negro Women was asked to sponsor Wednesdays in Mississippi for a second summer in 1965.

Chapter Twelve

Mississippi, Crucible of Change

IN JULY 1965, I was the first black lecturer at the summer Institute on the Desegregation of Schools at the University of Mississippi. Dr. Roscoe Boyer, head of the Department of Education at the university, had received a federal grant to prepare teachers and administrators for desegregation. Faculty member Kate Wilkinson, who had been one of our WIMS "angels" in Jackson, had participated in the YWCA School for Professional Workers, which I directed. She and Dr. Boyer asked me to offer some of the first classes—to help participants understand the civil rights movement, the Civil Rights Act of 1964, and the essential role schools played in achieving full civil rights for every child.

The federal grant stipulated that both the faculty and the student body be integrated. Though an impressive number of white teachers, principals, and superintendents had signed up for the course, no blacks had. They were afraid. After some cajoling, Kate and Dr. Boyer finally persuaded the principal of a black school to attend. He in turn convinced one or two others to come along. The seventy-five-dollar per diem allowance for participants was big money compared with the paltry salaries most school personnel of any color were paid in Mississippi. Without that incentive, I don't believe many blacks would have set their fears aside to come.

Though significant strides had been made in many parts of the state since the previous summer, Kate and Dr. Boyer were anxious about what might happen the day I checked into the faculty club, where Kate had arranged accommodations. I would be the first black guest ever to stay at the Ole Miss Faculty Club. Kate and Ann Hewitt created a kind of buffer for me, occupying the two rooms on either side of mine. As soon as I arrived I sensed that their anxiety had been justified. The campus was full of reminders that it had not been very long since James Meredith was the first, lone black student to enroll. I recalled the terrible battle he had gone through, and Dr. Boyer showed me the still visible stains on the sidewalk where the blood of many had been spilled on the brutal night of Meredith's arrival.

The next morning, as I entered the classroom to conduct the first session of the institute, Dr. Boyer received a call from an irate university official on the other side of the campus. The caller asked Dr. Boyer how I got there and what I was doing. Dr. Boyer advised the caller that the chancellor of the university had approved my appointment, and he dismissed the protest. Indeed, Chancellor John D. Williams had hosted a dinner party in my honor at his home on the first evening. As word of his approval spread across campus, it was like a miracle. The pervasive sense of unease seemed to dissipate.

I learned a lot at Ole Miss. I was astonished, for instance, that when I discussed the report of the U.S. Commission on Civil Rights and its recommendations about school desegregation, the white people in the class, all educators, were convinced I was reading from a Communist document. They could not believe that anyone in the United States of America could speak "officially" in such terms.

After class I often met privately with individuals who wanted to discuss issues at greater length. In one of these meetings a white teacher expressed her fear about having both black and white children in her classroom because, she worried, the white children would "contract syphilis." I asked her what age group she taught. When she said second grade, I suggested that perhaps she had forgotten how syphilis is passed from one person to another; I didn't think this would be a problem for second-graders. She didn't seem to have the slightest idea of what I was talking about. She kept saying, "But they'll all go and sit on the same toilet seats!" After I offered an elementary lecture on the nature of venereal disease, she began to see how unfounded her fears had been, but it sure was a struggle!

I found that it always helped our discussions when we moved beyond civil rights to look more broadly at the costs—to everyone—of segregation. At that time the majority of the participants, white teachers, earned five or six thousand dollars annually. When I told them about the generally higher teachers' salaries elsewhere in the nation, my Mississippi teacher-students were incredulous. How could anybody earn eight or nine thousand dollars a year as a teacher? That was unimaginable in the South, where two separate school systems had to be maintained with barely enough resources for one. As institute participants thought about this, they began to see the sense of a unified system.

Toward the end of my stay I talked with the class about how they might work with their colleagues when they returned home. I hoped they would not see desegregation as a great controversial issue they had to shoulder alone. Rather, I suggested, they were delegates at the institute and should relate as much as possible of what they had learned to their fellow teachers. At the end of my short course nearly all of them recognized that it was the first time in their lives they'd ever heard a candid, nonbelligerent discussion of civil rights and desegregation.

Dr. Boyer arranged a breakfast meeting with the superintendents of schools who were participating in the institute. That turned out to be an educational process for all of us. None of those top men in education had ever sat at a breakfast table with a black person, much less a black woman.

I was especially struck by the words of the superintendent from Natchez when he said that he had some real problems with desegregation. "If you ask what I'm going to do when I go back," he said, "I'd have to tell you that I'm not going to do anything. I'm going to leave things as they are. But I chose the best teachers and the best principals that I had, and I brought them to this course. I have a feeling that they will begin things, and eventually I'll be able to say to the board of education, 'You see, this is what the people want.' When that time comes," he concluded, "I'll be ready, and I'll have the people on my staff ready to support it."

That taught me something. Just as there were some people who were trying to block desegregation, there were others, like this man, who saw its inevitability and were willing to think creatively about strategies that might sustain progress. I also learned that the obstacles imposed by racial segregation in the South reached beyond the black community. The white community too had been handicapped by its isolation from the rest of society.

On my last day at Ole Miss the dean of women asked me to meet with a few young women who were organizing freshman orientation for the following September. Because more black students than ever before would be registering, the dean wanted to be sure that their interests were considered in the arrangements for orientation. Pleased to have this opportunity, I met first with a group of white coeds.

When I arrived, they were preoccupied with plans to celebrate Miss Homecoming, or Miss Mississippi, or Miss Something Else the same week as freshman orientation. The girls let me know that they didn't have time to worry about how they could help freshmen, especially black freshmen, as they arrived on campus. Next, I

talked with two black women—outstanding students, I was told—
who spoke of the very difficult time they had had as entering freshmen the previous September. When I discussed these two separate
encounters with the dean, she invited the two black students and
the white students to meet with me. It was the first time white and
black students had sat down together to think about how freshman
orientation might welcome newcomers of different backgrounds.
The conversation seemed to open new vistas for all concerned.
There was a new mood!

That same summer saw the return of Wednesdays in Mississippi.
Citizens, mothers, and community leaders concerned about civil
rights and human relations once again traveled to the state in
WIMS teams. As in 1964, the northern women met with and listened to their southern counterparts and, on their return home,
shared their experiences widely. The Mississippi women who participated were influential Negro and white women representing a
broad range of southern opinion. Militant segregationists were the
only ones who weren't involved. All told, forty-seven women from
the North, the West, and the East made the trip south that second
summer.

The interracial aspect of the WIMS project was given much
higher visibility in 1965 than had been possible the previous year.
This time black and white staff members lived together, and
Negro and white women from communities across Mississippi
were encouraged to join WIMS teams in public places whenever
possible. This was of immeasurable value, Mississippi women told
us, as the sight of Negro-white relationships was still rare. At the
end of the second summer one leading Mississippi woman wrote:

> After two summers of vigorous activity, WIMS has established a
> pattern and method of operation that should not be allowed to dis-
> appear. It should be enlarged and applied on a much larger scale—

all over the South, certainly, but also in other divided and simmering communities. A catalogue of "Wednesdays" achievements probably cannot be compiled, simply because they did too much and the things they did have yet to end. But if you look back over the last two years and mark every forward step in Jackson community relations, you will find that a "Wednesday" lady has somehow been involved.

Throughout the 1960s Mississippi served as the NCNW's crucible, a place where we could test and refine self-help programs. After the WIMS program was established, whenever I went to Mississippi, I tried to go to a place I had not visited before to learn what people needed. Whenever possible, we responded to these needs. Over time the NCNW developed a hunger program, a housing program, help for teenagers, a health program, and a careers program. These projects inspired our work elsewhere in the United States and, a decade later, in Africa.

When we first went into Mississippi in 1964, we met some middle-class women who didn't seem to want to get their hands dirty but we were wrong. Church women like Jane Scutt and Jesse Moseley worked across racial lines to support the movement. These ladies had offered food and bedding to the Freedom Riders when they came through in the late fifties. But they kept themselves invisible. They did not publicize their support of what others called "rabble-rousers."

A few years later, when Mississippi poverty programs were being seriously threatened by conservatives, I was proud to see our traditionally timid ladies rise up in protest. They organized an NCNW section in Jackson and decided that one of the most pressing community needs was for a twenty-four-hour child-care and information service. The center would provide standard day care programs but also help children who'd wandered away from home or who were neglected and needed a place where they could find care. The NCNW group first rented and later bought a house, furnished it, and set it up with a staff of nine or ten. Some of the staff were retired teachers, others were teenagers; all were volunteers. Even a few white women volunteered at the NCNW center. NCNW members got a local emergency food program to contribute sustenance for the children and cajoled other organizations into donating different kinds of supplies. They kept a twenty-four-hour-a-day service operating entirely with privately raised funds.

Later, when the local television station became so blatantly racist that authorities threatened to rescind its license, the same NCNW group, with Barbara Barnes of the YWCA, black and white women together, monitored the station and challenged its qualifications to hold a license. The station changed its policies.

From its very beginning, Head Start was a perennial issue for the Mississippi NCNW. Throughout the sixties nearly 40 percent of the national Head Start programs were in Mississippi, mostly under the aegis of the Mississippi Child Development Group (MCDG). When racist state officials advocated withdrawing the MCDG's federal funding, the NCNW joined the struggle to keep the group in business. On another occasion Mississippi Governor John Bell Williams, opposing any federal programs that furthered integration, announced that he would veto Head Start unless it required that all Head Start teachers be "fully qualified." Until then, Head Start had been extremely effective in hiring local people and paraprofessionals who worked under the supervision of highly trained professionals. If the governor's requirement went through, it would disqualify the vast majority of Mississippi's Head Start staff and leadership, most of whom were black.

The Southern Regional Council, in league with the Mississippi Council on Human Rights, convened a public hearing. I was invited to serve on the panel to examine witnesses at the hearing. Twelve hundred people came from across the state to testify. One of the most memorable witnesses was an eighty-year-old grandmother. She told the panel that she had no training, but when Head Start came to her town she volunteered and felt she had been able to help a lot of children. With black parents struggling so hard and working such long hours, many children needed simple, loving care, and that was what she provided. Though she couldn't teach them their letters or numbers, she told us, she could give them the care of a loving grandmother. She prepared food, taught manners, and showed the children the difference between right and wrong.

Other volunteers talked about children who were handicapped, who could not read, who were blind or deaf. They told how those children were discovered and helped through Head Start—and how without it, they would have been left to wither. Moving testimony went on for several days. These people knew firsthand the value of Head Start—to the children it served and to the adults whose caring it engaged.

James Farmer, an old friend who had led the Congress of Racial Equality and was now an assistant secretary of Health, Education, and Welfare, arranged for us to summarize the testimony for HEW Secretary Elliot Richardson. Because the Head Start program was 100 percent federally funded, Secretary Richardson had the authority to override the governor's veto. He did, and the Mississippi Head Start program was rescued one more time.

Still, the battle continued. Many Mississippi authorities found Head Start threatening because they understood its power among the majority black population. They rightly suspected that by engaging so many black families and volunteers in its work, it was fueling the political awakening among blacks. In little towns across Mississippi, when people got involved in Head Start, it seemed only natural to encourage them to register to vote.

The drive to register voters opened other avenues of action. One day Fannie Lou Hamer came to visit me in New York from her home in Ruleville, Mississippi. They were in a tough situation, she said. Thelma Barnes, a prominent black woman, had run for Congress in Washington County, and even though the district was more than 70 percent black, Mrs. Barnes lost. Many people had come to Mrs. Barnes afterward and said, "I wanted to vote for you, but Mr. So-and-so offered me twenty dollars to vote for the white candidate, and I just needed money so bad." Even worse, just before election day white landowners all of a sudden had offered people jobs in the fields. Of course the people couldn't give up the chance for work, but it meant that they had to be in the fields from sun up to sun down on election day, even if they had registered to vote. The Friday after election day they were all let go. Their jobs were gone, and a white person—not Mrs. Barnes—had been elected to "represent" them in Congress.

Seeing my incredulity, Mrs. Hamer explained: "You see, Miss Height, down where we are, food is used as a political weapon. But if you have a pig in your backyard, if you have some vegetables in your garden, you can feed yourself and your family, and nobody can push you around. If we have something like some pigs and some gardens and a few things like that, even if we have no jobs, we can eat and we can look after our families."

I began to understand what Mrs. Hamer meant. "Maybe we could set up a pig bank," I thought out loud. In my work at the YWCA I had been impressed by the Heifer Project, which donates livestock to needy families around the world so that they have the means to feed themselves. So in 1967, with expert advice from a retired Iowa farmer and the assistance of the Prentiss Institute, the National Council of Negro Women purchased fifty-five Yorkshire pigs—fifty females and five males—to start the pig bank. Participating families were trained to care for pigs, to establish cooperatives, and to work together to improve the community's nutrition and health. Each participating family signed a "pig agreement," promising not to sell the pigs and to bring back two piglets from each litter to deposit in the bank. That way more and more families could receive pigs over time.

As families carried out their responsibilities under the pig agreement, many confessed that they learned more than they ever knew about food, water, hygiene, and their own health. Years later, after the king of Swaziland saw an NCNW film that included the pig bank, he asked for help in developing one. NCNW sent John Davis, an extension worker who helped with the training of families in Mississippi, to Swaziland, where he taught rural women how to run a pig bank and market their pigs.

In the fall of 1965, soon after the second Wednesdays in Mississippi summer, the WIMS project changed its name and its focus—but not its initials. Team visits stopped, but northern and southern women remained actively engaged in fighting racism and poverty through the NCNW's Workshops in Mississippi. The goal was to reach and assist more and more groups of hard-core poor women.

The first workshop was held in Jackson in November 1966. Though only twenty-five women had been invited, sixty showed up. They came from fifteen Mississippi communities reaching from north to south and from east to west. They were animated about their need for housing, community centers, and school breakfast and lunch programs. They talked of finding more women for volunteer service, of their desire to bridge the gap between those who had received the benefits of education and those who had not. They spoke of the responsibility of women who had a better education and a good job to work for the general good, because they had access to information and knew how to use it. They made clear that many of the most dedicated women were too poor to give their time and energy as volunteers in the conventional sense, speaking eloquently of how Negro women had to attend birthings, nurse the sick, bury the dead, and always make something out of nothing.

Two months later Annie Devine of Canton chaired a second workshop in Oxford, Mississippi. The theme was how to write grant proposals. A wide range of experts came to teach the participants how to appeal for money. Many of the experts had grave misgivings. They doubted that much could be accomplished in an area that seemed to call for so much previous education and expertise. Among the forty-three participants, a few had a regular source of income as a teacher or beautician, and a few others owned a business. But most could only be classified as "economically deprived."

To the amazement of the experts, by the end of two and a half days the women had outlined, drafted, and critiqued proposals for day care centers, community centers, enrichment programs for teenage girls, and school breakfast programs. The Oxford workshop demonstrated that WIMS connections could help isolated rural Mississippians meet specific, answerable needs through tapping available federal resources. Fannie Lou Hamer announced that she would like to bring poor white people from Sunflower County, "who feel exactly like we feel and they need this kind of help too," to the next NCNW workshop.

Six months later, at the invitation of the U.S. Department of Agriculture (USDA), the National Council of Negro Women convened a third rural training workshop, this time in Indianola, in the heart of the Mississippi Delta. Fannie Lou Hamer served as host-moderator, and I was the discussion leader. Thirty-one rural poor women, fifteen representatives of federal, state, and local agencies, and nine members of the Sunflower County Community Action Program had assembled. Some who had said they would come dropped out in fear of reprisal, but their places were quickly taken by others who had faith that the National Council of Negro Women could help them. With annual incomes of six hundred dollars or less, these women looked to us to understand their deprivation and to connect them in a meaningful way with the otherwise faceless government bureaucracy on which they depended.

Ann Hewitt, our advance person, arranged for the group to be housed at the Travel Lodge in Indianola. When we arrived, we were told that our small grant from the Office of Economic Opportunity (OEO), which was to cover the cost of the workshop, had been vetoed by the governor because he thought NCNW was subversive. A Colonel Harper, the county clerk—and a friend of the governor's—brought the news. But the women were gathering, and all our plans were set. Polly Cowan rose to the occasion, saying that we could not let these women down. She arranged for her family foundation to cover the cost.

The women began arriving. They ranged in age from midtwenties to early seventies. Some were welfare mothers, some were elderly who lived virtually without income, some had lost their jobs because they had tried to register to vote. Those who worked either chopped cotton or, if they were lucky, worked in domestic service. They stayed in motels that hitherto had catered only to white guests, and they took their meals with white government officials. For them, living in a motel for two days and working in tandem with white people was something like going to school for the first time. The fear of driving up to the motel to register and stay was enormous, but for most it was overcome by the desire to "find out." Besides, the small lodge over the wholesale warehouse seemed very luxurious. They took little time adjusting to the pleasures of staying in a room with no more than three occupants, where the bathroom had hot and cold running water, real sheets were tucked under mattresses of kapok and ticking instead of corn husks, and each person had a whole bed to herself. Like the other "consultants," they were being paid a daily stipend of fifteen dollars.

I led off the program by advising the women to feel free to say whatever they wanted, but never to say "I." We did not want to create any scapegoats for reprisals. The participants were to say "we" or "some people" when presenting a problem. We simply had to help them protect themselves.

Colonel Harper never left our group all day and even joined us for a hot lunch at a local church. After a young woman told her story about being sterilized after having a child in the hospital—without her knowledge—he angrily interrupted. He did not want these outsiders sending memos back to Washington about things that were not true, he protested. I told him that in our experience it was hard to get fifty black women together without someone telling that story.

As the women overcame their private worries, they blossomed, freely sharing their knowledge of individual, family, and community problems in the Delta. The government people brought their knowledge of the structure and methods of their own agencies, and the WIMS team provided a bridge between the agencies and the women.

On the first day the women and the officials met separately to figure out how best to communicate with each other, how to make themselves clearly understood and how to go about solving problems. On the second day there was an open and constructive interchange. First, each representative presented his agency and its programs—food stamps, welfare, job training, minimum wage, Social Security, old-age benefits, health, Medicare. The women, in turn, described their experiences with each program.

"How can you buy food stamps when you don't have enough income?" "When minimum wage came in, our hours were shortened, so now, instead of more adequate pay, we do double the work in half the time." "What do you do if 'the man' took out of your pay for Social Security for the past ten years and you just found out he hadn't paid it to the government?"

Questions were asked, problems dissected, answers found. The disparity between the day-to-day reality of the women and the design and delivery of the programs intended to help them was clear to all. The USDA representative of the food stamp program, for instance, was delighted to announce that the cost of food stamps was being dropped from two dollars to fifty cents for twelve dollars' worth of food for people with minimal incomes. Expecting applause, he was surprised when his announcement was met by silence. One woman spoke up. She was sixty-two and had not had work since she registered to vote; because there was no record of money being paid into her account during the years she had worked on a cotton plantation, she was not eligible for Social Security. "What do you do if you have no income?" she asked.

The official admitted that could be a problem. But then he explained the difference between cash and income, concluding, "You may not have cash, but you must have some income."

"I wonder where mine is hid," said the woman, "'cause I sure can't find none." When he told her he had been across several counties and found only one person who had no income, the woman replied, "Mister, you have just met another!"

Through it all, the women and the government representatives showed mutual respect and an eagerness to close the communication gap. By the end of the workshop everyone understood more clearly the connection between services and people and the value of having both deliverers and recipients work together to solve problems.

One of the women described the importance of the experience:

> We have learned here we can better understand each other when we talk together. We've learned we can work together and even sit together. We've learned we can eat together. Maybe we can learn to live together and die together.

At the end Colonel Harper asked all to rise and "give Dr. Height and her group thanks! They brought us together," he added. "Mrs. Hamer and I even got together." From that point, NCNW had a new friend.

The Sunflower County workshop reflected the unique combination of factors that led to the success of the WIMS program. Since 1964 WIMS had drawn together Negro and white women from the North and the South, volunteers and professionals. It had been the medium through which the knowledge and strength of all could be directed to providing the women of Mississippi with the tools for their own development. The contacts and skills growing

out of team visits and workshops had built confidence, understanding, and cooperation among the government, the white community,
and Negro women. Inspired by the results of the Workshops in
Mississippi, the National Council of Negro Women took steps to
organize a nationwide Commission on Community Cooperation.
The idea was to entice new talent into the fight against poverty
and discrimination by training women who were socially isolated
and giving them opportunities for creative community action.

What I learned in these projects turned out to be useful in
unforeseen ways. In the late 1970s, for example, President Jimmy
Carter appointed me to the Commission for the Protection of
Human Subjects of Biomedical and Behavioral Research. The
other fifteen members were professionals in fields like medicine,
ethics, law, health, and education. I was a public member, and I
brought to the commission what I had learned face to face with
poor women. I could be the voice of women who knew that their
rights had been violated. I had something to contribute in the
shaping of policy recommendations and pressed for policies to be
written so that they were understandable at low levels of literacy.*

Underlying all the discussions in Mississippi was the urgent need
for decent housing. "When I cook in bad weather, I have to put on
my raincoat, hat, and boots," said one participant. "If anyone
comes to see me, they think I'm on my way out, but I'm just trying
to stay dry and get supper for the kids." Following the tradition of

---

* In the work of that commission I came to appreciate more than ever the importance of letting people teach us how to help them. I had long believed that prisoners of color were exploited as the main guinea pigs in drug experiments
involving human beings. But as we visited prisons across the country, I found the
opposite was true: very *few* black prisoners had the opportunity to participate in
such experiments—and they felt that they were discriminated against. The
largely white subjects of the experiments were housed better and fed the best of
foods—and they won earlier probation and sometimes release. I listened and
learned.

creative approaches to low-cost housing begun years before by Mrs. Bethune, NCNW seized an opportunity in 1967 to make one of its finest contributions to community development.

The acute need for housing in Mississippi had been brought to our attention at one of the first WIMS workshops. At that time NCNW's housing expert, Dorothy Duke, explored available federal, state, and local housing programs to see which might be tapped. She concluded that local housing authorities were best suited to provide more housing. She had also observed that many needy families had a strong desire to own their homes. Based on Mrs. Duke's findings, the NCNW drafted a proposal for an experimental program that could meet specific needs of Mississippi families and provide incentives for them to maintain their homes themselves. By making it possible for people to become homeowners rather than just tenants, the program would ultimately reduce their need for federal subsidies. Unita Blackwell, a civil rights leader who had attended our workshop, was employed to work in partnership with Mrs. Duke.

When we presented our proposal to officials at the U.S. Department of Housing and Urban Development (HUD), we were received with polite but obdurate skepticism. Because our proposal was "too people-oriented," we were told, it failed to meet HUD requirements. Not wanting us to leave empty-handed, however, the HUD people kindly referred us to the Office of Economic Opportunity.

The OEO officials were intrigued by our idea. Their enthusiasm led to several months of intensive negotiations with representatives of HUD and OEO, the Ford Foundation, the Mississippi Research and Development Center, the National Association of Housing and Redevelopment Officials, the Mississippi Home Builders, and a host of Mississippi housing experts and local officials. For the first time in state history public officials and private businesspeople sat in conference with representatives of a national black women's organization to discuss—as equals—how to meet the housing needs of the state's poorest black people.

Dorothy Duke, Unita Blackwell, and I talked with HUD Secretary Robert C. Weaver and shared our desire to help meet the needs expressed by the women in Mississippi. He assigned Joseph Burstein, general counsel, to explore the possibilities. "If the government subsidizes rental housing," Burstein reasoned, "why not subsidize homeownership for low-income families?"

After our meeting in Washington, Mrs. Blackwell turned to me and said, "I reckon if we come up here again to these fine offices, I should wear stockings."

Under "Turnkey III," as it was called, families who qualified for public housing were selected to move into their future homes without a cash down payment but with an agreement to give maintenance work "sweat equity" of two hundred dollars. NCNW organized the Homebuyers Association, which trained members to manage and maintain their homes on a cooperative basis.

The interest and support of both the national and the Mississippi Association of Home Builders were crucial. Francis X. Collins, former president of the Mississippi Home Builders Association and a member of the board of the National Association of Home Builders, not only was one of the most energetic supporters of the NCNW effort but was prepared to take risks and knock down the wall of prejudice against public housing. His enthusiasm was compelling. He enlisted the Hancock Bank of Gulfport and the First National Bank of Biloxi, which together handled the financing. And federal officials developed the legal basis for a lease-purchase plan that would enable low-income families to take possession of homes as buyer-occupants under the public housing rental program. The program was structured so that if participating families' incomes rose above the limits for public housing, they were given opportunities and incentives to purchase their homes under an appropriate FHA-insured mortgage or other financing arrangements.

In September 1967, HUD Secretary Weaver gave NCNW full credit for initiating the pilot project of 200 homes at North Gulfport, Mississippi, and called it a "precedent-making development." The North Gulfport project contained 200 detached three-, four-, and five-bedroom homes, plus centers for day care, recreation, and other community services. By June 1972, 6,637 homes in 85 municipalities were participating in what came to be called the Homeownership Opportunities Program.

By the time the program was up and running in North Gulfport and Indianola, Mississippi, NCNW housing staff had become as informed and experienced as any low-income housing specialists anywhere in the country. With the support of the OEO and Ford Foundation grants, NCNW moved on to Raleigh, North Carolina; St. Louis, Missouri; San Antonio, Texas; Elizabeth City, New Jersey; Oklahoma City, Oklahoma; and New Orleans, Louisiana, to encourage public-private partnerships promoting low-income housing. By the end of the project, 18,761 units had been constructed at an estimated value of $407 million.

In October 1968, Secretary Weaver thanked the NCNW for its initiative. "You have pioneered an experimental program in public housing which may well establish a pattern for the nation," he wrote. "And while I am proud of your magnificent accomplishment, I am not surprised by it. You have always been in the forefront."

When HUD Secretary George Romney toured the area after Hurricane Camille in 1969, the only site intact was Forest Heights, the Gulfport development. It had been saved because Ike Thomas, a resident, risked his life to close the floodgate. He was asked why he did so. His answer was simple—and eloquent: for the first time in their lives, they had something of their own. HUD developed a film entitled *Something of Their Own*.

NCNW's work in Mississippi is our best example of how self-help can become a reality. For many years now it's been impossible for us to have a small meeting in Mississippi. Wherever we convene, women come from all over the state to be part of our work. In fact, because of the way one thing led to another in Mississippi in the sixties, there are more local sections of the National Council of Negro Women there than in any other state.

Not every dream has come entirely true, of course. One example was a project we hoped would help teen mothers. In the sixties, two members—Willie T. Rashberry and Kate Wilkinson—suggested that the NCNW purchase the former Okolona Junior College, which had closed after some civil rights tragedies on the grounds. It was a beautiful, ninety-acre site on the highway.

Some of the Okolona city fathers had already approached the Episcopal Church, which owned the grounds, offering more than a quarter of a million dollars for the college. They wanted to turn the property into a country club. But after hearing the women's proposal, the diocesan board voted to turn back the first offer. They provided the property for use by NCNW at one dollar per year.

We got full funding of a proposal for an educational center for teen mothers and their children, and the Tupelo School District agreed to admit the mothers as students so that they could finish their education. But no sooner had the program been fully developed and staffed than a local congressman protested that NCNW was bringing prostitution into his backyard. The funds were withdrawn, and NCNW had to return what had not been spent.

Even so, we did not give up. The buildings were put to good purpose. NCNW had child-care programs, and some of the space was provided to Head Start. NCNW headquarters carried the program for six years. The NCNW Mississippi women managed to purchase the property and restore some of the buildings, and they now look forward to using it as an educational center for youth and adults.

Throughout the civil rights struggle many groups came into Mississippi. NCNW never left. We stayed by, and we moved from one project to another, from one area to another, until we had a beautiful garden of experimental ventures blooming in practically every corner of the state. Whether it was carrying books and art supplies to the freedom schools during Wednesdays in Mississippi, keeping Head Start on track, setting up pig banks, or building houses, we were helping people meet their own needs, on their own terms. Women knew that if they joined the National Council of Negro Women, they were going to help themselves by helping others.

In a 1968 newsletter sent to everyone who had ever participated in a WIMS program, Polly Cowan wrote:

> Every day brings more exciting developments, each in its way the outcome of the work all of you began. If *you* had not had the courage and the interest to go to Mississippi during the worrisome summers of 1964 and 1965, the women of Mississippi would not have asked the National Council of Negro Women how they might help themselves.

Chapter Thirteen

Living up to Our Promise

P ASSAGE OF THE Civil Rights Acts of 1964 and the Voting Rights Act of 1965 turned out to be bittersweet for many African Americans. The initial jubilation was overtaken by disillusionment as the legislation failed to erase the fundamental causes of disenfranchisement of black Americans. Black women continued to have to provide for themselves and their extended families many services that white women took for granted. They carried on nurturing and nursing, teaching and training, providing social and spiritual uplift, while trying to eke out enough to stay alive. But even though they continued to bear major responsibility for the welfare of their families, black women were shut out of traditional community work. No matter how well qualified for leadership and service, our women were still all but invisible in community decisionmaking. Crucial decisions usually were made miles away by white governments and businesses that had little regard for their impact on black communities. As economic pressures tightened, the black woman found herself trapped in a triple bind of racism, sexism, and poverty.

In 1966 the National Council of Negro Women tried to loosen that bind by turning black women's frustration into positive action. NCNW had finally received tax-exempt status and with it two major grants to help recruit and train Negro women. We called the effort Project Womanpower, and its goal was to bring six thousand Negro women into volunteer community service. If black women were mobilized, we figured, they would bring about changes in their communities that could begin to correct some of the injustices still rampant in our society.

With generous Ford Foundation support, we launched our training program, knowing that success would depend on our ingenuity. The black woman who might be inclined to commit time and energy to a project such as Womanpower sought information, the sharpening of her skills, and association with others who had similar interests. She expected to be challenged and to take on major issues. And that's precisely what Project Womanpower volunteers did.

The first vanguard of recruits was made up of ninety women from thirty communities all over the country. They were housewives, factory workers, teachers, nurses, office workers, welfare mothers, college students, and a few older retired women. Their ages ranged from eighteen to sixty. We brought them to Nyack, New York, where they received instruction from NCNW staff and volunteers, plus professionals, including the psychiatrist Dr. Alvin Pouissant. When the first ninety returned home, they recruited and trained more women to join them in the struggle for better housing, improved schooling, community development, and consumer ventures.

In Mississippi a woman said that she had never before met with her sisters in this way. Now she had found out that many of the things done to her were illegal and that there was such a thing as a "fair hearing." She brought this knowledge to her neighbors, and a welfare rights group was born.

In Lorain, Ohio, a community council was created and surveys were made for community development in an all-black area that had no paved roads, sewage, or other utilities. When school desegregation led to violence in Boston, our women spearheaded an information service and provided legal and medical services as well as food, clothing, and shelter to victims of civil disorders.

The experience with Project Womanpower equipped NCNW to grow another seed that had been sown at the 1964 Women's Interorganizational Committee meeting in Atlanta. Sargent Shriver was setting up the Women's Job Corps under President Johnson's Great Society program. Jeanne Noble, who was assisting him, had told him of the history of the coalition* on civil rights issues, and Mr. Shriver asked if we might bring the same power to bear to help young women in poverty. With a combined membership of twenty-seven million women, our four national organizations offered a formidable force!

When the leaders of the organizations gathered to discuss how to respond to the administration's request, it was obvious that we still lacked a proper name. The idea of the wick and the candle that had emerged in Atlanta had caught on, so we decided to continue to call ourselves WICS; this time the acronym would stand for Women in Community Service. Mary Halloran, former colonel of the Women's Army Corps, was the first executive director.

The objective of WICS was to funnel young, poor women into the government's Job Corps, which would train them in academic, vocational, and social skills to help them find and keep good jobs. Volunteers worked long hours searching out girls aged sixteen to twenty-one who could benefit from the Job Corps programs. They visited homes, talked to parents, contacted school officials and social workers—anyone who could help them find qualified girls. Once the girls were found, it was not just a simple matter of

* The National Council of Negro Women, the National Council of Jewish Women, the National Council of Catholic Women, and Church Women United.

recruitment and screening. All too often there were hurdles that made it difficult for recruits to seize the chance at a fresh start, from failure in school and responsibility for dependent children to miserable living conditions in crowded, substandard housing.

But the volunteers were undaunted. They worked with thousands of young women, getting them into the Job Corps, staying with them while they were in training, and continuing to counsel them even after they got jobs. They gathered wardrobes for girls who had none. They started grooming and family planning courses. They helped girls overcome health problems. In one Texas town WICS volunteers started a literacy course for adults when they discovered some fathers were not signing the consent forms for their daughters because they could neither read nor write. Girls who were not selected or did not want to go to the Job Corps were referred to other community agencies.

Just one year after the program began, WICS volunteers had established more than 289 screening centers in fifty states and the District of Columbia. Twenty-two thousand applicants had been referred to the Job Corps, more than nine thousand young women were enrolled in eighteen residential centers, and four thousand eligible applicants were awaiting placement. Some graduates were already earning more than three times what they had earned before. Equally gratifying were the new relationships among the volunteers. Women who had had no contact or equal exchange before—black, white, and brown, Protestant, Catholic, and Jewish, poor, middle-class, and affluent—learned what it could mean to work on a common cause. In 1969 the coalition was further strengthened by the addition of the American GI Forum and the League of United Latin American Citizens, whose goals were to enhance opportunities for young Hispanic women.

As we found young women to help, we found and helped each other too. In the end our diversity proved an extraordinary stimulus to discovering common ground. It was gratifying when a high-level administration official described us as "an illogical organization . . . a fantastically varied group of women who are not experienced in this type of work. They are volunteers. They are all the things that experienced organizations traditionally avoid. But they have one unusual attribute—they are overwhelmingly successful."

Through our experience in Mississippi we had learned much about the devastating reality of hunger in the United States. Many rural schools had no food service at all. Annie Devine, a longtime activist in Mississippi, argued that hungry children cannot learn, and she led NCNW to establish a school breakfast program in Canton, Mississippi. After the Civil Rights Act passed, NCNW made a study of school lunch programs in cooperation with the NAACP Legal Defense and Education Fund, whose Jackson office was directed by Marian Wright Edelman, founder of the Children's Defense Fund (CDF).* Entitled *Their Daily Bread*, the study found pervasive hunger in northern cities and in schools across the rural South. When asked what was different about their newly integrated schools, black children in the South often replied, "We get lunch."

Eventually NCNW brought together sixty-four national organizations—some two thousand citizens—for a National Convocation on Hunger. People from the heart of the hunger belt met with leaders from the worlds of education, business, and social services. In 1969, at President Richard Nixon's White House Conference on Food, Nutrition, and Health, reports from NCNW workshops and data formed the basis of the main working paper. The stories of

---

* In 2001, at the Children's Defense Fund annual conference, Marian Wright Edelman honored women who had participated in Wednesdays in Mississippi. That NCNW program inspired "Wednesdays in Washington," CDF's own work mobilizing advocates for child welfare. And in Bellagio, Italy, I co-chaired, with John Hope Franklin a CDF-sponsored retreat that produced the Black Community Crusade for Children. I quoted the motto Mary McLeod Bethune had given NCNW: "Leave No One Behind." The scholar Cornel West, hearing it, asked whether NCNW would object to the group's using "Leave No *Child* Behind." I did not object, believing that Mrs. Bethune would want to do whatever she could to stimulate greater concerted action for children.

real people collected from a wide range of churches, shelters, and other facilities brought to life the reality of hunger in the midst of this land of plenty. I cherish a note from Dr. Benjamin Mays, who gave a keynote speech at the hunger convocation. He wrote a single sentence: "I like what you do and the way that you do it."

Mississippi had also taught us that many people of limited educational background were fearful about registering to vote. They believed, for instance, that if they had a parking ticket that hadn't been paid, they'd be arrested if they tried to register. Many felt much the same way about the decennial U.S. census. Minorities and other marginalized people tend to be fearful of being counted. But when you don't get counted, you don't get represented— either by elected officials or when decisions are made on the allocation of federal resources based on population.

In the mid-1960s the NCNW began to address these issues. In big cities, where large numbers of blacks often are lost in the undercount, NCNW women set up systems for helping people get counted in the census. We tried to allay their fears and to let them know how important it was for them to be counted. We did the same for voter registration. Many people either didn't know their rights or didn't know how to exercise them. So our women went into the streets to explain the hows and whys of voting.

Once, in Harlem, a woman on welfare asked me all kinds of questions. As we talked, a drifter interrupted, complaining about how long it had been since he'd had a job. He said he saw no need to vote because it wouldn't make any difference. The welfare woman shook her finger at him. "If you get up and get yourself registered to vote, you might be able to do something for yourself," she declared. "You'd better try it!" And so he did—he registered to vote. That was the way we liked to work, helping neighbors talk to their neighbors, encouraging people to pull themselves up by their own bootstraps.

One of our best voter registration projects, WMCA Call for Action, was in New York City. Founded in 1965 by Ellen Strauss, it

brought together volunteers and the radio station as a central information and referral service. Through it, NCNW volunteers pressed
for extensions on the time requirements for registration and for
expansion of the number of places where people could register. We
were a major factor in getting firehouses designated as registration
sites. The following year, when the League of Women Voters
decided to expand its registration program, the chairman of the
New York Board of Elections referred the league to the National
Council of Negro Women because he thought we had developed
the best information available. By 1970 three-quarters of our nearly
two hundred local sections had voter education and registration
programs, and all that work paid off. A few years prior, a survey by
the Joint Center for Political and Economic Studies showed that
black women had the best voting records of any group in the country, including white males.

In 1967, as we approached the end of our third decade, the NCNW
leadership decided that it was time to take stock, to see if our projects and programs were responsive to the rapidly changing needs
of the black community. Under the terms of the Project Womanpower grant, we brought together women who had been working in
many different communities with the heads of our twenty-four
national affiliate organizations to examine how we were living up to
our promise.

After three days of work, we discovered anew that different
organizations had different goals. Teachers worried about education, nurses about health, and labor union people about jobs. But
unless we worked interactively on all of these goals, we'd be
unlikely to reach any of them. Unless we thought about ourselves
with a sense of wholeness, we risked losing the potential power of
our combined skills and knowledge. In the final report of our meeting, we confirmed that our objective was to implement the goals of
each affiliate national program through collaborative efforts. These

words meant more than just "let's cooperate." Each of us saw that if she wanted to help a child, she must work with the health people and the education people and all the others involved in that child's life. If we were to be of genuine service to our communities, each of us had to take the others' concerns to heart.

Reflecting the sense of urgency, we called the report of that meeting *Two Minutes to Midnight.* A few months later the theme of NCNW's 1967 National Convention, "Women—The Crisis in the Black Community—Direction and Decision," reflected our new sense of mission. And the following years turned out to be a period of phenomenal growth for the NCNW. Between 1965 and 1980 our annual budget soared from a few hundred thousand dollars to several million. We launched some forty national projects concerning employment, youth, housing, consumerism, hunger and malnutrition, civil rights, volunteerism, women's issues, and family life.

The NCNW's response to teenagers in trouble was Operation Sisters United, a program developed with funding from the U.S. Department of Justice. The idea was to give courts a rehabilitation alternative to detention for juvenile female offenders. With our extensive network of volunteers in cities across the country, we could work with girls in one-to-one relationships at centers that also provided educational and group counseling. Operation Sisters United would be picked up by other organizations across the country.

In 1970 the NCNW opened the Women's Center for Education and Career Advancement in New York City. Its purpose: to encourage and train young minority women who were stuck in entry-level jobs because of inadequate skills. At the time more than half of the black women aged twenty-six to sixty-four who lived in metropolitan New York worked, many simultaneously carrying heavy family responsibilities. But black and Hispanic women were concentrated in the lowest-paying jobs.

The idea for the Women's Center came from Helen Rachlin, who had served on the staff of the National Council of Jewish

Women. She had several young women on her staff who were bright and well motivated but whose skills were far below par. (One of them who later came to work for me demonstrated the problem perfectly. I had asked not to be disturbed and overheard her say to a caller in her lovely, helpful manner: "Oh, dear, Miss So-and-so, Dr. Height aren't available at the moment.") What we needed, said Helen Rachlin, was a "Project Pygmalion" to help young women— especially those affected by poor education in some southern and rural areas—prepare for a higher level of employment.

The Women's Center was set in the Wall Street area to reach minority women where they worked. We also reached out to those who lived uptown. If a young woman in Harlem took the first step of coming down to the Women's Center, we discovered that such evidence of motivation meant that real commitment to training and employment usually followed. The center featured general education and basic skills, career counseling, and training geared toward gaining and keeping jobs. It was open to women and men of all races and ethnic backgrounds.

After a year or two, in cooperation with Pace University, we developed a special degree program that featured an advisory group of businesspeople. These successful men and women served as on-call counselors, each spending up to a day a week with a student, attending classes with her and talking about course content. The corporate volunteers loved this work as much as the students did.

Under the aegis of the Women's Center, we set up a program called Debtors Anonymous to help young women learn how to handle money. We found that many black and Hispanic women were wary of seeking advancement even when they had the skills because so many had unfortunate credit histories and feared losing their jobs if they were "found out." Debtors Anonymous was based on the mutual support and anonymity that had proved so effective in Alcoholics Anonymous. Members came together weekly to talk about how to get out of debt, how to budget, and how to set and achieve long-term financial goals. They studied the cost of credit, consumer protection laws, and comparative costs of goods and serv-ices. They had credit card–burning sessions and testimonials when members cleared their debts. Each member had a "credit pal" whom she could call if she felt the urge to splurge. At the height of the program we had almost a thousand calls a day from people who wanted to join.

The Women's Center's program became a prototype for others across America. By the time the center celebrated its twenty-fifth anniversary in 1995, it offered individual career counseling, a résumé writing and interview workshop, a program on entrepre-neurship for women living in public housing, a training program for displaced homemakers, a session on financial aid for black and Latino high school students, and an employer-requested seminar on "Working Parents and New York City Public Schools" to enable working parents to make effective decisions about their children's education. Now independently incorporated and funded by the New York State Department of Labor, private corporations, and foundations, the Women's Center has trained more than twenty-five thousand people.

Mary McLeod Bethune said in 1935 that the time had come to "harness the womanpower" among us. She had a special way of explaining the potential of such cooperation: "If I take a finger and touch you, you won't even know you've been tapped. If I take two fingers, you will know that something touched you. But if I bring all of those fingers together in a fist, I can give you a terrible blow!"

Collaborating and coalition-building were the very essence of Mrs. Bethune's way of work, and I have believed in these practices all my life. Seldom have I witnessed their effectiveness more clearly than in 1997, after President Bill Clinton enthusiastically nominated Alexis Herman to become the nation's first African American secretary of Labor—only the fourth woman in the agency's eighty-five-year history.

I had met Alexis Herman in 1972 through A. Philip Randolph and had come to love her as a daughter and to have the highest respect for her professionalism, wisdom, and commitment. She had become director of the Labor Department's Women's Bureau before she was thirty years old. She had been chief executive officer of the 1992 Democratic National Committee and served as the DNC's chief of staff. During President Clinton's first term she had distinguished herself as director of the White House Office of Public Liaison. In short, she was extraordinarily well qualified for the post of secretary of labor, yet the confirmation hearings did not move. It was clear that some of the opposition to her was gender-based, some designed to embarrass the president, and some to divide and weaken the progressive community. I knew that the kind of opposition forming against Alexis Herman was formidable. It could prove damaging to any nominee. We had to organize an equally formidable coalition on her behalf. It was not hard to do because through her own work she had built several constituencies.

I soon found a groundswell of interest, and it was not long before we built a strong coalition* of concerned organizations and individuals who generated thousands of letters and calls demonstrating grassroots pressure to confirm Alexis Herman and keeping the White House commitment to her strong and uwavering.

The key to the confirmation was the support of Senate Republicans, who were the majority party at that time. When the confirmation hearing finally began in the Senate Labor Committee, Alexis Herman was introduced by two powerful Republicans from her home state of Alabama, Representative Herbert Leon "Sonny"

* Those who joined the battle to get Alexis Herman confirmed included: Wade Henderson, executive director of the Leadership Conference on Civil Rights; Marcia Fudge, national president of Delta Sigma Theta Sorority; Yvonne Scruggs Leftwich of the Black Leadership Forum; John Sweeney, national president of the AFL-CIO; Nancy Zirkin of the American Association of University Women; William Lucy, president of the Coalition of Black Trade Unionists; and C. Delores Tucker, chair of the National Political Congress of Black Women.

Callahan and Senator Richard Shelby. But what ultimately ensured her confirmation was support from an unlikely source—Mississippi Republican Senator Trent Lott, who knew her work in Pascagoula, Mississippi, where she had helped displaced shipyard workers. Wade Henderson, Nancy Zirkin, and Richard Byrd, director of the National Association of Neighborhoods, and I met with Senator Lott's staff. After that meeting opposition to Alexis Herman began to fade. On April 30, 1997, she was confirmed as secretary of labor.

I believe that Alexis Herman is a shining example of what women of color can achieve despite the odds. More important, her confirmation reaffirmed the extraordinary power of coalition politics—the great strength of many groups working with a unified purpose. On the day Alexis Herman was sworn in, there were so many friends, supporters, and well-wishers present that they overflowed the assigned space. Her distinguished record of service as secretary of labor speaks for itself.

Over the decades the NCNW demonstrated the truth of Mary McLeod Bethune's words. And although the NCNW's accomplishments were themselves a tribute to her vision, it seemed to many that there ought to be a more concrete and public memorial as well.

In 1958, three years after Mrs. Bethune's death, Dolphin Thompson, owner of a public relations firm in Washington, had come to see me. He told me about a monument on Capitol Hill called "The Emancipation Group," which depicted Abraham Lincoln with a slave breaking out of bondage. Set in a plaza called Lincoln Park, that monument was the idea of Charlotte Scott, a freed slave, who was sixty years old when she heard that Lincoln had been assassinated and pledged the first five dollars she had earned in freedom to build a memorial to him.

Mr. Thompson thought there should be another monument in Lincoln Park, one that would show that more than emancipation had happened in the lives of American Negroes, and he thought the sub-

ject should be Mary McLeod Bethune. I liked the idea and encouraged Mr. Thompson to take Elsie Austin, then executive director of
the National Council of Negro Women, out to see the park.

Miss Austin and Mr. Thompson then began to explore what sort
of congressional action would be required to create a memorial to
Mrs. Bethune. Ultimately, with the help of Representative Frances
Bolton, a strong Republican from Ohio who had been a good friend
of Mrs. Bethune's, we drafted what ultimately became a congressional resolution.

Mable Keaton Staupers, a charter NCNW member and pioneering leader, walked the halls of Congress with me. We took the idea
to Senator George A. Smathers of Florida, explaining that we
wanted to balance Lincoln and the slave with a monument that
would represent the many contributions that African Americans
had made to American life. Senator Smathers, a fine southern gentleman, nodded in agreement and then told us more about Mrs.
Bethune's life and work than we had told him. When he finished,
he said that if he took the lead in the Senate in support of this project, he would not be reelected. On the other hand, he said, when
he was running for office for the first time, Mrs. Bethune had
stumped for him: "I wouldn't be here today if she hadn't helped
me." So, he assured us, "don't worry about the Senate." Once he
found another senator to introduce the bill, George Smathers mobilized votes and supported it all the way.

In 1960 President Dwight Eisenhower signed into law the first
joint resolution passed by the Eighty-second Congress, authorizing
the NCNW to erect a memorial statue on public land in Washington, D.C. Negotiating the labyrinthine web of governmental red
tape and raising $400,000 in private funds took longer than anyone
expected. But there was a determination to put "Ma in the Park"!

For fund-raising, we tried all sorts of schemes.

We created little brown boxes that we sold to our members for
one dollar. The idea was that our members and their families and

friends would fill the boxes with coins and send them back to national headquarters.

We created Sweetheart Dollar Days in February one year—playing off Mrs. Bethune's favorite song, "Let Me Call You Sweetheart"—and invited everyone to contribute throughout the month. By this time our fund-raising goal had risen to $2 million because, in addition to the memorial statue, we wanted to create a Bethune Memorial Education Center. We wanted this to be a living memorial in every way.

During the height of the civil rights struggle in the midsixties we had to put the fund-raising on hold. Even our own were asking, "Should we give to a monument, or should we help raise bond money to get Dr. King out of jail?" But in 1971 the Ninety-second Congress passed, and President Richard Nixon signed into law, an authorization that granted the final extension of Public Law 86-484, stipulating that the monument would be erected "without cost to the federal government." It required the NCNW to certify on or before June 1, 1973, that the money was in hand to finish the memorial.

The greatest boost came from women of the United Methodist Church. Mrs. Bethune had been very active on the denomination's Women's Board. I was invited by Thelma Stevens and Theresa Hoover to an assembly where we discussed the Bethune memorial. Not long afterward I received a telegram saying that the United Methodist Women would contribute $100,000. I was so excited! For a moment I thought Western Union had printed too many zeros! Everyone in the office wanted to touch that telegram. We knew then that we would meet our goal.

With only a few months to go before our time ran out and some $135,000 still to be raised, we redoubled our efforts. Courageous women on the Committee of 400 accepted goals of $1,000 each, and we created the National Roll of Honor, a beautifully embossed book in which the names of all who donated one dollar or more were inscribed. Our last-minute appeals succeeded. The money was in hand.

To create the memorial we organized a competition under the criteria of the National Commission on Fine Arts. The winner was the sculptor Robert Berks, who would later create the bust of John F. Kennedy for Washington's Kennedy Center. He proposed portraying Mrs. Bethune passing her legacy to two children. After his idea was selected, he started visiting schools to find a boy and a girl he thought would be representative. He must have done a thousand drawings of black children. From these he developed a composite boy, but for the girl he wanted a live model. The one he finally chose was Harry Belafonte's younger daughter, Shari.

On July 10, 1974, the monument was unveiled. Some forty-seven thousand people came to Lincoln Park to pay tribute to one of the world's greatest women. The Bethune statue was the first memorial to a black American—and the first to a woman of any race—to be erected on public land in the nation's capital. Beautifully sighted by the architect Hilyard R. Robinson a few hundred yards across from Lincoln, Mrs. Bethune reaches out to a young boy and girl. The three figures stand on a base on which the topic sentences of her last will and testament are inscribed:

> I leave you love. . . . I leave you hope.
> I leave you the challenge of developing confidence in one another.
> I leave you a thirst for education.
> I leave you a respect for the use of power.
> I leave you faith.
> I leave you racial dignity.
> I leave you a desire to live harmoniously with your fellow man.
> I leave you, finally, a responsibility to our young people.

In 1986, to commemorate our first half-century, the National Council of Negro Women created the Black Family Reunion. Our inspiration was a PBS documentary by Bill Moyers, *The Vanishing Black*

Family. We didn't think Mr. Moyers's piece was about the black family at all. It was about teenage pregnancy. And it showed only black teenagers—overlooking completely the fact that the majority of pregnant teens are white.

I knew we couldn't counter Mr. Moyers's documentary with mere words. We needed to do something bigger to show the promise of family restoration as a fundamental strategy for overcoming black poverty and underachievement. It was time to take action.

I consulted my dear friends, our national family values hero Bill Cosby and his wife, Camille. They suggested that I talk to their publicist, Joel Brokaw. Joel reminded me that I was always saying what Dr. King had said: You need to do something that demonstrates what you want to accomplish—to "put people in action on their own behalf." That was why Dr. King did the marches, and why we now had to re-create the essential, uplifting black family experience to demonstrate what we were talking about.

We imagined an enormous, embracing family reunion that could reconnect people, bring together those who had advanced and those who had been left behind, reunite elders with youngsters and nuclear families with their relatives across the country.

We realized that our extended family has become ever more important. When I was growing up, every adult in our town looked out for every child. All the adults felt they could correct or encourage any child because each child's parents gave tacit permission to do so. Seventy years later it was time to honor and re-create that sense of extended family and community responsibility.

We wanted an all-encompassing, nationwide Black Family Reunion. We wanted a celebration that could serve as a rallying point for government agencies, private- and public-sector institutions, corporations, community-based organizations, and families of all compositions to work together on solutions to problems affecting the African American community. We emphasized the crucial connection between the strength of black family structures and social and economic progress.

As our ideas for the Black Family Reunion were developing,

one of our members, Dr. Vanessa Weaver, said she wanted to help the NCNW strengthen its ties with the corporate community. A psychologist on the management staff at Procter and Gamble, Dr. Weaver began by convincing her own corporation of the power of the Black Family Reunion idea. Procter and Gamble not only became our first full supporter but also lent us Dr. Weaver, who worked with us for three years while drawing her full salary from the corporation.

Washington, D.C., was the site for the first reunion, a festival dedicated to the history, tradition, and culture of the black family. On a beautiful September day in 1986, in pavilions decked out across the Washington Monument mall, we celebrated children, fathers, mothers, grandparents and in-laws, aunts and uncles and cousins. We offered music, games, art, poetry, and delectable food. Exhibits offered everything from information on job training programs and how to get a high school equivalency degree to blood pressure screening—all free of charge.

Two hundred thousand people turned out. They told us that they were, truly, "sick and tired of being sick and tired." They were tired of always being told what was wrong with them. A grandmother who spent much of the day watching plays and puppet shows and dancing with her eleven grandchildren said to me, "The best thing about a day like this one is that I can bring my kids out and they can see how many different things they can get into. You can get into gangs or you can get into good things. This day has shown them that they have a lot more choices than they think." A young couple who had never finished high school discovered that they could get diplomas by taking an exam. They started studying for the GED the next day.

So many people who attended the Black Family Reunion reminded us that when you know only that you have problems and do not realize your strengths, it's almost impossible to deal with the problems. Yet the black family has a history of demonstrating strength against the worst kind of oppression. Now, with growing economic problems, we needed to draw on that strength. The first reunion showed us that by lifting up our traditional values, we could reinvigorate and build on the historic strengths of the black family. We could find solutions to many of our problems.

After our first success in Washington, we rapidly expanded to other areas. Sometimes we picked cities, sometimes cities picked us, but we never went anywhere without the endorsement of our host-city officials. Procter and Gamble was our principal national sponsor, but others joined in too, making it possible for us to continue to offer everything for free. The last thing we wanted was for a parent of several children to have to choose which child to bring to the reunion because of cost; we wanted the whole family to come. And many, many came. By the close of our second season in 1987, the Black Family Reunion—its themes always centering on children, young adults, health, the work ethic, and family values—had taken place in Atlanta, Philadelphia, and Los Angeles, as well as Washington, D.C. We had reached more than seven hundred thousand people.

Even with such success, we had our detractors. Carl Rowan noted in his *Washington Post* column in September 1987 that "Dorothy Height and her National Council of Negro Women... are trying to revive the concept—and admiration—of the extended black family, whose bonds and pressures once were a powerful barrier against dropping out of school, engaging in crime, getting pregnant out of wedlock and using 'reefers' and other illegal drugs." However, he wrote, this "laudable crusade... is about as difficult as a mission to Mars."

In 1988 we added three more cities—Chicago, Cincinnati, and Memphis. At the end of that summer, the *Wall Street Journal* editorialized: "The National Council of Negro Women deserves much credit for daring to be anachronistic by promoting the institution of marriage and advocating a re-emphasis of traditional values in the black community.... Few other establishment black leadership groups... have moved family structure to such a core position in their policy agenda."

The values of so many black families I know—values of courage and commitment to progress no matter what the odds—will never be considered anachronistic by the National Council of Negro Women. By September 1992, more than ten million people had attended the Black Family Reunion celebrations. A year later we had more people at the Black Family Reunion in Cincinnati than there were in the entire population of that city! In Los Angeles nearly one million people came, and in Washington, D.C., more people attended the 1993 reunion than were at the thirtieth anniversary celebration of the 1963 March on Washington.

The Black Family Reunions awaken people to their rights, responsibilities, and opportunities. We have to lift people up and move them forward so they can conquer their feelings of powerlessness. I know we have black people—though some of them may not yet know this themselves—who are leaders. With the right kind of encouragement, these people could show their brothers and sisters the way.

Black Family Reunions have brought together not only families but generations. When young people come to a Black Family Reunion, they are exposed to the richness of our history. They get caught up in our music, theater, dance, and poetry. They begin to see what's gone before them—and the enormous potential that lies ahead. We must keep working together to save our families and our children. We are not a problem people, we are people with problems. By generating community energy to tackle our problems, the Black Family Reunion has become the most significant family movement in black America today.

Like the memorial in Lincoln Park, the Black Family Reunions embody the vision of Mary McLeod Bethune and her final, crucial imperative: "I leave you, finally, a responsibility to our young people."

Chapter Fourteen

Citizen of the World

EVER SINCE my participation in the World Conferences at Oxford and Amsterdam when I was twenty-five, I had felt a strong bond with women in the developing world. No matter what our circumstances or where in the world we live, we must daily fight against forces that wish to keep us down because of our skin color, our gender—or both.

My first opportunity to establish a tangible bond with sisters in another part of the world came in 1952, when I was invited to India to serve as a visiting professor at the Delhi School of Social Work, replacing Professor Eduard Lindeman, a distinguished social worker and philosopher, who had fallen ill. I was to teach the philosophy and skills of working with people in groups.

I arrived in Delhi on August 8, 1952. At eight o'clock the following morning I departed with three other faculty and fifty first-year graduate students for Alipur, a remote village not far from the border of Pakistan. The purpose of the trip was to help the students, who were from privileged families and had reached their advanced level of study because of that background, learn how to work with people of lower classes and castes.

When we arrived in Alipur, people were thronging to a ceremony in the central square. The women wore their finest saris. We dressed in saris too and joined the celebration. I had never been anywhere—even in Harlem—where I could look at the equivalent of two or three city blocks and see only colored people. In Alipur there must have been twenty or thirty thousand—very black Indians, paler brown people, mulattoes—all different shades. I had never seen anything like it.

In the central square, as was the weekly custom, the village leader brought the people up to date. He was a kind of living newspaper, delivering the news in what was really a "rap session." As he kept his rhythm, rapping on what he had to say, I knew it was about us, because every once in a while, he would speak an isolated English word or phrase—"social worker," for instance—and the people would cheer. At another point he said "American," and they cheered again. I felt truly welcomed by the people of Alipur.

And what a splendid group they were. The women looked like empresses in their saris, the rich darkness of their skin setting off magnificent jewel tones in their silks. All through my childhood the "beauty" of whiteness had been drummed into me. Yet at this moment in Alipur, how peculiarly wan and lifeless a white person would have looked.

Our first task was to turn a large field into living quarters. The students were about half men and half women, and for most of them this was a brand-new experience. None had ever worked outside, or with their hands. They were used to having servants do everything. None had ever been involved in such adventurous work with the opposite sex. Even though we had separate men's and women's camps, some of the women students stayed awake all night at first, worried because men were sleeping in the next field!

On the first day one of the students asked, "Why did they send you out here?"

I asked what she meant, and she replied, "Well, I came to get a master's degree, and I didn't think they would send an inferior person. I thought they were sending an American."

"I am an American," I said.

"But you're not an American," she insisted. "You're a Negro."

"Is it that you don't think I know what I'm doing?" I asked. "No," she replied, her brow wrinkled. "I like you, and I like what you are doing, but when I finish my education, I want to be able to get a job, and I just don't know why they would send an inferior person."

We soon were caught up in an interesting discussion about what it means to be an American and what it means to be a black American. I explained that being Negro simply meant that I was a part of Negroid humanity, but as a person and a citizen, I was an American. Thousands of miles away from home, I wanted to stand up for my country. I believed more than ever that it was possible to bring about change at home and that I could help to make America be what I hoped it would become.

We found that we learned a lot just by going into neighboring villages to talk to people, though I had to rely on student interpreters because I spoke no Hindi. One evening I met a little boy named Ramaprita Singh. Ramaprita spoke some English and offered to lead me back across the fields to the place where we had pitched our tents. As we walked, guided by a path of cow dung, he said, "Miss Height, do you speak Hindi?"

"No," I said.

A worried look crossed Ramaprita's face. "If you don't speak Hindi," he asked, "how will you be able to help us? How will you know when we are happy or sad, or what makes us happy and what makes us sad?"

"I guess I will have to count on friends like you to tell me," I replied.

He shook his head. "But we can't tell you how we feel unless you know our language." Starting the next day, for the rest of my stay—the full school year—I got up at 5:00 A.M. four days a week to study Hindi for an hour and a half so that I could do my job as Ramaprita expected.

When we were ready to begin our work with children, we went to an open field where we hoped a few children would come to meet us. Imagine our delight when hundreds ran out to greet us. They were eager to see us because they'd never met anyone like us before.

I was asked to introduce myself and to let the children know I would be working with them. "I'm from America," I said. I decided to teach them a song. For some reason, I chose the little action song:

> *Little Tommy Tinker*
> *Sat on a clinker*
> *And he began to cry,*
> *"Ma, Ma, what a good boy am I!"*

As I sang, I went through the motions of sitting on a clinker, then jumped up when I got to the "Ma, Ma" part. In the United States this is not a number that I would put on the best-songs-to-teach-a-child list, but the Indian children loved it. Even the very little ones, who didn't know what one word of the song meant, would hop up and down when they got to the "Ma, Ma" part. As long as we were in Alipur, anytime I walked through the streets, some child would jump up and shout, "Ma, Ma."

Little Tommy Tinker taught me a wonderful lesson. It was a perfect icebreaker because the kids could throw their arms up in the air and jump up and down. My success with that song led me to teach them many others. It also taught me to relax a little. I found that music was a good means of reaching people in Alipur and establishing the rapport essential to moving forward.

When we returned to New Delhi, I lived at the YWCA residence. At that time Indira Gandhi was the chairperson of the YWCA Committee on Volunteer Training. I was intrigued that a Hindu played such a prominent role in the Young Women's Christian Association. I learned that she was impressed by the YWCA volunteer training program because we didn't simply train women for traditional roles, like hospital work, but prepared them for public affairs. We taught parliamentary procedure and how to run a meeting, and also how to be active leaders in their communities.

My work in India made me see and understand poverty as never before. In the streets of Delhi there were homeless people everywhere, with no shelters, no soup kitchens—nothing. I remember a woman who had attached herself to a corner on the sidewalk near the School of Social Work. I saw that woman pregnant, I saw her after the birth of her baby, and I saw her trying to feed her child from her withered breast. Students tried to assist people like her, but it was like putting a Band-Aid on a hemorrhage.

Before I left for India a friend had given me a diary and told me to write everything down, "because after a while you won't see it." In Delhi I came to understand what she meant. When you look at so many faces of suffering, after a while you don't see them. Their misery is just there—overwhelming, beyond anything you can imagine changing.

While I was still in India, the Third World Conference of Christian Youth was held in Travancore Province, and I was pleased to be able to attend. Travancore had the most Christians and the most Communists of any province in India. It also had fifteen thousand unemployed college graduates, most of whom had a major anti-American attitude. I discovered that there is no better way to understand international politics from a non-American vantage point than to be exposed to disgruntled students!

I was invited to the Soviet consulate in Travancore to see some propaganda films. One film about the United States featured an ignorant black man shuffling across the shabby porch of a farmhouse. The clear implication was that this was typical of American blacks, and one of the Indian students said it confirmed what he believed about how blacks lived in America. I will never forget how shaken I was. My experience in India gave me a very different feeling about many things I thought I had understood, including what Russian communism was all about. But it also taught me that people in India and China were looking to communism more as a means of social change—a way to redistribute wealth, open opportunities, and address social welfare—than as a political philosophy.

In 1955 I visited Africa for the first time. A YWCA colleague, Ruth Lois Hill, invited me to join her in Liberia to work on leadership training for women following my participation in the Centennial Conference of the World YWCA meeting in England.

I always learned far more from the participants in training sessions overseas than they did from me, and Liberia was no exception. The women there taught me the importance of making information available in a way that allows people to make it their own. Though many of the questions posed by the Liberian women were the same ones women were raising in the United States, there were fundamental cultural differences.

In Africa, for instance, respect for age is a cultural norm. In any given group, no woman would challenge another who was older than she. I admired this respect for elders tremendously in principle, but it made it very difficult to get across the idea that, when the work of an organization needs to get done, it is the role and responsibility each carries within the organization—not her status in the community—that matter. The Liberian women taught me that you cannot disregard cultural patterns or historic ways of looking at things simply to have a more businesslike organization. "Starting where they are" is more than a cliché.

In the first training session I asked the women to describe the obstacles that stood between them and the good life. Each woman's answer depended entirely on her economic circumstances. Poorer women tended to focus on practical homemaking and workplace issues, while women who were better off thought more in terms of opportunities to express their views or other more abstract kinds of advancement.

With my training as a social worker, I knew how to reach poor people at home and what to do when I found them. But in Liberia the social distances between economic classes were so great that it was very difficult to get a chance to communicate with people at the bottom. When I was able to talk with some of the lower-class women, their alienation came through. I believe that Liberia's troubles are sadly rooted in the huge gap between the haves and the have-nots. When people are so far apart, what else can follow but the kind of wrenching civil strife in which Liberia has been caught up for nearly a decade?

My exposure to the developing world was rounded out in 1959, when I was invited to join an unusual group on a tour of Latin America. After Vice President Richard Nixon's chilly reception there in 1958, George Denny, the producer of a popular radio program called *Town Meeting of the Air,* decided to set up a World Town Meeting. Denny's idea was to take a group of thirty-five Americans to several Latin American countries to talk with their local counterparts about issues of mutual concern.

Once again, I think the experience was far more significant for us than it was for the people we met along the way. There was only one other person of color in the group: Edith Sampson, a prominent Chicago judge and constitutional lawyer, also an adviser to Mrs. Bethune. Because the Supreme Court decision to desegregate schools was still fresh in people's minds, Judge Sampson and I often were put on the firing line.

For instance, in Montevideo, Uruguay, where people had thrown tomatoes and eggs at Vice President Nixon, we braced for fireworks and were not disappointed. People flocked down from the hills, loaded with questions about the racial situation in the United States. It was headline news that in Prince Edward County,

Virginia, schools were closing rather than allow black and white children to learn together. "We understand you've closed all the schools because the whites don't want to go to school with black people," Uruguayan students said. We tried to explain that the important thing was that the Supreme Court had given a unanimous ruling in favor of desegregation nationally. We stressed that the school closings were a temporary phase of protest happening in one county of one state. It was hard to get this across. To the people in the outside world the news was that the United States was choosing to close schools, rather than open them to people of color.

As discussion intensified, I realized that these students mistakenly thought that every black child in the United States was in a segregated classroom, and since these classrooms had been closed, they assumed blacks would get no further education. I pointed out that neither Judge Sampson nor I had ever attended a segregated school, and that "there are millions of black people all over the United States who have never attended a segregated school." Edith told about her undergraduate and law school education in the Midwest, and I told about going to completely integrated schools in Pennsylvania and New York. We did not deny the impact of segregation, nor the fact that there was resistance to the court decision. And we could see among the Uruguayans glimmerings of understanding about the nuances of our situation. It touched me that these small pieces of our personal histories suddenly became an important part of our national story.

After our session at the university, Edith and I began getting calls from radio stations and newspapers for interviews. People invited us to their homes to talk to gatherings of friends. Because so many Latin Americans are people of color, they seemed to trust Edith and me. People wanted to ask not just about race but also about U.S. policy toward countries like Cuba. They followed us everywhere we went.

Most of the white members of our group had never been in a situation where people were questioning them—sometimes even in a hostile manner—because of racial policy and unequal treatment in the United States. I think some feared that Edith and I might wear out and they'd have to carry on. Few had ever experienced such anti-American feeling or had thought very much about how they would answer the questions about race that were constantly fired at us. Our team members also said that they couldn't get over the loyalty that Edith and I expressed for our country, and they marveled that we were able to find the balance between acknowledging that the United States still had racial problems to solve, on the one hand, and pointing out the progress already made and confirming our hopefulness about the future, on the other.

In 1960 I was invited by Anna Lord Strauss to join the Committee of Correspondence, an unusual group of women inspired by Thomas Jefferson's notion that people could change the world if they kept in good correspondence. Eunice Hunton Carter was already a member. The work of the committee was to develop and sustain international connections, to carry and bring back messages. As members traveled, they kept the names of women they met abroad. When a member returned from a trip, she would produce a newsletter and send it to everyone she'd met. After a while the committee began bringing groups of women from different countries to the United States. They wanted me to lead discussions and help them learn how to appreciate cultural differences and deal with conflict.

Shortly after I joined, the committee proposed that I spend several months studying the training needs of women's organizations in West Africa. This was a fascinating opportunity, as people in these newly independent countries were just beginning to think about the roles women might play in nation-building.

I went first to Sierra Leone for a meeting of women leaders from neighboring countries. Living and working with African women in close quarters for four days gave me a wonderfully different perspective than I'd gotten as an outsider just visiting.

At the close of a meeting it was local custom to ask a senior person to summarize the proceedings. Though I often found little resemblance between what I thought had happened and what the summarizer reported, I soon learned that everyone considered the elder's recapitulation to be the final word. The woman who reviewed the meeting in Sierra Leone was eloquent. "The women from our four countries have met together, and the men have been worried about it," she said. "The men should be worried, but not about whether we are going to take over their shoes. We don't want to take over their shoes. But we may take over their socks. It's not going to be the same as it used to be." The group cheered.

I realized that many of the Africans had never before held a women-only meeting. This was the first time many of them had openly discussed common problems. The elder concluded, "We've talked these days about wastage! The wastage of our women and of our babies who are malnourished. Our daughters who don't get an education are wasted, and we've decided to do something about it."

From Sierra Leone I went to Ghana, arriving just at the moment of independence, as Kwame Nkrumah was being elevated to the throne. I stayed at the home of the minister of foreign affairs, where I got a liberal education around the dinner table. The minister reminisced about the old days when Ghana was the Gold Coast. He told about the great cocoa crops they had once harvested and how the cocoa industry then had been taken over by outsiders. He spoke also of an even earlier era, when the Europeans divided up territory as if they owned it, with no regard for the Africans who lived there. "When nations were divided like that, the people had to go with the country," he said sadly. "It's just as if you were selling a house. All the mice in the house go with the house." That was the way Africans had been treated.

After working with several women's organizations in Accra, I spent a weekend with a youth group in the Ashanti region. They had a fascinating flag—a field of red, with nothing on it but a mosquito. When I finally found the courage to ask them to explain the flag, a lad of about fifteen was happy to respond. "The flag means that but for the mosquito, the white man would have it all." I returned his smile and asked no further questions.

From Ghana I went to Nigeria, where I organized the Nigerian Council of Women, which is still active. Nigeria also was celebrating its independence from Great Britain. It was thrilling to witness the change from colonial to indigenous rule. I lived with a couple who brought me into the center of activity. My host was about to become chief barrister, and the family engaged in lively debates about whether he should wear the white wig, in the British tradition. I couldn't help seeing how difficult the transition to full independence would be. Although some have given the British credit for their "indirect" colonial rule, which is said to have prepared people more effectively for independence than the French "direct rule," neither system truly prepared Africans to run their own affairs.

A small incident brought this home to me. My skin parched by the relentless African sun, I went into a chemist's shop in Lagos to buy some face cream. Shop clerks now were the "new Africans," young Nigerian women with little or no training. When I asked the young lady behind the counter if she had Pond's cold cream, she said, "No," indifferently, as if her thoughts were a thousand miles away. I scanned the shelves. When I spotted some Nivea cream, I explained that Nivea was a fine substitute. While she wearily wrapped my package, I couldn't help thinking how differently the transaction might have gone in an American pharmacy. The clerk would have said, "We don't have that, but we do have this," because she would understand that her job was to sell her inventory and, if possible, to please the customer in the process. In the Lagos shop, not only was the inventory strange, but the whole system of merchandising—selling for a profit and customer service—was totally alien. Who was there to teach her? I wondered. How could the outside world understand how much newly independent African people had to learn to do simply because they had not had the exposure or training before?

My next stop was Guinea, where the head of state, Sékou
Touré, had just declared that all currency, except what he had
printed the day before, was useless. My hotel was crowded with
people who were stranded. They didn't have any of Sékou Touré's
money, so they couldn't go anywhere.

In Guinea's case, the colonial power—France—had left the
scene quite abruptly, and the nation, in disarray, was slipping
quickly into the Soviet orbit. The leftward tilt was manifest in a
Communist women's march through Conakry, which I attended
with Marie Gadsden, a member of the rapidly shrinking U.S. diplomatic delegation. We were struck by the angry tone and the anti-
American slogans. Obviously Americans, we were no doubt
suspect, and as the whole city was in turmoil, there was little that I
could do there.

When I got home, I told the Committee of Correspondence
about the energy I had felt among the African women. Eager to
take part in the reconstruction of their newly independent nations,
they wanted help with leadership training and with organizing and
developing affiliations between urban and rural women. They were
impatient to strengthen their institutions, including schools and
child-care facilities, but they needed long-term help. I recommended that the committee assign a full-time person. Fortunately,
Sara Lee Owens, with whom I had worked at the YWCA, was available. She subsequently spent several years in West Africa, endear-
ing herself to its women.

As independence swept across Africa, African Americans were
increasingly aware that the United States needed to rethink its policy toward the continent. During the colonial regimes we had
taken a hands-off approach. But now that so many countries were
independent, they needed support.

In 1962 Roy Wilkins, then executive secretary of the NAACP,
organized the Negro Leadership Conference on Africa with help

from the U.S. State Department. He brought together a group representing numerous national organizations and asked me to be cochair, along with Martin Luther King Jr., Whitney Young, and A. Philip Randolph. The conference took place over three days in November 1962 in Harriman, New York.

At its conclusion, we adopted a resolution urging the U.S. government to adopt a dynamic course to raise the international status of the twenty-eight new African states and liberate the remaining colonial territories. We suggested that effective American aid would be the best countermeasure against the Soviet influence there.

On South Africa, the resolution was blunt. It criticized the United States for condemning apartheid yet refusing to support a United Nations call for sanctions against that nation. The situation in South Africa, Roy Wilkins declared, "demanded something more than deploring resolutions coupled with business as usual."

One outstanding African representative, Chief Simeon Olaosebikan Adebo, had just arrived in New York as Nigeria's ambassador to the United Nations. Some time after the launching of the Negro Leadership Conference on Africa, Chief and Mrs. Adebo assembled us all at their home in New Rochelle to discuss how Africans felt about U.S. policy. He knew that we were clear about this in relation to South Africa, but he wanted black Americans to think more precisely about how the United States was relating to other parts of the continent too. He urged us to be aware of policies that affected the utilization of raw materials throughout southern and central Africa and to understand the political and military objectives that governed—and sometimes impeded—food distribution to needy regions. Above all, he wanted us to know how U.S. policy played into these complicated issues. While we concentrated on getting American business out of South Africa, he cautioned, we must also be aware of what was going on elsewhere.

Our new attention to Africa did not escape the government's notice. Before long I was appointed a consultant to a State Department advisory panel on Africa. I found it puzzling that even though we had all of these new, darker countries in which we had to staff embassies, there were very few people of color in the Foreign Service. When I asked why, I discovered that Negroes who applied for the Foreign Service weren't even being considered. Appalled, I called the attention of the other panelists to these gaps. After the panel gave its recommendations, a special effort was made to recruit and nominate qualified African Americans for the Foreign Service.

In 1966 I was invited to participate in a study mission to Israel under the aegis of the American Jewish Committee. I was one of nine Negro Americans, all of whom were involved in the search for answers to human and civil rights problems at home.

We were touched and inspired by the melting pot of peoples and cultures wherever we went. Whether it was the leader of a Druze village, an Arab student at a street restaurant, a student at Bar-Ilam University, a woman leader in a kibbutz, or a chambermaid at one of the hotels, all those we encountered seemed to embody a certain spirit of purpose, a strength of feeling born through suffering and a continuing thirst for education and knowledge. What we encountered during that remarkable trip gave us all new inspiration to carry back to our struggles at home.

I took very much to heart what I learned on my travels abroad. Women of color around the world have common problems and common dreams. Whether affluent or needy, living in the northern industrialized world or the developing South, educated or illiterate, we all want to improve the quality of life for our loved ones and our communities. We want to participate in our nations' development. We long for loving child care and access to nutritious food and good health for our families. We seek training and skills for better-paying jobs. We expect equal wages for equal work.

Women of color everywhere are often the backbones of their families. They have to work—often alongside their men in the fields or factories—and they also have to provide the emotional, intellectual, social, and spiritual support their men and their children need. In the developing nations of Africa, Asia, and Latin America, women are the producers, vendors, and preparers of food, the staunchest supporters of education, the people on whom so much of the future seems to depend. And yet black women universally have been denied education and barred from political power. The systematic denial of women's central role in nation-building has been as costly to the nations concerned as it has been harmful to women and their families.

What I learned in my travels made me more determined than ever to involve the National Council of Negro Women in women's struggles abroad as well as at home.

Chapter Fifteen

Making Common Cause

MARY MCLEOD BETHUNE had always wanted the National Council of Negro Women to be global in outlook. She felt strongly that black people had to be part of the struggle for peace everywhere. She had traveled with W. E. B. Du Bois and NAACP leader Walter White to San Francisco in 1945 to witness the founding of the United Nations, and she was proud that the NCNW held observer status at the UN ever after. For years NCNW had gathered great women from Africa, Asia, and Latin America to discuss common concerns.

In 1975, as we prepared to celebrate the one-hundredth anniversary of Mrs. Bethune's birth, we decided to build on her global vision. For forty years the NCNW had served to unite more than four million women in the struggle for civil and economic rights in the United States, bringing attention to the inequities suffered by black people in housing, education, employment, health, and food and nutrition. Now it was time to encourage women of color all over the world to come together to develop a blueprint for self-help programs that could work universally to lift women up.

In July of that year the U.S. Agency for International Development (USAID) approved our request for funds to develop an international program. Before the ceremony awarding several such grants to private voluntary organizations, the agency's administrator, Dan Parker, told me that he took "special pride and pleasure" in our grant, since he strongly believed that the NCNW's community development work at home should be shared beyond our borders.

Five months later the United Nations was to host the first worldwide conference of women in Mexico City as the kickoff for International Women's Year (IWY). To the NCNW this seemed to be perfect timing: We could honor Mrs. Bethune's one-hundredth birthday, contribute to the gathering in Mexico, and launch our international program all at once.

The IWY conference in Mexico City actually was two events: the official meeting of government-appointed delegations—many of which were predominantly male—and the unofficial "Tribune," an unstructured gathering of women open to anyone who wished to register. Some six thousand women from 132 countries participated in the Tribune.

Not surprisingly, there was controversy about having so many men on the official delegations. Some women argued that there should be none at all. I disagreed. If only women had come to the conference, if they had left behind all the men of influence in their countries, they'd have been talking to themselves. The final "plan of action" adopted by the conference wouldn't have meant much. The reality was that the power positions at that point were held by men.

As a black American woman, I have confronted both racism and sexism. I have learned that if you have only blacks talking about the future, or only women talking about the future, you don't have a model for change. If you want real change, you have to listen to— and be heard by—people who are different from you, especially if they're the ones you need to help you bring about the changes you're seeking.

A great value of the IWY conference and the Tribune was the way they helped women understand their differences. There was a strong anti-capitalism, anti-imperialism thrust, and Western women were forced to recognize the disparity between their lives and the experience of women in less developed countries. While American women, for instance, were talking about advancing in their careers, women from the developing world talked about how to create activities that could simply produce a little income or food.

NCNW saw the proceedings as an opportunity to make common cause with all women of color and to share stories of heartache and moments of triumph over racism, sexism, and poverty. We convened an international seminar, bringing women from developing countries in Africa, Latin America, and the Caribbean together with women from rural communities in the United States. Our twenty-eight-day session was in three segments—in Mexico City, in Mississippi, and in Daytona Beach, Florida. It proved a rare opportunity to lay the basis for the worldwide network of which Mary McLeod Bethune had dreamed.

In Mexico NCNW took a large hotel suite so that the seminar participants could come together regularly. There were supposed to be only thirty in the group, but we never were fewer than fifty in number, as people who heard about the sessions decided to attend. Our "official" participants included everyone from lawyers to home economists, from a tribal chief to a member of Parliament, from a midwife to an officer with the Organization of African Unity—all terrifically competent women who knew what their countries needed.

After the conference in Mexico, NCNW brought fifty women to Mississippi to see firsthand what the National Council of Negro Women was all about. Our first stop was Jackson, where the group met Patt Derian, one of our "angels" during the Wednesdays in Mississippi project in 1964 and later the first assistant secretary of State for human rights, in President Carter's administration. Patt spoke as a white southern woman of how white women in Jackson had known that awful things were going on but did not feel responsible because none of the "nice" people they knew were dealing with the "Negro problem." The WIMS teams had encouraged women on both sides of the color line to find out what really was happening on the other side of town.

The day after we were received by the governor's wife for a special tour of the state house and mansion, we met with Aaron Shirley, a black doctor. He cautioned our visitors not to misunderstand that hospitality. He had been trying for months to get state support for a badly needed health clinic, and he had learned that the people at the state house were far better at making grand gestures for visitors from afar than they were at getting anything done for needy people in Mississippi. A young black fellow who represented the governor's office was present. Dr. Shirley intentionally put him on the spot. Then someone asked the young man how old he had been in 1964. Eleven, he said, adding that he had attended a freedom school visited by one of the WIMS teams.

In the Mississippi Delta we visited a housing development where there is a bronze plaque bearing my name. It adorns the Height Community Center. Later a delicious luncheon was catered for us by a local woman who told us her story. She had been put out of work, had lost her husband, and had twin boys to feed, so with her meager savings she started a catering business. Stories like these were important for our guests to hear. Although many had visited the United States before, they had never spoken to people like the ones they met in Mississippi. When they did, they lost their innocence. They no longer believed that everyone in America walked on streets paved with gold.

In Ruleville, Fannie Lou Hamer took us to see the pig bank. By 1975 the fifty young sows and five boars we had purchased in 1967 had produced two thousand pigs, providing many families with a plentiful source of protein. It was a holiday weekend, the Fourth of July, and a huge family reunion had just roasted one of the pigs.

Mrs. Hamer commented that not long before no one would have thought of bringing their kin from all over the United States to a reunion in Mississippi. But here they were, seventy or eighty strong, and the local family was feeding them all.

The last segment of our seminar journey was at Bethune-Cookman College in Daytona Beach, where we celebrated Mrs. Bethune one-hundredth birthday. It was a joyful occasion until the very last day, when a terrible thing happened. One of our most distinguished visitors, Madame Siga Sene, vice president of the Economic and Social Council of Senegal, was wrongly accused of shoplifting a $1.59 can of talcum powder. When she picked up the can to read the label, the store clerk panicked and called his supervisor, and the supervisor called the police.

Madame Sene's interpreter, Madame Diallo, tried to explain that Madame Sene was not taking the powder, that she had money and was fully prepared to pay for it, but the store workers would not listen. When the police tried to arrest Madame Sene, Madame Diallo made such a fuss that they finally let her go, but she was badly shaken. We called the store to protest, and when we could not reach the manager, we called the city council—and also the State Department and the Senegalese embassy. When we finally tracked down the store manager, we insisted that he and his staff make a public apology.

The next morning the manager, supervisor, clerk, and owner of the store came out to Bethune-Cookman College, where we arranged an open session before the whole body of women. The owner spoke first, then called on the store manager, who tried to apologize. He asked what we intended to do. Slowly and regally, Madame Sene rose. Speaking in French, with Madame Diallo interpreting, she said that the manager may have stated his position to us, but he probably had not made his position clear to his employees. She respectfully requested that he do so. He might also do well, she suggested, to bear in mind that money had no color. Then she accepted his apology.

One of the worst things about the incident was that when Madame Sene had tried to explain who she was and what she was doing, the sales clerk kept saying, "How do I know what she said?" When Madame Diallo tried to explain, "I am an interpreter and I am telling you what she said," the clerk just shook his head. He couldn't believe that black people could speak French, much less both English and French.

The incident was a poignant reminder, as we celebrated Mrs. Bethune, that all was not yet well in the world for anyone of color, especially women. We still had a long way to go to reach racism at its roots.

One important aspect of the seminar had been to engage our visitors in the planning for our NCNW international program. Having observed the NCNW's work in rural Mississippi, we asked them to propose ways we could be of help to them, wherever they lived. The next step was an exploratory visit to southern Africa.

Our target area comprised Botswana, Lesotho, and Swaziland, fondly known as the BLS countries. All landlocked, they lived in the shadow of South Africa and its apartheid policies. Though the countries were rich in raw materials, the people were very poor. And because three-quarters of the able-bodied men worked in the mines in South Africa, women had to do much of the work that men would do in other societies. They carried leadership roles and dug ditches, and they grew the food, raised the children, and built the houses for their families.

We had to enter each BLS country by way of Johannesburg, and our stay in South Africa reminded me very much of Mississippi in 1964. Because of the world attention on them, and because our visit was sponsored by the U.S. government, everyone tried to be as gracious as possible when our biracial team of four arrived at the Johannesburg airport. Shortly after we got settled in at our hotel, a contact who lived in the black township of Soweto arrived to take me to her home for tea and a tour. I asked if one of my companions, Margaret Hickey of the State Department, could join us. My Soweto friend spoke in hushed tones. Being white, she said, Miss Hickey would need a permit to enter Soweto.

Miss Hickey asked how, if she could not move about in the black township, I could move in white areas. Our friend explained that "it had been indicated" that I was to be treated as if I were "an honorary white, or honorary European," during my stay. This explained why, upon arriving, each of us had been asked to submit four passport photos, and an airport clerk had said to me, "Your picture will soon be in the hands of every district police chief. The word will have been received that you are to be treated well."

Botswana gave us a reception fit for royalty. The Botswana Council of Women was on the tarmac in full force, brightly arrayed, singing their welcome. They took us immediately into their care, presenting a moment-by-moment schedule of activities.

As we set about explaining the goals of our program, we found that our notion of "self-help projects" was different from what our hosts expected. When we'd ask women what they would like us to do, more often than not they'd tell us first what they hoped we would give them. They needed a mortuary or a nursery. They wanted buses. They wanted money to build buildings. We had to make it very clear that we could offer ourselves and our services, but we had neither the wherewithal nor the intention to purchase large-scale equipment or launch building projects.

The lady mayor of Gaborone arranged for us to go to the edge of the city, where several thousand families, poor squatters from rural areas, had gathered. It was a desperate place, a terrible eyesore. Though the mayor and other urban Botswana women genuinely wanted to assist these rural poor, they had little in common on which they could build a supportive relationship. Here too, the toughest part of our job was to listen well and then try to help people see how we could fit into their efforts to resolve the massive social and economic problems.

Toward the end of our visit we sat down with some of Botswana's women leaders to evaluate what we had learned. We agreed that the problem of child development wasn't just a question of having a nursery or a school; it also was a matter of nurturing at many stages. The moment we did that we could see a wide range of opportunities for NCNW to become involved. We could help mothers understand how children grow and mature, what their nutritional requirements are, how they learn.

In Swaziland we saw a wonderful example of a home-based, decentralized sewing cooperative that had been developed with women who could neither read nor write. To keep their accounting straight, they had created a system using chips. Each member of the cooperative got a red chip for each garment she completed. When she'd turned in three garments, she got a blue chip, which represented three red chips plus a dividend. If she produced ahead of schedule, she got a special bonus—a chip of a third color. At the end of the week each member's chips were counted and translated into currency.

Women who had been denied formal schooling functioned in this system as if they were fully literate. They even set up a small committee that operated like a credit union. If someone wanted to venture a little further, to expand or diversify her output, she applied to the committee for seed money or extra raw materials. The committee would determine her creditworthiness. A central office distributed raw materials, set production schedules, kept track of everyone's output, and managed marketing and sales.

This seemed to me to be a wonderful way of making cottage industry work, in contrast to having people just make something to peddle on the street, a model under which many would often deny themselves food in order to buy raw materials. The scheme represented exactly what we had tried to do in Mississippi—find new, practical ways to help people improve their lot. When Mrs. Hamer spoke to us about the nutrition deficits in Sunflower County, we had set up pig banks and community gardens. These were enterprises that people could manage successfully.

There was another part of our Mississippi experience that was very useful in Africa. Early on we had discovered that if you cannot get local people to take the lead from the beginning, the project most likely won't get done—and certainly won't stay done. In Africa the number of different languages spoken presented a major problem in this regard. Whenever we went out into villages in the countryside, we had to have an interpreter. This is a tiring way to try to establish relationships, but it's also very good discipline. You select your words carefully when you have to ask yourself, Is what I'm about to say worth hearing again in another language? You learn very quickly how to tighten up what you have to say!

Just getting around turned out to be another major challenge. There was no such thing as the kind of transportation that was needed—not just by us, but by the women we wanted to serve. Public conveyances were crowded, unreliable, and not always likely to go where people needed to go. If you wanted to be sure about getting around from village to village, you had to have a rugged four-wheel-drive vehicle.

That we were black Americans coming to help was a great novelty. Madame Dombi, the wife of the Botswana ambassador, said after our visit, "You know, we were so glad, because you're the first black American group that we ever had any contact with." Lady Khama, the British wife of Botswana's head of state, couldn't understand why we called ourselves the National Council of Negro Women. One evening at a gala reception she asked, "Aren't you segregating yourselves?" I assured her that we welcomed all women, but we were concerned primarily about what was happening to black women and their families. But then she asked, "Why don't you just call yourselves the National Council of Women?" I realized then that she didn't understand our country or our people. A few moments later her daughter joined the conversation and pressed once again. "Why wouldn't you just call yourselves the Council of Women of the United States? You're just women. If your country is a democracy, why do you have such a segregated organization?" I explained that the United States is a pluralistic society, a democracy in which each group can celebrate its own identity.

I sensed in these two women an awkward blend of pride—as highly placed citizens in a newly independent, relatively successfully integrated African society—and uneasy awareness that white expatriates still held more than their share of important positions. And their questions brought home to me once again the depth and transparency of racism here in the United States. When a black American traveled abroad to offer a service to citizens of a developing country in the 1950s or before, people sometimes questioned the offer because they knew their visitor had been devalued at home. Would-be beneficiaries had to make sure that whoever was coming to serve them truly had enough "power" to be helpful. Understandably, they saw white Americans as having higher value because they were closer to bases of power. The thinking seemed to be, if you send a powerless black out here to help us, then it must mean that you want to hold us back.

Now, in the late 1970s, people in Africa overwhelmingly let us know that they were proud to have us there. I remember the first time I addressed a large group, of five hundred or so. I said, "I bring you greetings from your sisters and brothers in the United States of America," and the crowd went wild. People knew exactly what I was talking about, and they responded with thunderous applause. When people made presentations to us, they would say things like, "We give you this because you are our sisters. Though you have been gone from your homeland many years now, we are glad that you have been there, that you have been able to get some of the benefits there, and have come back to us."

Most important, we communicated our openness to learning how we could be of help. We did not have a fixed program, nor did we intend to impose one. Our purpose was to support local women in any way we could to boost their own capacity to solve their most pressing problems.

The dark power of South Africa, with its evil system of apartheid, was a tremendous weight on all who labored in southern Africa in the years before Nelson Mandela triumphed. The economies of the BLS countries then were almost totally dependent on South Africa. Botswana and Lesotho did not even have their own currency; they used the South African rand. In spite of these handicaps, people sensed that they could change the situation. They were energetic and hardworking. They had a sense of purpose; they set goals. Above all, everyone had a terrific spirit. People said, "We're going to make it," and, I believe, they're well on their way.

Though it was clear to me after that first visit that we still had a lot to learn before we could be helpful, I also sensed that whatever the National Council of Negro Women could do to help people organize their efforts and mobilize their resources would be a valuable contribution. Today NCNW is still the only African American women's private voluntary organization registered with the U.S. Agency for International Development. We work through African partners, transferring skills, information, and modest financial resources to the women who are building the future in Africa.

One of our tactics is known as "twinning." Twinning agreements between the NCNW and women's organizations in African countries have as their stated goal helping and learning from each other and increasing contacts and communication between African and African American women of all educational, professional, economic, and social levels.

Thus, in 1979 four women leaders representing the Women's Associations of Senegal and four from the National Union of Togolese Women were guests at the NCNW convention in Washington, D.C. Following the convention the women traveled, divided into two teams, to selected cities and to the Navaho Nation, observing NCNW projects and the programs of other organizations focused on leadership and service to women and children.

In 1980 I led a delegation of thirty in an exchange visit with our twinning partners in Togo and Senegal. Banners across the streets in Senegal said, "Welcome Home, Sisters." His Majesty the President of Togo, in receiving our delegations, spontaneously presented to me invaluable elephant tusks. Thanking President Edeyama, I promised to take his message of goodwill to President Carter, but said I would take the tusks to NCNW. That was the only word that hit the press back home. Because of restrictions on exports of elephant tusks, President Edeyama himself took care of this gift all the way—and thanks to him, the tusks are on display in the lobby of the NCNW's building.

I signed the twinning agreement with the Senegalese women in a special session of the Parliament in Dakar with thousands of women wearing different colors of the same cloth. What a beautiful sight! I sensed and felt the power of our twinning partners in their home countries. I was glad that they had met a wide range of people while in the United States. They had been special guests at the Carter White House, and they had been received by mayors across the country, but they had also seen much more of our society than that.

One exceptional example was a seminar hosted by Avon Products in New York. I had invited a group of women from many fields to meet with the African women leaders. The Americans introduced themselves, and when it was Carolyn Reid's turn, she simply said, "I clean houses," referring to her work in household employment. The African women asked Mrs. Reid more questions than they asked anyone else. After the session Madam Kekeh of Togo, a judge, was joined by other African women who said they never had sat around a table with a woman who would clean houses. They seemed to realize that they could be more helpful if they knew more about women workers. They were surprised that Mrs. Reid was included and that she spoke with such pride. I hope this experience made a difference.

*

The United Nations Decade for Women, 1975 to 1985, was a watershed for women's empowerment. In three landmark conferences the United Nations brought together more than twenty thousand women representing every occupation and every point of view imaginable. I was involved in each of the conferences, but an event at Copenhagen stands out.

The mid-decade conference took place at the height of the cold war. United States bashing was routine at the time, and this was one in a series of UN conferences in which the same topics resurfaced— prominent among them criticisms of Israel and its actions in the Occupied Territories and denunciations of the apartheid-riddled states of southern Africa. Both subjects were a battleground between the United States and the Soviet Union. The Soviets tried to insert the phrase "Zionism is racism" in every UN document related to Israel, knowing that the United States would then vote against it.

In Copenhagen I got a taste of the strategy firsthand. We were a proactive delegation, led by Alexis Herman, then director of the Women's Bureau of the U.S. Labor Department, and Sara Weddington, special assistant to the president for women's affairs. Working with women from African countries, we crafted a resolution on racial equality. The resolution was presented by Alexis Herman, who pointed out that in a world where the majority of people were colored a resolution dealing with sexism alone would not be sufficient. Racism had to be included. There was great rejoicing, especially among women of color.

But political operatives of the Eastern Bloc saw the resolution and maneuvered to insert the odious phrase "Zionism is racism." Our State Department prevailed on us to help. Vivian Lowery Derryck and I had become close collaborators with some of the African women. We tried individual to individual to establish rapport and common bonds around issues of peace and justice and women's dual burden of working inside and outside the home. Many of the African women knew the YWCA, and many were eager to start organizations like NCNW in their own countries.

Yet when it came to this phrase, "Zionism is racism," we couldn't see eye to eye. As hard as we worked to win African support, when amendments were voted, we lost. One of the hardest things I have ever had to do was withdraw the resolution, as requested by our government, given the amendment to include the reference to Zionism. It was one time when hard-line nationalist politics won, beating out our deepest convictions and careful coalition-building.

In July 1989, I convened NCNW's first "Cradle of Civilization Symposium" in Cairo, Egypt. It was something brand-new in Egyptian-American relations: a delegation of two hundred fifty African American men and women meeting for four days with two hundred Egyptian counterparts to discuss common problems. Then prominent educators, historians, social scientists, and political officials engaged each other on a wide range of issues, from reducing poverty to community empowerment.

The NCNW delegation was made up of distinguished Americans from many fields. The Reverend Jesse L. Jackson Sr. was there, and so was Jesse Jackson Jr., who was later elected to the U.S. House of Representatives from Illinois. Representative Donald Payne of New Jersey was part of our group, as were Diane Watson—then a California state senator and now a congresswoman—and Comer Cottrell, founder and president of Pro-Line, the largest black-owned business in the U.S. Southwest. Along with Dr. Laila Takia, a member of Egypt's Parliament, these people played key roles in examining the political issues affecting both countries. Dr. Asa Hilliard Jr., a prominent Egyptologist from the United States, exchanged views with noted Egyptian specialists.

Egypt welcomed us royally. That nation's first lady, Suzanne Mubarak, opened the symposium, setting the tone for our lively discussions, and a group that included Reverend Jackson, members of Congress, and myself attended a private meeting with her husband, President Hosni Mubarak. Boutros Boutros-Ghali, soon to become secretary general of the United Nations, joined me in hosting a gala dinner. He reminded the fifteen hundred attendees of the close ties between Egyptians and African Americans and introduced us to Sam Nujoma, the recently elected president of the newly independent country of Namibia.

The issue of women in development was a prominent theme at the symposium. Egyptian and American women found much common ground, and their fruitful discussions led to the formation of the first section of NCNW based outside the United States. The symposium also allowed NCNW to forge useful new links between historically black U.S. colleges and Egyptian institutions of higher learning. And it led to a multiyear program, funded by the U.S. Agency for International Development, that was designed to develop and strengthen private voluntary organizations in Egypt. Ten years later a second Cradle of Civilization conference allowed such nongovernmental organizations to focus on social development issues and their role in helping to solve problems through the active participation of community members.

As I listened and learned through our discussions in Egypt, I was particularly struck by something I had not recognized before. In the United States, Egypt is usually characterized as part of the Middle East. But in our visits we were hearing from people who expressed great pride in the fact that Egypt is in Africa, and that Egyptians are Africans. As African Americans, we were interested and gratified to discover that important bond.

Chapter Sixteen

A Place in the Sisterhood

D URING ALL my years with the YWCA and the National Council of Negro Women, I was also affiliated with a third national women's organization, Delta Sigma Theta Sorority. Today I hold institutional memory and perspective that few others share. It is an awesome feeling. Delta was a sisterly arena that tested and nurtured my leadership capabilities—a network of sisters extending to the east, west, north, and south, across the oceans and seas. My years of involvement have afforded me wisdom I would never otherwise possess and given me an even greater thirst for knowledge and for new ventures to be of service to others. The power of sisterhood for African American women is a very strong force indeed.

Delta Sigma Theta was founded in 1913 at Howard University. It is an organization of college women pledged to ideals of academic excellence and public service. From the very start it was committed to principles of interest far beyond the campus confines. In March 1913 the twenty-two founders of Delta Sigma Theta marched down Pennsylvania Avenue in support of women's suffrage.*

I had wanted to be a member of Delta Sigma Theta ever since high school, when Deltas Lula Johnson Howell and Edna Kincheon came to Rankin to organize the Girl Reserves and told me about the sorority. I finally joined in 1939, while I was working at the Harlem YWCA, and in 1941 Dr. Elsie Austin, the eighth national president of Delta Sigma Theta, knowing of my background in social work, appointed me to design and chair an action program.

I proposed that the sorority undertake what came to be called the Job Opportunity Project. Its objective was to keep the members of Delta Sigma Theta informed about career opportunities and to take an active hand with employers to open jobs to women. It was an important crossroads in the sorority's history. At the time the whole issue of human rights was coming to the fore. Many women were well trained but lacked the opportunity to use their abilities in appropriate work. One Delta member appointed to the project committee summed it up as "equitable exposure of Negro women to job opportunities."

Many Delta chapters embraced the concept immediately. Others—overlooking the unique potential the sorority had for advancing women—questioned the need for the sorority to involve itself in work that other organizations were already doing. And some members were simply satisfied with the many other social activities and local service projects in which they were engaged. Yet wherever chapters committed themselves to making the Job Opportunity Project work, its impact was effective—and in some instances outstanding.

Because of that, I was surprised to receive a call from a dear

---

* Several of the founders were still active during my day: Ethel Black, Bertha Pitts Campbell, Myra Davis Hemmings, Vashti Turley Murphy, Naomi Sewell Richardson, Eliza P. Shippen, Florence Letcher Toms, and Madree Penn White. As Delta's president, I provided for all founders to be part of our national conventions. The richness and value they contributed cannot be overestimated.

friend who had sponsored my membership in Delta. Muriel Rahn, a beautiful, popular singer and actress, said she had been following my work on the project. At the time she was quite ill—near the end of her life, as it turned out. But she had called to chastise me.

"Dorothy," she said, "you are taking all of the fun out of the sorority." I was astonished. Hearing those words from her made me feel a little guilty. But I also felt that I had to tell her the truth.

"As I understand it, our sisterhood has a purpose," I said. "We don't have a sisterhood for the sake of sisterhood. I believe that in the sisterhood we are to enjoy ourselves and at the same time do some service that helps others. In fact, I believe we can have fun being of service!"

Many members seemed to agree with me. And at the 1944 Delta national convention, held at Wilberforce University in Wilberforce, Ohio, I got a surprise. Without a word to me, during a late business session Helen Work of Fisk University nominated me to be vice president of the sorority. I was half asleep when a soror tapped me and said I had better pay attention. I did so just as Helen Work supported my nomination by noting that the Job Opportunity Project reflected the spirit and determination of the founders who had marched for suffrage down Pennsylvania Avenue. To my surprise, I was elected vice president to serve with Mae Wright Downs—later Williams—who became the ninth national president.

Three years later, in the lower level of the Second Baptist Church in San Antonio, Texas, I was elected the tenth national president. My platform had called for eliminating the exclusion of members using the "black ball," for moving to admit members by majority vote, and for opening membership to women of all races. This platform could not be adopted without revising the Delta oath, which specifically referred to women of color.

Back in Washington I called the distinguished Mary Church Terrell, who had written the oath. With hardly a moment's hesitation, Mrs. Terrell agreed that Delta women should not belittle people of any race and that they should encourage others to take the same just stand. For me, her spontaneous response was an unforgettable moment!

I came into national office at Delta Sigma Theta with the benefit of years of national experience with the YWCA of the USA. In addition, I had long been active in national and international leadership with the United Christian Youth Movement. Those experiences were good preparation for what was to come.

The convention that elected me in December had voted to hold the next meeting in August 1948. Thus, the next national convention was just eight months away. To the challenge of preparing so quickly I added another objective: vowing to get Delta moved out of the church basement.

The 1948 convention was slated for St. Louis, Missouri, where I knew that no hotels would accept us because of segregation. Local Delta members had already made a commitment to a church, but learning of my resolve, they agreed to work with me. Our convention theme was "Human Rights from Charter to Practice," and that helped us persuade Mrs. Eugene Ross McCarthy, a member of the national board of the YWCA, to use her influence with city officials. As a result, Delta Sigma Theta Sorority became the first black group to hold a convention at St. Louis's Kiel Auditorium.

Mary McLeod Bethune, an honorary Delta, was the keynote speaker at that national convention. Her eloquence moved Delta women, led by the national treasurer, Beatrice Penman, to raise $4,700 to help purchase a headquarters building for the National Council of Negro Women—its first official home. The collaboration between the two organizations was the very embodiment of Mrs. Bethune's insistence upon collaboration and coalition-building.

From NCNW's beginning, Delta has been an affiliate. Mrs. Bethune felt free to call upon us for help and support in many important endeavors. In 1951 there was a UNESCO conference on women's rights in Port-au-Prince, Haiti—a conference that ultimately helped Haitian women win the right to vote in national elections. Mrs. Bethune invited me and Laura Lovelace, my counterpart at Alpha Kappa Alpha Sorority, to be NCNW delegates to the conference. While I was in Haiti, I organized the first international Delta chapter with the leadership of Madeleine Bouchereaux, a Haitian whom I had met at the United Nations.

I always tried to reflect the Bethune message of collaboration. NCNW itself is a member of the Black Leadership Forum, the Leadership Conference on Civil Rights, and Women in Community Service (WICS). WICS is itself a coalition,* and its presidency rotates among its five member organizations. When it was NCNW's turn to hold the presidency of WICS, Dr. Thelma Daley, Delta's sixteenth national president, served in that capacity. So there was a great deal of productive cross-fertilization.

Fairly early on in my Delta presidency I realized that the sorority's growth and development required the continuity and expertise of a professional staff. I was pleased when Patricia Roberts Harris (later a U.S. ambassador, secretary of Housing and Urban Development, and secretary of Health and Human Services) agreed to become our first executive director. I had known Pat Harris since her undergraduate days at Howard University, and it would come as no surprise that her tenure was a high point.

When I decided to name a national project director to help give focus and direction to the sorority's program, Pat Harris suggested Jeanne L. Noble, who was then working on her doctorate at Teachers College at Columbia University. She was an inspired choice. As national project chair, Jeanne Noble led the creation of a five-point program centered on education, health, volunteer service, international awareness, and public affairs. Her work laid the foundation for Delta's modern course. In 1958 Jeanne Noble herself was

---

* WICS is made up of the National Council of Jewish Women, the National Council of Catholic Women, Church Women United, the American GI Forum Women's Auxiliary, and the National Council of Negro Women.

elected national president of the sorority. And in the ongoing, collaborative world I have tried to foster in the spirit of Mrs. Bethune, in the 1990s she became the founding dean for the NCNW's Dorothy I. Height Leadership Institute.

Our coalition-building also included men. In 1952 Alpha Kappa Alpha, Delta Sigma Theta, Sigma Gamma Rho, Zeta Phi Beta, Alpha Phi Alpha, Kappa Alpha Psi, Phi Beta Sigma, and Omega Phi Psi—the eight Greek-letter, college-based sororities and fraternities that are largely African American—held their conventions simultaneously in Cleveland, Ohio, incorporated as the American Council on Human Rights. It took a full year to plan the event, but that process was exceedingly valuable, since we learned how to laugh about our rivalries and work together as sisters and brothers. That convention reinforced our conviction that those who had the advantage of education should use it responsibly on behalf of others and work to secure human rights.

To preside over that convention, I came to Cleveland straight from India, where I had been a visiting professor at Delhi School of Social Work. In the course of the first night at the Cleveland hotel, I awakened feeling terribly thirsty—but afraid to drink the water out of the spigot. The next morning, when I was about to brush my teeth, I laughed at myself. I hadn't realized, in my sleepiness, that I was back in the United States. The water was safe.

Before I became president of Delta Sigma Theta, the sorority had initiated a project intended to provide books to people in rural areas who had little or no access to a library. Somehow it had never gone very far, so after I took office I decided to translate the concept into action. I appointed Maude Watkins, a New York librarian, as chair of the library project. Virginia Lacy Jones, the distinguished librarian at Atlanta University, identified four counties in northwest Georgia that would benefit from the service.

Ultimately Delta sent a Ford van into Carolton County, Georgia, where it was loaded with books and dispatched into the countryside. The bookmobile completely dispelled the notion that only white people use libraries and black people would not do so even if they had the opportunity. People, white and black, came from miles around whenever the van's musical horn was sounded in their area. The Bible was most in demand. And the bookmobile carried more than books. It delivered everything from patterns for children's clothes to personal messages from one part of the county to the other. It became a point of communication. And it brought the black and white communities together because it was an equal opportunity lender.

When the popular demand was clearly established, Delta told county authorities that we did not think a private organization should continue to provide for rural citizens what the state provided for white citizens in more densely populated urban areas. Our message got through. Before long the State of Georgia had extended library services to poor people, white and black, in rural areas throughout the state. And when Patricia Harris presented the bookmobile to the county, she received overwhelming thanks from county officials and a throng of black and white citizens.

Now that's what I mean by public service. Delta could have gone on forever just providing books to people in rural areas, but instead we dealt directly with the fundamental issue. Services in the State of Georgia were transformed because of the Delta bookmobile. And a year later the project was honored by the American Library Association for making "a distinguished contribution to the development of enlightened public opinion on an issue of continuing importance."

Not everyone, however, had such an enlightened view of Delta. In 1954 we decided to hold our national convention in New York City. First, Pat Harris and I had to find a venue. Wherever she went, with the blessings of the city's Convention Bureau, she was well received. But I am darker-skinned than she, and whenever I turned up, all the possibilities that had been suggested to her suddenly evaporated into thin air.

We found a real friend in Paul Beltz of the Convention Bureau.

He made our cause his own. After much research, he recommended the Astor Hotel.

Pat Harris and I went there together. The manager was very gracious. But when he announced what it would cost us to hold our convention, the total was outrageous. I examined his calculations. He asked what I thought. I looked him square in the eye: "I think you have found a nice way to tell us that you do not wish Delta Sigma Theta, a group of women of color, to have a convention at the Astor Hotel."

His face turned bright red. I added that we had the option of meeting in Miami, Florida, and would rather go there, knowing it was segregated, than allow ourselves to be exploited in New York, which had a State Commission Against Discrimination.

Back at the Convention Bureau, Paul Beltz found that the Roosevelt Hotel was willing to accommodate us, but the International Bandmasters had a hold on the dates. Over the weekend, Roosevelt manager Robert Tilt contacted hotelier Conrad Hilton—a good friend of the bandmasters—on his yacht, and Mr. Hilton interceded on our behalf.

In the end the convention was held at the Roosevelt Hotel. It was the first convention held by a black organization in a downtown New York hotel. It was so successful that it opened doors that are still open today.

In 1954, when my term ended, we were busily solidifying Delta's infrastructure and focus, recruiting professional staff, and charting new plans for public service. We were also raising funds to pay off the mortgage on our first headquarters.

Two years before Delta's board had determined that we should look for suitable quarters. The day after the board acted, a Sunday, I happened to be with Dorothy Harrison, Delta's national treasurer, when we spotted a *Washington Post* real estate advertisement for a building at 1814 M Street NW, in the heart of downtown Washington. We immediately contacted the owner. Seeing two African American women, he told us he would have to have five thousand dollars the first thing the next morning in order to even consider our bid. Imagine his surprise when a group of African American women arrived that Monday fully prepared to buy his building for fifty-two thousand dollars.

Eventually the sorors paid off the mortgage—and later they sold the building for several times the purchase price and acquired a greatly expanded headquarters. But as my term drew to a close, with all the planning and fund-raising still under way, the sorority decided not to change horses midstream and voted to extend my term for two additional years. I was pleased to accept the challenge.

Looking back on my life in Delta Sigma Theta brings elation and a sense of accomplishment. To belong to an organization like Delta signifies that you are truly your sister's keeper. Your sister is not only the one who pledged with you or "made" you. She is the woman who cannot adequately feed her children because of insufficient income. She is the woman in Africa, Asia, Europe, and the Americas trying to eke out a living for herself and her family. She is all over the world. For as long as I live, pride and sisterhood will sustain my active concern wherever women are striving for equality and justice. That is the legacy that Delta Sigma Theta has left me.

Chapter Seventeen

Building a Legacy

T HE ELEMENTS of one's legacy that may endure are impossible to know; history will decide. But there is one tangible gift I am proud to leave to future generations of African American women, their families, their organizations, and their communities.

On December 8, 1995, the National Council of Negro Women took ownership of 633 Pennsylvania Avenue NW in Washington, D.C., thus establishing not only a permanent headquarters for the council but also a home for the National Centers for African American Women and the Dorothy I. Height Leadership Institute. Mary McLeod Bethune must have smiled down on us that wintry morning, because from the day she founded the National Council of Negro Women sixty years before, she always said, "I want our women to have a strong presence in the nation's capital." Now, with this beautiful building midway between the Capitol and the White House on America's Main Street, we do. How this came to pass is the story of many dreams, stubborn trust in them, and a lot of hard work.

Thirty years ago, when we were getting the legislation to memorialize Mrs. Bethune in Lincoln Park, I realized that we had to do more than erect a statue if we were to empower our constituent organizations to carry on in her tradition. We had to establish as a living tribute a center of learning and inspiration, a place that would embody and enhance the many contributions Negro women and their organizations make to American life. I wrote an essay about this idea, and on October 5, 1962, Senator Jacob Javits of New York kindly introduced it into the *Congressional Record*. It began:

> Mary McLeod Bethune belongs to all that is finest and best in America. Her life and work inspire the kind of service and activity so vital to the enrichment of the continuing education of adults for leadership at home and abroad.

The piece went on to describe a center that would perform many functions. It would house historical archives of Negro women's organizations and activities. It would include a training center for women community leaders and an appropriate reception center for the many foreign visitors who seek firsthand contact with Negro women's organizations. It would be a clearinghouse of information and services to encourage communication among people of many backgrounds and a headquarters for the National Council of Negro Women and the other women's organizations that would share the facilities and equipment. All through these years we have been moving toward the heart of this idea.

A handsome six-story structure, 633 Pennsylvania Avenue was built in the late 1850s in the heart of the city. In 1871, the building became the St. Marc Hotel, one of Washington's most elegant, and the residence of many congressmen. An abutting building housed Mathew Brady's National Photographic Art Gallery and studio, where many prominent people, including Abraham Lincoln and sixteen other presidents, had their portraits taken.

When the Central National Bank bought 633 Pennsylvania Avenue in 1888, the architect Alfred Bult Mullett was commissioned to renovate the old hotel. Mullett, who had recently designed the Old Executive Office Building next to the White House, added a new facade and twin six-story towers to the building's west side, turning it into one of Washington's most delightful landmarks.

Nearly half a century later, when Mrs. Bethune first came to Washington to join President Roosevelt's National Youth Administration, she lived in a small rented apartment. But as her influence grew, she realized that she would have to find more spacious quarters to accommodate the demands of her new life in government service and those of the expanding National Council of Negro Women. She found just what she wanted in a beautiful stone building on Dupont Circle, which was owned by Cissy Patterson, the publisher of the *Washington Times-Herald*. When Mrs. Patterson learned who wanted to buy her building, she immediately took it off the market, announcing publicly that "Negroes will never be on Dupont Circle."

A grand Victorian at 1318 Vermont Avenue was Mrs. Bethune's second choice, and in December 1943 she received authorization from the board of directors of the National Council of Negro Women to buy it for $15,500. With a $10,000 donation from the Chicago magnate and philanthropist Marshall Field in hand, Mrs. Bethune summoned women across the country to help raise the remaining $5,500. Council members organized dozens of fund-raising dinners, fashion shows, teas, and bake sales. Daisy Lampkin of Pittsburgh chaired the national campaign and got the Pittsburgh Pirates to donate a portion of the proceeds of one of their ball games. Flushed with success, she spread the word that all one needed to do was ask.

The house at 1318 Vermont Avenue, built in 1874, was three stories high and three bays wide. It featured a long staircase, beautiful pocket doors with maple burl veneer panels, and varnished mahogany stiles. A chandelier of prism-cut glass hung from an ornate plaster medallion in the front parlor, and a decorative plaster cornice bordered the twelve-foot walls. Above the white marble fireplace, a huge mirror reached to the height of the cornice. Soon after she bought the building, Mrs. Bethune arranged for a prominent local artist to paint a mural depicting African American community life on the wall of the front parlor.

The second and third floors of the house were used for office space and as living quarters for Mrs. Bethune and important visitors. From 1943 until 1954, when Mrs. Bethune lived at 1318 Vermont Avenue, important plans were laid and memorable decisions taken in its paneled boardroom. Many of Mrs. Bethune's contributions to public life—on behalf of civil rights, women's rights, fair housing, equal employment opportunity, young people, the World Health Organization, and Project Hope—were initiated at the house. It was there that she hosted her "Black Cabinet" during the Roosevelt administration and received distinguished visitors like Eleanor Roosevelt, Mary Church Terrell, and Vijaya Lakshmi Pandit, the first delegate of India to the United Nations. At a time when black and minority persons were denied admission to many public facilities, everyone was welcome at 1318 Vermont Avenue. Flags of all nations stood on Mrs. Bethune's grand piano, proclaiming her belief in the oneness of humankind.

Even before Mrs. Bethune began making her own history at 1318, she had recognized the importance of preserving materials pertaining to the history of black American women. She asked Sue Bailey Thurman to lead an archives committee. Mrs. Thurman already had founded a scholarly NCNW publication, the *Aframerican Women's Journal*, to make black women aware of their heritage and the need to preserve it. She and her mother, Sue Ford Bailey, had supported numerous endeavors to encourage historic preservation.

In the *Aframerican Women's Journal*, Mrs. Thurman urged readers to search their attics for documents, artifacts, and relics for the museum she would establish at 1318 Vermont Avenue. Over the years she gathered an impressive lot of goods, including a collection of dolls by Meta Warwick Fuller, the sculptor, each doll designed to help tell the story of the distinguished African American woman it portrayed and the times in which she lived. Mary McLeod Bethune, Mary Church Terrell, Sojourner Truth, and Marian Anderson were among them.

After Mrs. Bethune's death in Daytona Beach, Florida, in 1955, 1318 Vermont Avenue became known as Bethune Council House, in loving memory of its illustrious occupant. This was Mrs. Bethune's last Washington residence and the first national headquarters of the National Council of Negro Women. When each of us became NCNW president, Vivian Carter Mason and I lived in the quarters Mrs. Bethune had occupied.

On January 27, 1966, when Washington was nearly paralyzed with unprecedented cold and a two-foot snowfall, an oil leak in the basement at 1318 started a smoldering fire. None of us inside the building noticed it, but a staff member, Conchita "Nikki" Nakatani, saw smoke billowing from the house as she walked back from the post office. As the entire rest of the staff of the council at that time—Ruth Sykes, Catherine Threats, and I—were inside, Nikki ran in to alert us and called the fire department.

The firemen had to use masks to enter, then chopped through the living room floor and tore down the doors to let all the smoke come out. They made a terrible mess! They had to cut off the water and the electricity, and somehow in the process managed to destroy both the grand piano and the chandelier in the living room. Even the sturdy tree that had graced the front bay window was ravaged.

After the fire, our staff and volunteers kept working—without heat, water, or toilet facilities. We'd trudge down the street to the Lutheran Church, which graciously offered the use of its rest rooms, and in spite of the subfreezing weather, we made do with electric heaters. No one wanted to leave. So much of our history had happened there! Not only had it been Mrs. Bethune's last residence and the first headquarters of the NCNW in Washington, but it also was where our involvement in the civil rights movement began, the place from which we went to Mississippi, the place to which women from all over the world had come to celebrate our work and become part of our lives. That history took hold of us. We felt that if we left, we would be giving up far more than the building. We worried that somehow our past would disappear, just as the venerable plant in the bay window had withered and died.

But in the end we had to accept that it was unsafe to continue operating there. Within weeks of the fire the building was declared uninhabitable and would soon be officially condemned. The repairs and remodeling required to render the building safe were beyond anything we could afford. Our insurance covered fire, but not the damage caused by firemen or the ensuing burst pipes. Because the house hadn't burned, there was very little we could recover in the way of insurance payments.

We had no choice; we had to move on. Fortunately, through friends at the National Council of Jewish Women, we were able to rent office space on Dupont Circle. In an odd way the move seemed providential, given Mrs. Bethune's first choice for a headquarters in that very area. From our eighth-floor suite, we could see her favorite building across the park, and every once in a while I'd look down on it and send my own message to the late Cissy Patterson. How horrified she would have been to see us on the circle!

Though the NCNW's new offices were far more spacious and efficient than the old, we never lost our attachment to Bethune Council House. A few years after the fire we decided to see what would be needed to preserve and restore 1318 Vermont Avenue. We thought that if we purchased the house next door, we could knock down the wall between the two, double our space, and thus create a suitable permanent headquarters for the council. When our attorney started negotiations to buy the house next door, the asking price was around $50,000. Within six months it shot up to $125,000, and we had to abandon that idea.

The consultant we commissioned to study how 1318 Vermont Avenue might be used advised us not only to preserve the building but to use it as a repository for documents and artifacts related to black women's history. In November 1972 we were notified that the area surrounding 1318 Vermont Avenue had been placed on the Department of the Interior's National Register of Historic Places, which meant that additional federal money might be available for rehabilitation and restoration. We negotiated a loan from the D.C. Redevelopment Land Agency and, in February 1975, were able to place $137,600 in escrow to cover the cost of renovating Bethune Council House. We wanted to turn it into a cultural center.

We recruited an architect, who proposed a beautiful but very modern facade. When a neighbor protested the modernization of the building, we turned to two preservation specialists for guidance. What a blessing! One of the specialists, Terry Lamb of the company Architechnique, wound up supervising the entire project.

Mr. Lamb was meticulous about reclaiming as nearly as possible the original character and integrity of the building. In what sometimes seemed like a global scavenger hunt, he searched all over for appropriate design elements. Some of the wood paneling came from Germany. In an antique shop we found a chandelier that once had hung in the White House. In 1976 the annual report of the Bethune Collection on Black Women's Organizations noted that "work on restoration of Council House is proceeding quite slowly because of technical difficulties related to labor, architectural, and construction problems.... A trickle of small contributions comes in on a day-to-day basis (but not daily)." The same report also announced that the Bethune Collection had been officially recognized as a program of the American Revolution Bicentennial. As such, it won a grant from the Bicentennial Commission headed by Senator John Warner of Virginia.

Early in 1976 I was invited to speak at the University of Iowa as part of a Black History Month series. At dinner afterward with the president of the university and several faculty members, I met Bet-

tye Collier-Thomas, an outstanding historian whose special interest was women's organizations and the church. I was drawn to her
vivid description of the work she had done on the women's club
movement and the AME church. I told her something about
NCNW, our growing archives and collection on black women's
organizations, and some of our dreams for the collection. Dr. Collier-Thomas told me that she had recently completed a study leave
and was at the point of making decisions for the following fall. She
was intrigued by the promise of the material we had gathered, and
supported by a small grant from the National Endowment for the
Humanities, she agreed to come to Washington to resurrect and
revive the archives and museum project. "This is a place of great
spirits," she said. "It is a place that contains and preserves history.
Our history, the history of Afro-American women. And we are
responsible for its maintenance, its preservation."

Our desire was to develop 1318 Vermont Avenue as a site where
the public could come to learn about the contributions to American
life of Mrs. Bethune in particular, but also of Negro women generally. The Bethune Foundation at Bethune-Cookman College in
Florida focused on Mrs. Bethune's contributions to education, but
during the years she lived in Washington, 1318 Vermont Avenue
had become the focal point of her public life. When Dr. Collier-
Thomas accepted the position of director of NCNW's Historical
Development Project in October 1977, she brought invaluable
skills to our aspiring institution.

Shortly after she began her work, Dr. Collier-Thomas discovered a cache of cardboard boxes in the carriage house behind the
main building. Armed with a flashlight, boots, and unflagging
enthusiasm, she uncovered and cataloged the rich collection of
documents and photographs of black women that had been assembled and stored there thirty years before by Mrs. Bethune's
archivist, Sue Bailey Thurman.

Once again the word went out that the NCNW was collecting
history. Under Bettye Collier-Thomas's leadership, the scope of

the Bethune Collection on Black Women's Organizations broadened to involve grassroots participation in a national search and discovery of the notes, letters, official documents, minutes, and memorabilia of black women and their organizations.

Dr. Collier-Thomas also began compiling oral histories, recording memories of living participants in black women's organizations. Together these efforts led to the establishment of a permanent national archive and research center on the contributions to America of black women and their organizations. The expanded, cataloged, and lovingly preserved Bethune Collection was NCNW's way of battling the manifest neglect of blacks in white history books.

In early November 1979, the National Council of Negro Women officially opened the Bethune Museum and Archives at 1318 Vermont Avenue and simultaneously hosted the first national scholarly research conference on black women in Washington, D.C. There were some one thousand participants. They discussed the fact that traditionally historians have turned to official records and newspapers to discover the contributions and influence of leaders in a society. But through the nineteenth century and well into the twentieth, women were not allowed to vote, much less hold office, and if their names appeared in print, it was considered a scandal. Since conventional methodology had thus failed to turn up women of influence, many had been led to believe that women played no significant roles in social movements. Participants in the 1979 conference discovered that if they asked the right questions of different materials, they found women in all sorts of important roles: founding orphanages, leading the antislavery movement, and contributing to social welfare in countless ways.

In recent years, with additional funding from the National Historical Publications and Records Commission and the Institute of Museum Services, the National Council of Negro Women has been able to establish and maintain reference files on the location and status of each document in the Bethune Collection. The archives have become a repository for research into all facets of the black woman's experience in America, from slavery on, and they operate as a clearinghouse for scholars. We have sponsored lectures and symposia and offered technical assistance to organizations that want to develop their own archival programs. Once Dr. Collier-Thomas had developed the program, Guy McElroy became the full-time archivist, and the NCNW established the Bethune Museum and Archives as a separate corporation. In 1982 Congress designated Bethune Council House a national historic site, and NCNW received an award from the American Institute of Architects for the first phase of the building's restoration.

At about the same time the restoration of 1318 Vermont Avenue began in earnest, the building at 633 Pennsylvania Avenue was undergoing restoration, this time by its new owner—Sears, Roebuck and Company. Having housed a ragtag succession of small businesses during the Depression and succeeding years, the once glorious building badly needed repair. When Sears bought the property in 1983, it actually comprised three buildings: the tall, turreted structure facing west that was originally the St. Marc Hotel, and two smaller buildings facing south that had once housed the Gilman Drugstore and Mathew Brady's photography gallery and studio.

Because it was the first privately funded restoration project on the avenue, it was closely watched by the Pennsylvania Avenue Development Corporation (PADC) and the Department of the Interior. When completed, the renovated Sears House splendidly preserved the past, with its gleaming white oak woodwork, barrel vaulted ceilings, fluted cast-iron columns, a striking marble staircase with glass footlights, and many other irreplaceable architectural details. Though much of the earliest character and spirit of the building were brought back to life, its new purpose was to house Sears's government relations operations, and so the renovation also provided for the conveniences and comfort found in a modern office structure.

I celebrated my eighty-first birthday in 1993, ten years after the restoration of these two remarkable buildings. At the time I was trying to sketch out a strategy for making real the dream that had driven me for nearly sixty years: the creation of a complex of national centers for African American women. The organization I imagined would be the first of its kind, a rich repository providing African American women with crucial links to leadership, ideas, resources, services, and education. It would serve as a nerve center for the exchange of ideas and for action. I knew that many women shared my vision, and I felt confident that the time was ripe to make it real.

Nearly thirty years after passage of the Civil Rights Acts of 1964 and 1965, their benefits had failed to trickle down to everybody. We had more African Americans in corporate life and more elected officials than ever before, but we also had record numbers of people of color living in poverty. Nearly half of all black children subsisted at or below the poverty line. The gap between the worlds of white and black had widened, and so had the gap between the relatively wealthy and the grindingly poor within our own black community. We had been split asunder, unnaturally distanced from one another, and we had lost some of our lifesaving resilience as a result. The time had come for African American women to come together to recapture our courage and reunite our communities—to work powerfully together to see that everybody got a chance.

I remembered the many times we'd begun to work on legislation for social or economic programs that could help us, only to hear people say that we were a "special-interest group," that all we wanted was to "rely on government." People who said this apparently had no appreciation of black history. We live in a country whose leaders go around the world extolling democracy and concern for human rights, and yet many here at home still cannot enjoy the simplest benefits guaranteed by the Constitution because of endemic, institutionalized racism. Institutional racism is more than debilitating—it is disastrous for the nation. It is long past time to end it, completely, everywhere.

Our young people ask why we have to keep trying to solve the problem of racism. Other people move on to other problems, but if you're black, you don't have that option. Your options are clear and limited: you either give up and go into drugs, or you work on racism for the rest of your life. In our society every step African Americans take is seen in political terms. Look at the political parties. The Democrats seem to take us for granted, and the Republicans seem to count us out—except for temporary flirtations when they really need us. We've learned that we have no permanent friends. We just have permanent issues, and we have to keep working on them.

I found a recent survey of the twenty-somethings deeply disturbing. When asked what their greatest concern was, most blacks in the survey said "racism." But not one white mentioned racism as a concern. When the few blacks who didn't mention racism were asked why, they said racism would be around forever and they preferred to give their attention to concerns about which they "could do something."

We think we have segregation because of prejudice, but I believe it is the other way around. We have prejudice because of segregation. Having been separated for so long, too many white people, like the twenty-somethings in the survey, aren't even aware that we live in unconnected worlds. These are the people who say we have "no problem," and they are the biggest problem of all. During the civil rights movement, when Bull Connor put his foot on the neck of a woman lying on the ground, or when dogs and fire hoses swept away innocent children, a kind of righteous indignation gripped the country. But now, in the spring of 1993, that sense of outrage was gone. Now whites wondered what our problem was.

It was time for African American women to come together to

inspire our sons and daughters to believe that change is possible and to dare to make it happen.

It was time for black women to bring our unique genius to finding solutions, to rebuilding our communities and the nation. I resolved that all of us, black and white together, could "do something" about racism. It's what I had been doing all my life. Now we had to support our youth on both sides of the color line who were willing to dare to continue the job. I had been encouraged by the number of young college women who had been coming to me in recent years, saying, "We want to have a hand, we want to take an active part."

I decided that it would be to these young women, their younger sisters and their own daughters to come, that the National Centers for African American Women would be dedicated. But first, we needed a home.

Chapter Eighteen

Home at Last

THE NATIONAL Council of Negro Women today embraces thirty-eight national organizations and two hundred fifty community-based sections. All told, the NCNW has a worldwide outreach to more than four million women. As an "umbrella" group, the council encompasses many distinct and diverse purposes. But always, it is committed to women of African descent and their families and communities. Its great strength has been that it builds leadership skills in women by emphasizing self-reliance, unity, and the commitment to working collaboratively.

I have never doubted that as long as its leaders remain true to the organization's principles, the NCNW will continue to be the strong voice of African American women. And in recent years we have endeavored to build an even stronger foundation for its stability and growth.

On the weekend of June 11–13, 1993, the NCNW gathered sixty-five African American women—scholars, national organizational officials, selected NCNW leaders, and experts from government and the private sector—to make plans for NCNW's future. Out of these and the board's deliberations, a new paradigm emerged: NCNW could best serve its affiliates and members as a resource, clearinghouse, capacity builder, and advocate. As a result, at the national convention in 1995 the delegates voted to establish the National Centers for African American Women and the Dorothy I. Height Leadership Institute and to modify and strengthen NCNW's management structure.

I expected that the new millennium would demand leaders who could motivate as well as manage, who could both raise funds and lift hearts. Launched in 1996, the centers would be able to teach those skills and many more:

- The Bethune Program Development Center would feature research-based program models in education, health, and family issues and encourage local leadership by African American women.
- The Economic and Entrepreneurial Development Center would provide technical assistance to help establish women-owned businesses and advance employment and economic opportunities.
- The Research, Public Policy, and Information Center would bridge the digital divide, providing broad access to research through technology.
- The International Development Center would build and support partnerships between African and African American women's organizations.
- Finally, the Dorothy I. Height Leadership Institute would train women and youth for participation in organizational and civic life.

Our next challenge was to find a place that could house this constellation of organizations. Mary McLeod Bethune's call for

Negro women to have a strong presence in the nation's capital was always with us. And since the early 1980s there had been calls at annual NCNW conventions for a "Buy a Brick" campaign to raise money for a national headquarters. An appropriate headquarters building would not only offer a concrete symbol of our unity but also enable us to meet the demands of the new information age.

In 1991 President George H. W. Bush signed a bill that made 1318 Vermont Avenue a unit of the National Park Service. A federal advisory commission was established to maintain the Bethune Museum and Archives for the public interest. When the Park Service acquired the building, it paid $632,000—the appraised value of the property. The NCNW voted to use the equity from this purchase to initiate a Fund for the Future. Its principal aim: the acquisition of a headquarters building.

For almost four years, Steve Muddy, now with the real estate services company Grubb and Ellis, patiently worked with us in search of a suitable building. Sandra Fowler, an architect and friend, was always on the lookout. I believe we knew every available building in Washington! But in 1994, when 633 Pennsylvania Avenue came on the market, the quest was over. A pale pink citadel between the Capitol and the White House, it was grand in an elegant, womanly sort of way, spacious and beautifully furnished. And though the historic integrity of the entrance hall and public spaces was unsullied, tucked behind the conference and meeting areas were rooms full of up-to-the-minute communications equipment. The place was perfect, except for one problem— the price. Sears, the owner, was asking $20 million, a sum so far beyond our reach that even in my most ambitious dreams I couldn't imagine raising it.

Still, I couldn't get 633 Pennsylvania Avenue out of my mind. It haunted me, and nothing else we saw even came close to our specifications. In September I decided to see if I could reach the president of Sears to propose that the company give us the building as a charitable contribution. When I presented this idea to the broker, he smiled wanly and shook his head. Ours was not the first such proposition, and he suggested that we forget it.

At about that time Paula Banks, president of the Sears Foundation, Reatha Clarke King of the General Mills Foundation, and Elynor Williams of the Sara Lee Corporation agreed to host fundraising events in support of NCNW. While en route to Chicago for an event that Paula Banks was hosting, I shared with her our vision of 633 Pennsylvania Avenue—a building she knew very well. She also knew that Sears would not donate it. But we might be able to get a lower price, and she was very helpful in explaining how I could approach Sears. When I got back to Washington, she and Toni Fay of Time Warner—an NCNW board member—had a conference call, then helped me to draft an appropriate inquiry.

A few months later the price on the Sears building was reduced to $16 million. By December it had dropped to $11 million. Once again, my imagination was up and running. I decided to take a careful look at the roster of Sears's directors and found that we had at least two friends on the board, Nancy Reynolds and Sybil Mobely.

We had honored Sybil Mobely with our "Black Women Who Make It Happen" Award. Nancy Reynolds had represented the United States at the United Nations during the Nixon administration, and the NCNW had honored her for her work there. Sarah Moten and I called Nancy Reynolds. An answering machine announced that she was away, but I left a message. A day or so later she called me from Mexico, where she was vacationing. I told her of our interest in the Sears building and that I hoped she might put in a good word for us with Sears's management. She immediately called Sears's Chicago headquarters.

A few days later I went to the building to see the broker and found three men there, checkbooks in hand. They were developers, ready to write their checks. But the broker said he'd been asked to see whether he could work something out with me. "I've been told to give the National Council of Negro Women first option on this building," he explained.

Hardly noticing as the holidays whizzed by, I set to work designing a three-year campaign to raise $30 million. We were favored with a great team of leaders—Maya Angelou, Camille Cosby, and Susan Taylor. Maya Angelou graciously agreed to chair the effort. Bill and Camille Cosby provided a substantial lead gift of a building at 1218 Sixteenth Street NW in Washington, valued at $1.6 million. In early January 1995 we launched the Fund for the Future campaign. The prospectus called it "the most important new initiative of the NCNW in its sixty-year history." Jeffrey Thompson gave invaluable guidance.

Owning this building would be beneficial to the NCNW in many ways. For one thing, its location would allow us to maintain a prominent presence in the nation's capital. For another, it would mean both substantial annual savings on rental costs and new revenue from affiliate organizations that were interested in leasing office space. Moreover, the Fund for the Future would allow us to seize unprecedented opportunities. With the advancement of African American women to positions of leadership in so many fields, our historic organization was well placed to respond to the needs of the twenty-first century. To succeed we needed to consolidate and maximize our resources, reinvigorate affiliates and local sections, and prepare a new generation of African American women leaders. Our emphasis would be on developing national strategies for grassroots results.

Late in the morning of January 11, 1995, the broker called to say that he had another potential buyer for the building who was willing to sign an $11 million purchase agreement at four that afternoon. He needed to know whether or not we were going forward with the purchase of the building. I told him I would let him know well before 4:00 P.M.

I put down the phone, closed the door to my office, and said a prayer. I felt strongly that this was our building. It was meant to be the home of the National Centers for African American Women. I knew that if we didn't sign the purchase agreement that day, we'd be out of it. I said to myself, If I do sign the agreement today and we don't make it, that's not a crime. They'll just drop me and go on to the next buyer. I called the broker back and said I'd sign. Then I tried to reach Dovey Roundtree, our general counsel, but I couldn't find her anywhere. Perhaps that was just as well. She probably would have tried to talk me out of my plan—although later, she proved to be the greatest support. She and Ronald Jessamy gave us the best of counsel.

The agreement stipulated that I had to make a down payment of $500,000 by April 1, and that the deal would close on April 28. By that day I had to find the remaining $10.5 million.

In the ensuing weeks, we wrote letters, we made calls, and we gave speeches. We cajoled and badgered and pleaded. Some days it was hard to get even our strongest supporters to understand why this building was so important to us—and to our daughters and granddaughters. More than once during those bitter weeks I asked myself what I was doing. If the people who would benefit from this didn't want it, why was I working so hard? I had a very encouraging meeting with Dolores Jordan, mother of Michael Jordan, who in her prayerful manner reminded me of the value of holding on. And when one prospective donor was slow to fulfill his promise, Jeffrey Thompson, a master of financial matters, helped find a solution, as he has done for many years.

In September, at a corporate breakfast during the Congressional Black Caucus's annual legislative weekend, we had an opportunity to tell our story. Maya Angelou delivered an inspiring message. We won commitments and pledges of more than $1 million. Then, through Maya Angelou, we got in touch with Norman Lear. Many years before the NCNW had honored him for the positive way he had portrayed a household worker in the role he created for the actress Esther Rolle in the television sitcom *Maude,* and he had called me to say how pleased he was. He said our positive response had inspired him to think seriously about giving Esther Rolle her own show. I told him some real stories from our experience with household workers. A few weeks later he worked several of the stories I had given him into the script.

Maya Angelou encouraged me to ask Mr. Lear if he would join our Fund for the Future campaign as a "credit enhancer"—one of several ways people could participate. Credit enhancers agreed to assume a portion of our liability should the NCNW be unable to meet its mortgage payments, thus enhancing our credit with lenders. We had made proposals to several well-heeled individuals before I called Mr. Lear—Michael Milken, for instance, had been very interested, but his legal adviser apparently vetoed the idea—but none had yet stepped forward. Norman Lear agreed to become our first credit enhancer, with a guarantee of $1 million.

Through the kind generosity of our corporate friends, Procter and Gamble, Anheuser-Busch, and Time Warner, we were able to raise the $500,000 in earnest money that was due on April 1. We also had very supportive friends at John Hancock, which offered to give us an even larger sum. But as the all-important April 28 deadline loomed, we were nowhere near our $10.5 million target.

A few days before the deadline Vernon Jordan, a good friend who once headed the National Urban League and one of the most powerful lawyers in the United States, appealed on our behalf to Sears vice president Anthony Rucci, who came to Washington. He listened attentively as we told him what we thought we could do if we had more time. We also met with Daniel J. Garrison, a vice president for administration at Sears. He made it very clear that he wanted to know whether NCNW was serious. I shared our history and our vision for the future and the importance of the building for our work. When he left, he had a new appreciation for NCNW. Ultimately, Sears generously delayed the deadline.

This gave us a little breathing room. Another friend, General Motors vice president William Brooks, came to see me, following up on a promise he had made in Ghana, where I told him and Lavelle Bond of Procter and Gamble about our interest in this purchase. He agreed to host a reception in Detroit where I could tell the story of the national centers and the building we hoped would house them. I agreed to go to Detriot on October 26.

These were heartwarming developments. But as spring turned into early summer, the total raised and promised was still far short of what we needed.

Meanwhile, my attention temporarily turned to other matters. Minister Louis Farrakhan, leader of the Nation of Islam, called to say that he was mobilizing black men across the nation for a "day of atonement and celebration." He intended to bring one million men to Washington, and he hoped that I would support the march. Although I was well aware of the controversy surrounding Minister Farrakhan—and particularly some of his remarks about Jews—I immediately assured him of my support. I felt that he probably *would* attract a million men to Washington, and I wanted the Million Man March to succeed.

When I made my decision public, the phone started ringing. People called from all over to express their concern. One call, from some of my closest friends, came from Martha's Vineyard. "We are calling you from a house full of your friends," they said. "We beg you not to have anything to do with the Million Man March. You have never been tainted. Please don't do it."

Other people worried about the absence of women from the march, the "exclusivity" of it. Cora Masters Barry was host to a group of women, some of whom felt the march ignored women. But I had fought for years for the right to have women-only groups and meetings. That didn't mean that I was "against" men. Similarly, I knew the Million Man March was not "against" women.

Perhaps the least forgiving critics of the march were Jewish supporters who were helping me raise money for the Fund for the Future. Michelle Cowan, a good friend, did not hesitate to get to the point. "Dorothy," she said, "if you get involved with this march, I will no longer be able to justify Jewish support for the National Council."

"Well, then," I replied, "I guess I'll just have to find more African American support." I did not feel that my involvement with the march was in any way inconsistent with my beliefs or the positions on issues that I had taken all my life. I have never been racist or anti-Semitic. That was not an issue.

Still others—mostly whites—worried that coming on the heels of the O. J. Simpson trial and acquittal, the march would further widen the already disturbing separation between the races. Perhaps so, I suggested, but positive things sometimes emerge from polarization. When the divide becomes so deep, we have to examine anew the issues that separate us. When divisions between us are so clear, people are forced to think about what they really believe and to listen to people on the other side. If we listen carefully, we can reach a new understanding and higher ground. Why does the white community have such a hard time imagining this? Why is it so difficult to understand the depth of hurting in the black community?

The mid-October day of the march was glorious. Planes, trains, buses, and cars streamed into the city from all corners of the country, bearing, many of us believed, far more than a million men of color to the capital. Some were elderly, others middle-aged, and many, I was glad to see, were young men and boys. Fathers and sons, grandfathers and uncles, brothers all, gathered peacefully in a day of quiet triumph. Though much of white Washington stayed away or closed down for the day (in fear of... what? I wondered), this massive army of men comported itself with dignity and without incident. It was a day infused with the somber joy of redemption and recommitment.

Late in the afternoon I was ushered to a place of honor near the podium on the Washington Mall. When it came my turn to speak, I stepped to the microphone and said to the thousands of expectant faces, "I am here because you are here. Thank you for coming." That evening, to their credit, my friends called to apologize for their statements. "When I saw you and listened to you there, I wept," Michelle said quietly. "Of course you should have been there. I was wrong to think otherwise."

The march over, it was time to get back to fund-raising. Helen Love, manager of community affairs at Ford Motor Company, received a letter from Lavelle Bond. The letter suggested that "we in corporate America" have to "stop just talking about helping Dorothy and *do* something!" That inspired Helen Love to hold a luncheon with high-powered women in Detroit, who in turn pledged to raise $1 million. She also arranged for me to meet with Wayne Doran, chairman of the real estate arm of the Ford Motor Company. Helen admitted that it was a long shot, but I was willing to try anything. I agreed to go to Detroit on October 26.

I told Mr. Doran about my long and cordial association with Henry Ford II, who, among other things, had chaired my sixtieth birthday banquet in New York. Then I showed him a picture of 633 Pennsylvania Avenue and started to explain why we were so keen on buying it. He listened for a moment, then interrupted. "You've got to have that building!" he said. He asked me to continue, and as I got into telling him about our Fund for the Future campaign, I mentioned a conversation I'd had with a banker who had said, "Why do you have to be on Pennsylvania Avenue, Miss Height, why can't you be on a side street?" I had replied, "The National Council of Negro Women is not on a side street now, sir, we never have been on a side street, and we never will be." When I finished, the man said, "Miss Height, I am a fifty-seven-year-old white male, and with all of the privileges that I have had, I believe that I should try to help you if I can."

Wayne Doran asked Floyd Washington, his manager of financial analysis, to take on our case. Washington, one of the first African American MBAs out of the University of Chicago and a community leader in Detroit, assumed that this assignment would be like all the others; he would advise us on how to structure the real estate deal, then delegate any follow-up to a subordinate.

In a phone conversation the next day I explained to Mr. Washington that after nearly a year of negotiations with Sears, NCNW had agreed to pay $11 million for the building. I acknowledged that as a nonprofit organization, the National Council of Negro Women was not a prize candidate for an $11 million mortgage. At the conclusion of our conversation, Floyd Washington realized that this was going to be quite a challenge. He decided to take it on himself.

His first step was to see if he could get Sears to reduce the price still further. He told Dan Garrison at Sears that he thought he could get the banks to come around if the price fell to $9 million. Garrison said he would do his best to sell the board on the idea. In return, Washington would have to line up the financing posthaste. Washington agreed. Then he called the real estate broker and got him to reduce his fee. "Everybody has to bring something to the party to make this happen," he said.

In early November the Sears board agreed to reduce the price to $9 million, on condition that we have firm commitments for financing no later than November 30. After several frustrating days trying to negotiate a mortgage at Nations Bank, Washington approached John Hancock but met the same kinds of roadblocks.

After ten days and no progress, Garrison called Washington. "It looks like you're not going to make it," he said. Washington said that if Sears could come down to $8 million we could meet the November 30 deadline. Given the collateral value of the building and the Sixteenth Street property, the $1 million that we had on deposit credit and Norman Lear's guarantee of $1 million, he figured the acquisition of the building at $8 million (plus $600,000 in closing costs) could be funded with a $1 million cash down payment, a $3 million mortgage, and a $4.6 million bridge loan. But time was running out.

After a third bank turned him down, Washington talked with his wife, who reminded him of the sentiment on the Million Man March T-shirt: "If Not Now, When? If Not Me, Who?" He decided he'd have to get his own company—and the other two major U.S. carmakers—to put some money in the deal. If he could get Ford, General Motors, and Chrysler each to guarantee up to $1.2 million to secure the bridge loan, it might entice a few more individuals to become "credit enhancers."

On November 8, Washington wrote to the appropriate vice presidents at General Motors and Chrysler, inviting them to "join Ford in providing an equal $1.2 million guarantee for this loan." Washington knew that the General Motors man also was African American, though they had never met. He soon got acquainted with Rod Gillum of General Motors and Frank Fountain of Chrysler. Frank Fountain told Washington that he would have to take the proposal to his board of directors, since it required a special amendment. He would not get an answer before the first week of December.

But there was an even bigger problem. With little more than a week before the November 30 deadline, we still didn't have a bank. I told him we had a friend, Robert Brown, on the board of the First Union Bank of Washington. Why not try them?

The next day Washington called First Union. On a conference call with a vice president and two senior VPs, he said he'd already been through three banks and he was running out of time. Could they do the deal? One of the senior vice presidents said that if he could get the paperwork to them immediately and the deal was right, he could sign off on it by December 1.

Then Washington did something he'd never done before. He told them that, coincidentally, a number of African Americans had been instrumental in putting this deal together. "May I ask if any of you are African American?" A chorus of laughter broke out. "All three of us are," they said. And then, "if you can deliver Ford, General Motors, and Chrysler, we can make the mortgage." Washington called Garrison at Sears. "Give me until December 8," he said, "and I guarantee we will close." He still didn't have GM and Chrysler, but he believed they would come through.

Frank Fountain and Rod Gillum proceeded as promised: each agreed with Ford Motor Company to share the $4 million that NCNW needed. Chrysler took the action necessary with its board, and General Motors followed suit. Sometime after this Earl Graves of *Black Enterprise* magazine came to Washington. As a Chrysler board member, he said, he wanted to see what he had voted for. He was moved when he heard the names Dorothy Height and the National Council of Negro Women, but he was especially proud of the action of the board once he saw the building.

On the day of the closing—December 8, 1995, in the offices of NCNW's attorney, Ronald Jessamy—the deal almost fell apart. When Sears's lawyers saw the press release we had prepared, they told Floyd Washington the deal was off. They did not wish to announce all of the terms of their agreement with NCNW. We recast the press release immediately, and the closing was back on track.

A few hours later the National Council of Negro Women became the proud owner of 633 Pennsylvania Avenue and its six floors of magnificent furnishings. I hailed the extraordinary partnership among Sears, Roebuck and Company, First Union Bank, Ford Motor Company, General Motors Company, and Chrysler Corporation as a sterling example of "corporate citizenship."

After the closing, Wayne Doran called to ask how it had gone. I thanked him for all that he had done, and especially for Floyd Washington. Mr. Doran said it had been a pleasure, and then added, "Miss Height, I knew that what you were trying to do was important, but when you told me about that banker who said that you didn't belong on Pennsylvania Avenue, I decided I had to make sure that this deal worked." As a further gift, Mr. Doran arranged for Ford to provide for the management of the building during our first six months of occupancy.

When I called Floyd Washington to thank him once again, he said, "Dr. Height, you were there for us at the Million Man March, and so we decided to be there for you." Then he said, "You know,

Dr. Height, I hadn't paid much attention to you before, but I sure was impressed when I saw that you were one of only two or three women who got up and spoke out at the Million Man March. When you told me about the controversies and the people who didn't want you to be involved in the march, you said, 'Sometimes you've got to take risks to make things happen.' I realized then that I'd been managing risk in a corporate setting for thirty years, but you taught me what taking risks is really about. I realized that I can influence decisions and do deals like this over and over. That march was all about African American men standing up and taking charge, and so was this deal. I discovered that there are able black men all over the place who just don't realize what they can do."

I thanked him once again, and he said, "Thank you, Dr. Height, for letting me be a little part of history. This was my best assignment in thirty years at Ford."

I learned later that when Washington walked into his office the Monday after the closing, his staff remarked that they hadn't seen much of him for the last month. "You look like you've been on a mission," said one. That is exactly what it was.

I cannot describe the true significance of the partnership that brought us to this place. The fact that the leaders in a major industry entered into this with genuine interest and a sense of shared vision and purpose was a great stimulation not only to the NCNW board of directors but to the membership. As a symbol of our gratitude, we presented to each our highest award, the illuminated scroll of the "Bethune Legacy."

The inaugural celebration of the National Centers for African American Women and the Dorothy I. Height Leadership Institute took place in October 1996. African American women flocked to the nation's capital for three days of festivities. The actress Cicely Tyson and the broadcast journalist Renée Pouissant cochaired the opening ceremony, and first lady Hillary Rodham Clinton gave a stirring keynote speech. Among those who attended were NCNW supporters Susan Taylor, Maya Angelou, Camille Cosby, Betty Shabazz, Coretta Scott King, Dionne Warwick, Bishop Vashti McKenzie, and Gladys Knight, to name just a few.

For the first time in history, Pennsylvania Avenue was closed for an African American group. Our theme was "African American Women Get It Done," and we had a special new logo developed by Erika Cosby. With a grant from Time Warner, the NCNW published its first book under the National Centers for African American Women, entitled *Voices of Vision: African-American Women on the Issues*. Edited by Julianne Malveaux and Shirley Jackson, it contained contributions from more than thirty women on issues in education, health, economics, leadership, family, and public policy.

Throughout the inaugural we held a series of roundtables on the subject "Women's Work—A Global Call to Action." A luncheon cochaired by NCNW Advisory Committee chair Lavelle Bond and Philip J. Carroll of Shell Oil, corporate chair of the Fund for the Future, inaugurated the Leadership Institute and featured Ann Fudge, president of Maxwell House. Sears sponsored a gala at the Grand Hyatt Hotel, including a special performance by Maya Angelou and Ashford and Simpson.

During one of the receptions Frank Fountain, DaimlerChrysler senior vice president for government affairs, who had become chair of our corporate working group, whispered to me, "We are going to finish this off in three years," referring to our mortgage. He has given strong leadership to it ever since.

We still had to complete the multiple objectives of the Fund for the Future—raising money for the centers and the Leadership Institute, securing general operations support, completing the building fund and seeding an endowment. At the convention in 1999, NCNW Life Members, led by Gertrude Peele, called for "burning the mortgage." Paying it off would free up more funds for program work.

Across the country, members, friends, and supporters sponsored fund-raising events.* And before long we decided to lauch a major annual fund-raiser. Patricia Brantley, chief development officer, suggested naming it the "Uncommon Height Gala." Joel Brokaw, the publicist, added a concept: "The Legends Celebrate the Legend."

The fourth gala in 2002 was hosted by Oprah Winfrey and the actor Danny Glover and chaired by Leland Brendsel, the head of Freddie Mac. Four first ladies—Lady Bird Johnson, Barbara Bush, Hillary Rodham Clinton, and Laura Bush—served as honorary chairs.

That evening the spirit moved. Johnnie Furr of Anheuser-Busch announced a major scholarship in my name. U.S. Representative Diane Watson of California shared legislation requesting a Congressional Medal of Honor for me. Impresario Don King presented a check for $100,000 and challenged Oprah Winfrey to join him. She did, announcing, "I love you, brother, but I came prepared to give two-point-five. That's million!" We will long remember how Oprah Winfrey moved from table to table, cajoling everyone to contribute. She laughed and shouted as she went: "You all want to be on the *Oprah Show*—well, here's your chance! Tonight we're having a birthday party!" Before we knew it we had reached the $5.4 million in cash and pledges needed to pay off the mortgage.

I am convinced that there was more than a little providence involved in NCNW's finding a home at 633 Pennsylvania Avenue. On February 17, 2002—long after we had bought the building—the cover of the *Washington Post Magazine* featured a photograph of two young African American women, the Edmondson sisters, with the headline: "They fled Washington to make themselves free and

---

* Ultimately, the fundraising showed one of the NCNW's great strengths. The "Buy a Brick" campaign expanded to other levels of support. Members, friends, people of all races and backgrounds contributed. Giving levels ranged from $10 into the millions. The building may bear my name, but it will also bear the names of all those who have contributed; they will grace its walls in perpetuity.

made history instead." The article recounted the story of the largest uprising of slaves in America, a failed attempt by seventy-seven slaves from Washington and environs to escape to freedom.

At the time enslaved persons had no legal rights in Washington, D.C. Even freedmen had no rights. They could not gather in groups of more than seven, were subject to a curfew, and were in constant danger of reenslavement.

In 1848 Emily Edmondson, fifteen, and Mary, thirteen, followed their four brothers on the abolitionist schooner *Pearl* in an attempt to reach the Underground Railroad. After being apprehended by a one-hundred-member posse, they were put in chains and led to the slave market in Washington. An angry crowd gathered to claim the fugitives, prompting a U.S. senator from New Hampshire to declare, "Today in France they are mobbing for liberty, and we are here mobbing for slavery."

The Edmondson sisters were sold at the market, and their new owners planned to ship them to New Orleans. But because of yellow fever there, they had to be returned to Virginia. Their father, a freedman, convinced the Reverend Henry Ward Beecher and his church in New York to purchase their freedom. Their story led Harriet Beecher Stowe to write *Uncle Tom's Cabin.* *

The Center Slave Market where the Edmondson sisters were sold was located on the corner of Seventh Street and Pennsylvania Avenue, where the National Council of Negro Women now stands. I believe it was providential that we had the opportunity to claim this site and to sustain upon it an active presence for freedom and justice. Never should this property leave African American ownership. It is ours to keep.

---

* The Stowes sent Emily and Mary to Oberlin College in Ohio. Mary, weakened by the effects of slavery, developed tuberculosis and died within a year. Heartbroken, Emily returned to Washington, D.C., to work with Myrtilla Minor, a white woman who educated slave girls and freed persons; her enterprise eventually grew into the Minor Teachers College. Historians contend that the *Pearl* incident, more than any other single event, escalated the antislavery debate.

Chapter Nineteen

A Family of Friends

I HAVE FOCUSED in these pages on the life's work that I was blessed to discover quite early on. And it is true that during the years when I was director of the Phyllis Wheatley YWCA in Washington, D.C., I devoted the daylight hours to that job, then worked long evenings and weekends with Mary McLeod Bethune and the National Council of Negro Women. I learned to work around the clock, something I have often done over all the years that followed. But I did have a private life as well.

As I have written, it always seemed to me that I grew up in a large, loving family. And over the course of my life I added to its members a number of dear friends who, although they may not have been related to me by blood, became, in the deepest sense, true members of my family circle.

It started back in Harlem in the midthirties, while I was in graduate school. During those years I lived with my friend Frankie Dixon, who herself was like a sister, and with Frankie's mother, Maude

Myers. Mrs. Myers and Frankie were always comparing me with Maurine Gordon—later Perkinson—who had lived with them as a student in high school and teachers' college. Maurine's mother had died when Maurine was just a child, and her father—like Mrs. Myers a devout Christian Scientist—had made the living arrangements.

"Mother," as Maurine called Mrs. Myers, kept us all in touch through weekly conference calls. But I didn't meet Maurine face to face until 1945, when I was directing a YWCA educational program on the West Coast. We often smiled that the whole world observed our meeting—at the Figueroa Hotel in Los Angeles at the very moment the whistles were blowing for VJ Day, after the atom bomb fell on Hiroshima.

From that day until her death in 2000, Maurine and I claimed each other as sisters. I got her active in Delta and in the National Council of Negro Women, and she worked devotedly in both. We shared social work experiences. We celebrated holidays, traveled, and worked together across the miles until she declared herself officially retired. She included NCNW and me in her will.

I added some more new family members after my nearly fatal automobile accident in 1941. At the time I lived in the annex of the Phyllis Wheatley YWCA, where I was the executive director. During my recuperation, I met a woman named Yvonne Ray, who quickly became one of my very best friends.

Yvonne was originally from Cleveland, Ohio, but had been living with an aunt in Virginia. She had made connections with wholesalers in the seafood industry and launched her own oyster business. Eventually her clients included most of Washington's leading restaurants.

When I had recovered and was ready to find an apartment, a highly respected Washingtonian, Charlotte Ridgley, let me know that she had created an apartment on one floor of her home on Tenth Street—close to the YWCA. Yvonne and I decided to take it together. And that was just the beginning.

Yvonne had a twin sister, Marjorie, who was married to a man named Robert Hall. Marjorie and Robert lived in Cleveland with the Earlys—Mable and "Aunt Bess"—and it was not long before they seemed like family too. Every visit I made to Cleveland—with or without Yvonne—was like homecoming.

Robert, Yvonne's brother-in-law, worked for the Pullman Company. Whenever his job brought him to Washington, he would stop in to see us. And when we weren't visiting back and forth, three- or four-way phone calls with the Early household brought us all together. Everyone made it a special point to keep in close touch with Marjorie, who had marked ups and downs. At the time we did not know enough to call it depression, although today that almost surely would have been the diagnosis.

One day Robert called to say he was in town and would stop by. We had been girding ourselves to tell him not to stop but to get home to Cleveland as quickly as he could. Marjorie had disappeared. She had left the Early house beautifully dressed and seemingly in good spirits, saying she had to run a quick errand. But she had not returned. Aunt Bess, the last person to talk with Marjorie, was simply devastated. The suspense was unbearable.

The next day Marjorie's body was found. She had jumped off a bridge. The tragedy and the depth of suffering it caused brought us all closer together than ever. Widowed, Robert kept his home with the Earlys.

In the fall of 1944, Yvonne and I moved to New York. We took an apartment at 464 West 152nd Street. I had joined the national staff of the YWCA of the USA, and Yvonne had taken a job with the United Service Organization (USO). But she was an entrepreneur at heart, and before long the desire to own her own business took hold. She purchased a grocery delicatessen store on St. Nicholas Avenue in the heart of "Sugar Hill," Harlem's most prestigious neighborhood, near the residences of Duke Ellington, Sy Oliver, and others.

Realizing that she needed help with her new enterprise,

Yvonne remembered Robert's skills in the management of an exclusive Cleveland club. With Aunt Bess's support, she persuaded him to come help manage the store. Robert moved in with a family in our apartment building. All of us had our own friends, male and female, and our separate interests. But we all came together for holidays and special occasions. Traditional gatherings at "464" were cherished by a circle of our close friends.

At first all went exceptionally well with Yvonne's enterprise. The neighbors were delighted to have the new owners at this convenient spot. But then Yvonne ran into trouble. When she applied for a liquor license, she found that something the previous owners had done had resulted in a restriction that prevented the city from issuing a license to her building for a designated period of years. Every effort to correct the problem failed—and without a license, the store could not sell beer. Such stores counted on beer sales, given the small edge of profit on groceries, and customers wanted one-stop shopping for snacks, delicatessen, and drinks.

Under so much pressure, Yvonne sold the store and took a job with New York's Mount Sinai Hospital. But she still possessed that great entrepreneurial drive. Her first failure was devastating and caused a deep sense of loss—and ultimately a nervous breakdown.

She was hospitalized for a long time. Robert and I made sure that one or both of us were always there on visiting days, and we always brought goodies to cheer her. Throughout Yvonne's ordeal I was thankful for my studies in mental health at New York University. They served me well. I could draw upon what I had learned in works such as *A Mind That Found Itself*, Clifford Whittingham Beers's autobiographical account of his confinement in a mental institution in the early part of the century. I knew I was dealing with illness, not disgrace.

We rejoiced when Yvonne regained her health. She had such a good work record that she was able to return to her job at Mount Sinai Hospital. Eventually, however, we realized it was time to make some changes.

Through my work at the YWCA I had gotten to know Richard Ravitch, who was a principal in the development of a luxury apartment complex on Twenty-third Street in Manhattan. During our many meetings he told me about the Waterside, as it was called, and I passed on the information to Robert and Yvonne. Finally, the three of us agreed to pool our resources and take a spacious three-bedroom apartment on the thirty-third floor overlooking the East River. Leaving Harlem was not easy, but the move seemed just right.

Over the years Robert and Yvonne became my support system. After Yvonne sold her store, Robert had gone on to manage another Harlem store and then to work for the Community Development Association in Brooklyn. As a gourmet cook, Robert kept us well fed at home and did any chauffeuring that was necessary. Yvonne handled the housekeeping and many other essential chores. Between them, they made sure that I never had to worry about even simple things like packing bags and being met at airports. They were a vital part of whatever I did.

For years I commuted between New York and Washington, carrying my job with the YWCA and my volunteer service with the National Council of Negro Women. For a long time I simply stayed in a hotel when I was in Washington. But after I retired from the YWCA in 1977, I found I was spending most of my time there, so finally I took an apartment in the District of Columbia.

After Yvonne died in 1978, it was just Robert and me. And whatever the situation or need, Robert was there. At different points in the ensuing years he said he hated being by himself so much and wished he were back in Harlem, as he missed his friends. Quite tactfully, I had to remind him that he was outliving them and they were not there.

In June 1995, my sister Anthanette lost her husband, Daniel Aldridge. It was not until I went to New York to his funeral that I gave serious attention to Robert's state of mind. I began to realize that it was not simply that he was lonely; his mental state was changing. He attended the funeral, but the next morning he did not feel up to going to the cemetery for the burial.

When I returned to Washington, Robert called, and he sounded so strange that I asked Sylvia McMurdoch of the NCNW New York staff to help him get to Washington. Reluctantly, he went to the hospital for an examination. Sadly, he was in the early stages of Alzheimer's. Robert, who had loved spending hours in the kitchen, no longer went in that direction. Increasingly, there was very little that he could do. It was my turn to be the caregiver. And having our roles reverse in this fashion was a privilege for me, since Robert and Yvonne both had always been there for me unselfishly.

In September 2001—along with Wade Henderson, executive director of the Leadership Conference on Civil Rights—I led a delegation to the World Conference on Racism in Durban, South Africa. Some friends were concerned that I was taking Robert on that trip with me, arguing that he might not even remember the occasion. But I am so glad to have had that experience with him. It was only one month later that Robert became very ill and died.

All told, I was blessed with more than fifty years of friendship with Yvonne Ray, Robert Hall, and Maurine Perkinson. And in the last few years, I have found even more extended family in Washington, D.C. Alexis Herman Franklin and I had long since claimed each other, back in the early seventies. More than ten years ago, at a private dinner, my friends Kent Amos and LeBaron Taylor shared their concern and interest in Carl Holman and me. They assured me that so long as they lived, I should not be wanting—a heartwarming moment I can never forget. LeBaron Taylor has since passed, but Kent and Carmen Amos have been there for me. Ronald and Sharon Harrison schedule regular times to sustain and lift my my spirits. Lavelle and Barbara Bond make a homecoming of every Black Family Reunion in Cincinnati. Maya Angelou, with her abundant capacity for caring, enriches my life. And Brenda and Courtney Miller are always on call.

When I look back, I am more thankful than I can say. These were truly friends who became family.

Chapter Twenty

"Temples Still Undone"

T HE IMAGE of the Sankofa bird, which flies forward while looking backward, seems to me to be a particularly apt symbol for my life.

I look back toward a past that spans nearly a century. I have lived through extraordinary times, when Americans of all backgrounds awakened to the racial, economic, and social injustices that betrayed the promise of our great country. Early in life I was exposed to youth and adults from around the world. I have worked directly with women and their governments on five of the seven continents. I have had the challenge of leadership in three major national women's organizations. Building on religious faith deeply rooted in my childhood and youth, I found my life's work. I am the product of many whose lives have touched mine, from the famous, distinguished, and powerful to the little known and the poor. The past has taught me many lessons—most especially that I have a responsibility to future generations.

Moving forward, I feel accountable to the boys and girls, the young men and women, who are creating new ways of effecting change. I urge young people to participate in their communities, to observe the issues and situations affecting their lives, and to share what they learn with each other so that they can continue to build a world that is better than the one they inherited. They must absorb the lessons of the past—not because there has been no change, but because knowing just how much *has* changed will give them the courage and energy to make it through.

I fear that too many of our young people know only where we are now, not how we got here nor where we are going. Too many see doors only recently opened and do not appreciate how they got pried ajar. I believe that all of us must keep working so that more and more of our children have opportunity, but we also must be sure that our youth recognize the preceding struggle. Our task is not unlike developing the memorial of the Holocaust. We too must never forget. We must remember our dead as well as our living. We must rekindle and keep alive the memory of our own history in people's hearts.

I was encouraged not long ago when a young woman I had counseled sent me a note thanking me for advising her not to allow her life to be driven by personal ambition alone. I had not used those exact words, but she got the message I pass on to young people.

These are the things I tell them. Ambition is essential, but when you are self-centered, you stand in your own way. You will accomplish a great deal if you do not worry about who will get the credit. You should enjoy the success of others as well as your own. Know yourself and set career goals worthy of the person you know you are. Hold fast! The road will not be easy. Success depends upon your stick-to-itiveness and the passion with which you pursue your goals. Give yourself a start and keep going. The surest path to success is through education in a society increasingly based in science and technology. Education is key.

*

Back in the days when we were working on segregation and overt discrimination, what we needed to do was very clear, and the all-too-apparent injustice we battled raised a righteous indignation across America. We declared: "Jim Crow must go." And now, legally, Jim Crow has gone.

But enforcement of the civil rights laws that were passed in the sixties is still inadequate. Affirmative action is threatened, and unemployment and underemployment are rising among people of color. Today we still have to deal with the same old issues, but from new angles. Now covert discrimination is the problem, and in many ways it is more difficult than the old overt variety. Now, after generations of unremitting poverty, there is an entrenched culture of poverty among some of our people, and dismantling it will take our most concentrated and committed efforts.

Unless we acknowledge that racism exists, we will never eliminate it. Language is such a carrier of values that there is a tendency to state problems in a way that makes us feel comfortable. In today's world, the word *diversity* is widely used. Unless we deal with the underlying problems of racism and sexism, diversity will have little meaning. If people define racism only as certain personal attitudes, then the only solutions they will seek are various ways of changing these attitudes. If, on the other hand, racism is seen as pervasive, fundamental, and systemic, then the solutions sought will be different and deeper in character.

Some people chide me for never giving up, no matter how hopeless the cause may seem. It's not that I am such an optimist. Life has taught me that in the face of man's inhumanity to man, we must try to exemplify man's humanity to man. I am glad that I was often in a time and place where I could do what needed to be done.

And I can bear witness to the potential over a life experience. Barnard College did not let me in, but New York University welcomed me. Many years later, both institutions gave me their highest honor. One white person hurt me, and another helped me heal. Many people declined to support us as we tried to raise the funds to buy our building—including three national banks that assumed African American women would fail. But six African American men in corporate leadership whom I had never met helped make our dream come true.

Through the last century we learned that it is in the neighborhoods and communities where the world begins. That is where children grow and families are developed, where people exercise their power to change their lives. Whatever national strategies we may develop now will always be designed specifically to improve grassroots community life. The Quakers say, "Let us center in." My dream is that each of the five National Centers for African American Women will "center in" the work of the National Council of Negro Women while, at the same time, pushing us to reach out toward the real action, which has to be in our homes and communities.

African Americans know how much our forebears contributed to building this nation, and we are proud of it. We know the value our ancestors placed on faith, kinship, education, and hard work. We cherish their ingenious inventions, their poetry and music, the grit and wisdom they have passed down to us. These treasures enrich our lives and sustain our faith in the future, and they are inextricably woven into the fabric of America.

For all our struggle for justice, there is still much work to be done. When Mrs. Bethune founded the National Council of Negro Women in 1935, she declared that "Negro women, the trained and untrained alike, stand outside of America's mainstream of influence, opportunity, and power." This daughter of slave parents and adviser to four U.S. presidents called for women in all walks of life to join hands in service to themselves, their families, their nation, and their world. Mrs. Bethune knew that there would still be struggles in the twenty-first century. But she also knew that the inner power never ceases to flow.

I believe it is the hand of God that led African American

women to establish a center on the corridor of power halfway between the Capitol and the White House on a site hallowed by our enslaved ancestors.

I was both uplifted and humbled when the building was named the Dorothy I. Height Building of the National Council of Negro Women. The dedication ceremony on Mary 26, 2003 included a litany of Moments of Praise by the Reverend Brenda Girton Mitchell, a prayer by Bishop Vashti Murphy McKenzie of the AME Church and the following Dedicatory Declaration by Maya Angelou:

> *This plot of everlasting earth is heavy with memory. Once Washington's Center Slave Market stood here. However, It has been transformed. Today, the majestic office of the National Council of Negro Women rises high above the infamous past. Its membership pledges to continue offering its services to the needy, the neglected, and the underrepresented.*
>
> *The building and the land have been obtained by the sweat and tears of slaves, the vision of Dr. Mary McLeod Bethune, the zealous commitment of Dr. Dorothy I. Height, and the devotion of countless African American men and women.*
>
> *It is dedicated to all people around the world who love freedom and who know that freedom can only be achieved by those who are willing to work for it, to cherish it, and to share it.*

From "Our House," we must always be a strong presence, an unrelenting force working for equality and justice until the freedom gates are fully open.

Acknowledgments

It would take another book the size of this one to thank all of the people who have helped me over the past ten years in writing this book. They have encouraged me and have demonstrated patience and tenacity, especially when pressures of work caused deadlines to be extended.

I offer special thanks to several persons without whose contributions this book may never have happened. Camille Cosby took the initiative and called together the first meeting with a literary agency and publisher to get the project off and running. Shortly thereafter, Maya Angelou, over breakfast at the Madison Hotel, inspired me and gave me the equivalent of a crash course on writing my story. Her foreword brings added value to this book, or to any book. Joel Brokaw has been a creative counsel and publicist throughout the work in progress. Ramona Edelin developed the first outline from my oral history in the Schlesinger Library at the Radcliffe Institute for Advanced Study at Harvard University.

Susan Goodwillie Stedman worked with me for countless hours to record, transcribe and write some nine decades of recollections and stories. For the intensive interview and research, I thank Rochelle Jones, who helped me place myself in each situation rather than making an organizational report. Angelica Broadus, as an elementary school pupil, prodded me at every family gathering, asking for my book.

Alexis Herman Franklin, Thelma T. Daley, Cheryl Cooper, Vanessa Weaver, Laverne Parks, Linda Morton, Angela Harper, and Rosslyn Casey were thoughtful readers whose questions and suggestions made the difference.

Patricia Brantley, Robin Breedlove, Wade Henderson, Brenda Miller, and Joyce Fourth gave invaluable editorial assistance. Esther Wynn was the keeper at every stage in the manuscript development. Several of these women spent so many late nights at my home, helping me research, draft, redraft, and organize that my housing association could have charged them membership. Michelle Holder and Mary L. Brown graciously supported every effort. Sylvia McMurdock assembled many historic pieces. Lola Early and Christine Toney kept the office services moving. Thanks to Ofield Dukes for his constant support of public relations and promotions. Special thanks to Sandra Green for her creative designs to enhance the promotion of the book.

Since 1985, the Black Leadership Family founded by Tom and Barbara Skinner has nurtured trusting relationships among my peers. I have found it has been a source of renewal and an experience in the essence of sharing.

I had to count on my sister, Anthanette Aldridge, my nephew, Bernard Randolph, his wife, Billy, and my nephew, Bill Briggs, for putting together material, especially from my early years.

Betty Stradford, Ted Lewis, Jason Johnson, Louis Myrie, Ed Adams, and Ray Wilson were generous with their photography. Sheila Flemming shared the invaluable historic resources of Bethune-Cookman College. Robert Parker, Cultural Resource

Specialist at the Bethune Museum and Archives, the only archives devoted to black women's history in the United States, proved an invaluable resource.

Delores Brinkley and Lillian Kimura found publications and program materials I had written when we worked as colleagues on the National Board of the Young Women's Christian Association. Beryl Carter, a former member of the National Board, reached into her archives of black newspapers.

Holly Cowan Schulman and Geoffrey Cowan came forward with friendly counsel and contacts to overcome a major obstacle. And last, but not least, the wonderful team at PublicAffairs—Peter Osnos, Kate Darnton, and Merrill McLoughlin—who brought great professional skill, sensitivity, and spirit with caring hands and eyes to shepherd this book to completion.

I am indeed thankful. Each one and all together they have made me sense the intrinsic value in my life's work and my accountability for the past and to the future.

Photo Credits

Graduation Day: Courtesy of Dr. Dorothy Height's files; *With niece in Harlem:* Courtesy of Dr. Dorothy Height's files; *Mother and her sisters:* Courtesy of Dr. Dorothy Height's files; *With Mary McLeod Bethune:* Courtesy of Bethune Council House Museum, National Park Service; *With her three sisters:* Courtesy of Dr. Dorothy Height's files; *At Mrs. Roosevelt's Val-Kill Cottage:* Courtesy of Franklin D. Roosevelt Library; *President Kennedy signs the Equal Pay Act:* Courtesy of The White House; *At the March on Washington for Martin Luther King Jr.'s "I Have a Dream" speech:* Courtesy of *Ebony* Magazine; *Robert Kennedy with Civil Rights leaders:* Courtesy of The White House; *The one woman in the crowd:* Courtesy of NAACP; *With President Lyndon Johnson in the Oval Office:* Courtesy of The White House; *President Ronald Reagan holds a White House reception:* Courtesy of The White House *With the Carters at The White House:* Courtesy of The White House;; *A briefing at Blair House with President Ronald Reagan:* Courtesy of The White House; *A NCNW meeting with President George Bush at the White House:* Courtesy of The White House; *President Bill Clinton presents me with the Presidential Medal of Freedom at The White House:* Courtesy of The White House; *The Black Family Reunion:* Photo by Betty Kleckley Stradford; *The National Council of Negro Women's new headquarters:* Photo by Betty Kleckley Stradford; *All decked out:* Photo by Betty Kleckley Stradford.

Index

DR. DOROTHY HEIGHT has received more than 20 honorary degrees, as well as the Congressional Gold Medal, the Presidential Medal of Freedom, the Franklin Delano Roosevelt Freedom Medal, and the Citizens Medal Award. Now ninety-three, she continues to serve as chair and president emerita of the National Council of Negro Women in Washington, D.C.

PublicAffairs is a publishing house founded in 1997. It is a tribute to the standards, values, and flair of three persons who have served as mentors to countless reporters, writers, editors, and book people of all kinds, including me.

I.F. Stone, proprietor of *I. F. Stone's Weekly*, combined a commitment to the First Amendment with entrepreneurial zeal and reporting skill and became one of the great independent journalists in American history. At the age of eighty, Izzy published *The Trial of Socrates*, which was a national bestseller. He wrote the book after he taught himself ancient Greek.

Benjamin C. Bradlee was for nearly thirty years the charismatic editorial leader of *The Washington Post*. It was Ben who gave the *Post* the range and courage to pursue such historic issues as Watergate. He supported his reporters with a tenacity that made them fearless and it is no accident that so many became authors of influential, best-selling books.

Robert L. Bernstein, the chief executive of Random House for more than a quarter century, guided one of the nation's premier publishing houses. Bob was personally responsible for many books of political dissent and argument that challenged tyranny around the globe. He is also the founder and longtime chair of Human Rights Watch, one of the most respected human rights organizations in the world.

For fifty years, the banner of Public Affairs Press was carried by its owner Morris B. Schnapper, who published Gandhi, Nasser, Toynbee, Truman and about 1,500 other authors. In 1983, Schnapper was described by *The Washington Post* as "a redoubtable gadfly." His legacy will endure in the books to come.

Peter Osnos, *Publisher*